How to Use This Book

Due to its extreme power, Adobe Photoshop can be a bit intimidating for beginning, and even intermediate, users. People working with Photoshop for the first time—regardless of their background—face a monumental challenge in learning to use this program, and people who are already familiar with Photoshop need fast access to information about the new version 5 features. That's where this book comes in.

Sams Teach Yourself Adobe Photoshop 5 in 21 Days provides a strong foundation for working with Photoshop's tools, palettes, and dialog boxes, but it doesn't stop there. This book walks you through all levels of examples—from beginning to more advanced—and teaches you the techniques you need to become an expert Photoshop user. Each chapter builds on the previous one, helping you tackle the program in bite-sized pieces. With relative ease, this method moves you from the most basic uses of Photoshop to some of the more complex.

Who Should Use This Book

If you have ever used graphics editing applications or if you've ever wanted to learn, then this book is for you. Whether you have no experience or limited experience, *Sams Teach Yourself Adobe Photoshop 5 in 21 Days* is the book to get you up and running quickly. This book focuses on teaching by example, so once you've worked through the tutorials, you'll fully understand both the tools and the techniques. All of the tutorials are designed to be fun and informative, and they'll definitely set off your creative spark. If you're looking for ways to be creative with Photoshop 5, look no further.

T. Michael Clark

SAMS Teach Yourself
Adobe
Photoshop 5
in 21 Days

SAMS

A Division of Macmillan Computer Publishing
201 West 103rd St., Indianapolis, Indiana 46290 USA

Sams Teach Yourself Adobe Photoshop 5 in 21 Days

International Standard Book Number: 0-672-31300-6

Library of Congress Catalog Card Number: 98-84023

Printed in the United States of America

First Printing: June 1998

00   99   98   4   3   2   1

Interpretation of the printing code: the rightmost double-digit number is the year of the book's printing; the rightmost single digit, the number of the book's printing. For example, a printing code of 94-1 shows that the first printing of the book occurred in 1994.

Printed in the United States of America

Trademarks

All terms mentioned in this book that are known to be trademarks or service marks have been appropriately capitalized. Sams Publishing cannot attest to the accuracy of this information. Use of a term in this book should not be regarded as affecting the validity of any trademark or service mark.

PUBLISHER
Jordan Gold

EXECUTIVE EDITOR
Beth Millett

MANAGING EDITOR
Brice Gosnell

ACQUISITIONS EDITOR
Karen Whitehouse

DEVELOPMENT EDITOR
Jennifer Eberhardt

SOFTWARE DEVELOPMENT SPECIALIST
Adam Swetnam

PROJECT EDITOR
Kevin Laseau

COPY EDITOR
Michael Brumitt

TECHNICAL EDITOR
Robert Reinhardt

COVER DESIGNER
Aren Howell

BOOK DESIGNER
Gary Adair

INDEXER
Kelly Talbot

PRODUCTION
Carol Bowers
Mona Brown
Ayanna Lacey
Gene Redding

Overview

Contents

About the Author

T. Michael Clark, a Canadian author published by New Riders Publishing and Sams, is the author of several books on imaging software and Web graphics and has worked as technical editor on other projects from Macmillan Computer Publishing.

A multi-award–winning digital artist, writer, photographer, programmer/analyst, Web site designer, and Internet veteran, Michael owns and operates the very popular "GrafX Design" Web site (http://www.grafx-design.com), which features free online tutorials for Photoshop, CorelDRAW, and Paint Shop Pro, along with other Web design-oriented topics and product reviews.

Michael is a moderator and associate member of Chris Dickman's "i/us" Association for Visual Professionals, where he lends support to Photoshop and Paint Shop Pro discussion groups. In addition, he is a frequent contributor to many Usenet graphics newsgroups. Michael's clear, concise teaching style, as displayed in his online graphics tutorials, as well as his graphic design talent, have garnered international acclaim within the Web community.

Robert Reinhardt is a multimedia installation artist, living and teaching in Toronto, Canada. After studying psychology, Robert earned a degree in still photography, combining his knowledge of digital technologies with his use of traditional media. He has taught graduate, continuing education, and seminar-based courses in digital media, as well as maintaining an online freelance consulting service at http://www.o-n-s-i-t-e.com.

Dedication

I'd like to dedicate this book to my lovely wife Pamela, who, instead of just shoving food under my office door at regular intervals, actually made sure I got away from the computers every once in a while. Thanks, Hon.

Acknowledgments

No project this size could be completed without the help of a great number of people. I'd like to take the chance to thank the following:

All of the people who visit the GrafX Design Web site on a regular basis. It's because of you that I keep coming up with new ideas and push myself, and the various imaging programs I use, to new limits.

The great people I get to work with at MCP including Beth Millett and Karen Whitehouse.

My favorite editor and best cyber-buddy Jennifer Eberhardt. Jennifer makes this work even more fun than it already is.

The tech editor, Rob Reinhardt, for making sure it all worked.

My two models: Marianne Dodelet and my wife, Pamela.

For providing me with some of the coolest imaging software around: Michelle Murphy-Croteau at Corel, the gang at Alien Skin, Shayne Jolie at Auto F/X, Dwight Jurling at Ulead, and Amy Morris at Adobe.

For providing me with some of her artwork and for being a big fan, Laren Leonard.

For providing a sample of his amazing actions to be included on the accompanying CD-ROM, Steven Alexander II.

Last, but certainly not least, I'd like to thank the amazing people at Adobe, including but not limited to John Leddy, Christie Cameron, and Marc Pawliger.

Introduction

Welcome to Photoshop 5.0

From its not-so-humble beginnings as a film-editing program, Photoshop has grown into the world's leading image editing software. With the advent of the Web, imaging software has gained a whole new audience. Due to its power, though, Photoshop can be a bit intimidating for beginners. Even people with photographic, artistic, graphic, and computer skills can be faced with what may seem a monumental challenge when encountering this program for the first time. That's where this book comes in.

Between the covers and on the accompanying CD-ROM, I'll walk you through the program. From the first day, when you'll learn to navigate the interface, to the final day, when you'll discover the secrets to using Photoshop for Web graphics, this book will give you the confidence and the skills to work with this powerful program at its fullest potential.

Each chapter builds on the previous one, helping you tackle the program in small, bite-sized pieces. This method will move you from the most basic uses of Photoshop to some of the more complex uses with relative ease. I encourage you to try all the techniques yourself so that you can experience the hands-on training.

Vector-Based Versus Pixel-Based Imagery

Before we get started with conventions, I'd like to give you a quick lesson in digital imaging. There are two basic ways to describe computer images: with pixels and with vectors. Photoshop is a pixel-based (also known as bitmap- or raster-based) program. In other words, it uses pixels, or small dots of light, to describe, store, and manipulate computer images. Vector-based programs, such as Adobe Illustrator or CorelDRAW, use mathematics, or vectors, to describe images. Although pixel-based programs are good for photograph-type artwork, vector programs are better suited for illustrations. Each type of program, however, can easily complement the other, and you'll see how these two programs can be used together throughout this book.

Conventions Used in This Book

Each chapter begins with a short list of topics to be covered and ends with a Quiz section that tests what you've learned. Also at the end of each chapter is a section called "Q&A," which provides answers to questions that go beyond the scope of the chapter but still pertain to the topic at hand.

Also in this book are Notes, Tips, and Cautions:

Note

A Note presents interesting information related to the discussion.

Tip

A Tip offers advice or shows you an easier way of doing something.

Caution

A Caution alerts you to a possible problem and gives you advice on how to avoid it.

Now if you're ready, let's get started with Day 1, "Introducing the Photoshop Interface."

WEEK 1

At a Glance

Whether you're working with Photoshop for the first time or you're trying to get up to speed with the features new to version 5, this first week will provide an in-depth overview for both types of users. This first week will cover the following:

- Working with Photoshop's interface: palettes, tools, and menus
- Learning to navigate via keyboard shortcuts
- Setting up your Photoshop preferences
- Working with the memory options
- Getting up to speed with Photoshop's new features, including the History palette, text editing, and more
- Finding out when and how to use the most common image file formats
- Taking photographs with a digital camera and scanning images into your computer
- Creating images from scratch
- Saving, exporting, and printing your images
- Understanding the various color models, color palettes, color depths, and calibration

1

2

3

4

5

6

7

DAY 1

Introducing the Photoshop Interface

Working in Photoshop is a pleasure. Adobe has spent a lot of time working on the interface and it's paid off. Whether you're a beginner or a more seasoned pro, the interface works with you instead of against you. After only a short time, you'll find that it becomes almost intuitive to work with Photoshop.

This first chapter covers the various elements that make up this easy-to-work-with default interface, as well as the ways to navigate in, around, and through it with ease. More specifically, you'll learn the following:

- The major functions of the various menus
- What you can do with the various toolbox tools
- How to work with Photoshop's palettes
- Navigation via keyboard shortcuts

Getting Acquainted with the Interface

Finding your way around Photoshop is quite easy (see Figure 1.1). The menus are well thought out, as are the toolboxes and palettes. As you work with Photoshop, you'll start to see how the menus, tools, and palettes are grouped together logically.

FIGURE 1.1

The default Photoshop interface.

Photoshop's menu bar ┘

Toolbox opens on the left by default

Palettes appear on the right by default

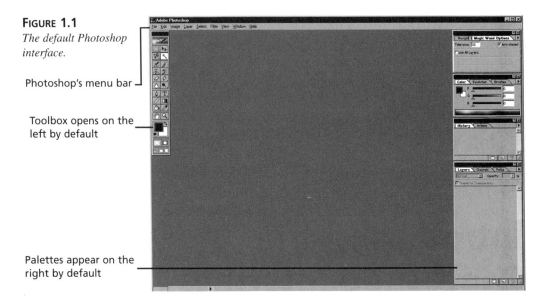

Along the top of the screen are the main menu selections. In the upper-left corner is the toolbox and down the right side of the screen are the palettes. We'll take a look at each of these in the following sections.

Menus

If you're used to working in a windowed environment, such as Windows or on a Mac, the first thing you'll notice when you run Photoshop is the main menu across the top of your screen (see Figure 1.2).

The menu begins, as most do, with the File entry. Going to the right, you'll see Edit, Image, Layer, Select, Filter, View, Window, and Help. In a nutshell, here's a brief description of each:

- **File.** For when you want to open, import, save, export, or print images, or set document preferences.
- **Edit.** The menu for copying, cutting, pasting, and so forth.

FIGURE 1.2

The Photoshop menu bar.

- **Image.** Access the various modes and adjustments, change the size and canvas size of your image, and more.
- **Layer.** Apply all the various Layer options including adding and deleting layers, and applying adjustment layers or layer masks.
- **Select.** Select all, Deselect, Reselect, Feather, Modify, Save, and Load your selections.
- **Filter.** The easy way to apply more than 90 special effects.
- **View.** Zoom in and out of your images, and align your images to grids.
- **Window.** How to open and hide the toolbox or any of the myriad palettes.
- **Help.** What to click when you don't know what to do.

There are, of course, many additional options for each of the various main menu commands. For example, when you choose the Sketch command from the Filters menu, a flyout appears with an additional 14 Filter options to choose from. I'll discuss several of these additional options as we work our way through some of the techniques included with this book.

Some of the menu command choices may not be available depending on certain conditions. For example, certain filters are not available in all color modes. If a choice appears in light gray, it is not currently available.

The Toolbox

By default, the toolbox (see Figure 1.3) rests in the upper-left corner of the Photoshop screen. You can, of course, place it anywhere on the screen that you wish. You could, for example, place it alongside the palettes if you find that you're often skating your mouse from one side of the screen to the other. One thing you'll notice as you move the toolbox around is that it seems to snap into place when you move it near the screen's edges or when you move the toolbox near the palettes. This is designed to make it easier to move the navigational elements around.

FIGURE 1.3

Photoshop 5.0's tool-box, broken down by category.

Selection tools

Painting and editing tools

Fill, Text, Pen, Move, and Grid tools

Color swatches

Edit modes

Screen modes

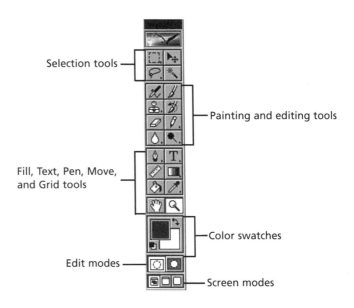

 Note   For a complete breakdown of the individual toolbox tools, see Appendix A, "Keyboard Shortcuts and Tool Documentation."

Breaking Down the Toolbox

If you look closely at the toolbox, you may notice that it seems to be broken into sections. This is no accident. These sections represent the different groupings of functions that are available from the toolbox. The six sections, from the top down, are

- **Selection tools.** These enable you to select areas of your image.
- **Painting and Editing tools.** For painting and editing tasks, these tools are like having a digital darkroom.
- **Fill, Text, Pen, Move, and Grid tools.** With these tools, you can fill areas, add text, or view a grid to help with placement.
- **Color swatches.** These change the current foreground and background colors.
- **Edit modes.** Standard and Quick Mask modes are contained here.
- **Screen modes.** These modes include Standard, Full Screen with Menu Bar, and Full Screen without Menu Bar.

1

As we work through the various tutorials presented in this book, you'll learn how to use each of the tools. I'll demonstrate selections, paths, text, and so on. One thing that you can try right now, though, is the switching between different Screen modes.

Zooming In and Out of the Various Screen Modes

You'll notice that the leftmost icon of the three Screen mode icons is pressed in. This icon sets the Standard Screen mode.

To begin, move your mouse over the icon and hold it there for a moment. You should see a small window pop up. It contains the words "Standard Screen Mode (F)." Because this button is pressed in, it means that this is the current mode. The (F) is a shortcut key. Pressing the "F" key in succession cycles you through the different Screen modes. Try it.

The second screen, Full Screen Mode with Menu Bar (F), shows whatever image you're working on in Full Screen mode. You'll still see the menu bar in this mode, too. To get to the third Screen mode, where even the menu bar is hidden, press the F key once again.

Tip

Even in Full Screen mode with the menu bar hidden, you may notice that the toolbox and the palettes are still visible. If you want a really uncluttered workspace, press the Tab key. The Tab key toggles the toolbox and palettes on and off (regardless of which mode you're currently in). With the third Screen mode (Full Screen Mode) selected and after pressing the Tab key, the only thing that'll be on your screen is the image you're working on.

Toolbox Flyouts

Clicking and holding the mouse on some of the toolbox selections brings out a choice of other selections. Any selection on the main toolbox that has a small black arrow in its lower-right corner produces a flyout in this manner (see Figure 1.4).

FIGURE 1.4

The Marquee tool flyout options.

Click and hold on any tool with a small
arrow to view the flyout options

The flyouts enable you to select other tools from the same option. These tools, although functionally the same, change the way in which you can perform a certain option. For example, the flyout seen in Figure 1.4 presents the five Selection tool options. The tool visible when I hold the mouse down is the Circular, or Elliptical, Marquee tool. By holding the mouse button down, I get four more tools that function similarly. The first option is the Rectangular Marquee tool. You'll then notice the Elliptical tool, but you'll also notice that it's grayed out because it's the current tool. After that, you'll see the Single Row Marquee tool, the Single Column Marquee tool, and finally the Crop tool.

These tools all perform similar functions, so, rather than display all the tools at once, Adobe hides all but the current tools in the flyouts. This is a nice way of uncluttering the screen, and yet it leaves all of the tools at your fingertips.

You should familiarize yourself with the different tools hidden under each of the flyouts because each of them has functions just as important as the tools that appear by default. As with the Screen modes, holding the mouse over a tool produces a small window that describes the tool and gives you the shortcut key, if any.

 Tip

> If you would rather not see the ToolTips, you can turn this option off. Choose File, Preferences, General, and click the Show ToolTips option.

After having selected a tool you can further modify its behavior. The options available for any tool appear in an Options palette.

Palettes

All the palettes are lined up along the right-hand side of the screen when you open Photoshop (see Figure 1.5). The different palettes are grouped as follows:

- **Navigation, Info, and Options.** The Navigation palette enables you to move around your image; the Info palette provides information about cursor placement, the color under the cursor, and selection info; and the Options palette provides options for the different tools.

- **Color, Swatches, and Brushes.** These palettes enable you to choose brushes and to select colors.

- **History and Actions.** Here you can review the history of changes you've made, as well as create and run actions.

- **Layers, Channels, and Paths.** These palettes enable you to create and delete layers, channels, and paths.

FIGURE 1.5

The default palette setup.

1

As with the menus and the toolbox, the palettes are laid out in a logical fashion. Unlike the menus and the toolbox, though, you have some choices in how the palettes are shown. You can tear palettes away from one another and lay them out differently than the default.

Separating a Palette

To separate a palette, simply click and drag its title tab. In Figure 1.6, I've separated the Channels palette from the Layers and Paths palettes (shown in Figure 1.6), and I've moved it to the left of the existing palettes. This way I can, for example, see the channels and the layers as I work on an image.

 Note
To replace the palette, simply drag it by its tab and drop it back with the other palettes.

As with the other program functions, I'll describe the various options available to you in more detail in the days to follow.

FIGURE 1.6

Moving the Channels palette from its default setup.

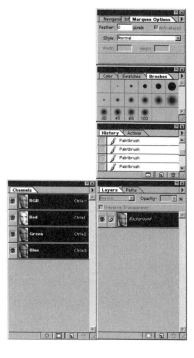

Shortcuts

Keyboard shortcuts are a software feature that many people rely on. I've been using a mouse since before most software even supported them and prefer to keep my hand on the mouse, or, even better still, on the graphic tablet's pen. Many people, though, like to use the shortcuts. Given that Photoshop has a shortcut for almost every available feature, I'll have to concede that it's a quick and easy method for applying options. I have even memorized a few over time. Ctrl+C, Ctrl+X, and Ctr+V (or Cmd+C, Cmd+X, and Cmd+V for you Macheads) have almost become second nature to me now that I do so much word processing.

The number of shortcuts available is almost as large as the total number of features and options. There are so many, in fact, that I'm not going to list them all here. What I will do is show you how and where they can be found.

In the menus, shortcuts are to the far right of a menu choice. In Figure 1.7, for example, you can see the shortcuts for the Edit menu options.

FIGURE 1.7

Menu keyboard shortcuts.

Shortcuts for the toolbox selections can be found by holding the mouse over a tool (see Figure 1.8).

FIGURE 1.8

Toolbox keyboard shortcuts.

Place your mouse above any tool to view its name and shortcut

After a second or so, a small ToolTip box appears below the mouse cursor. In this small box, you'll get a description of the tool and, at the far right, you'll see the tool's shortcut key.

Tip

To access an option via a keyboard shortcut, simply press the key or key combination listed. Note that the keyboard shortcuts are not case sensitive. Pressing Ctrl+n (Cmd+n) is the same as pressing Ctrl+N (Cmd+N). Of course, adding the Shift key changes which keyboard shortcut you access. Ctrl+D (Cmd+D) deselects a selection, while Ctrl-Shift+D (Cmd-Shift+D) reselects a selection. Note that the Ctrl key is analogous to the Command key on a Mac and that the Alt key would be the Option key on a Mac.

Note

You won't get the information for palette shortcuts this way, though. Any of the palette options that have shortcuts are found within the menus. Creating a new layer, for example, can be accomplished by clicking the small bent-cornered icon at the bottom of the Layers palette. However, you can also create a new layer with Layer, New, Layer. If you choose Layer, New, you'll see the shortcut (Shift-Ctrl+N for Windows, Shift-Cmd+N for Macintosh) at the right of the Layer choice.

Summary

Now that you know where the tools are, or more importantly how to find the tools, you'll be flying around this powerful, yet clean interface in no time.

You've seen how the menu is laid out at the top as with other window-based programs, where the toolbox is, and how to access the various tools within it. You've also seen how the palettes are grouped and how to change the groupings to fit your working needs. To help you maximize your time, you've also learned how some of the various shortcuts work.

Q&A

Q The figures in this book seem to have proportionally smaller text and icons than how they appear on my screen. Why is this?

A This is partly because of the difference in the resolution that I use and the size of my monitor. Certain options can be set, though. For example, you can change the size of the thumbnails that appear in the Layers, Channels, and Paths palettes. To do so, click the small black arrow to the right of the palette's name and select Palette options. In the dialog box that appears, select the thumbnail size.

Q It's great that I can turn off all my palettes while in Full Screen mode, but why can't I do this whenever I want?

A You can. Anytime you want to hide all your palettes and your toolbox so that you can concentrate on your image, simply press the Tab key. It toggles the palettes and toolbox on and off.

Workshop

Here's a quick chapter quiz. If you have any problems answering any of the questions, see the section directly following it for all the answers.

Quiz

1. Can I modify the work area in Photoshop?
2. How do you switch between the various Screen modes?
3. On the toolbox, what do the small black arrows indicate?
4. How do you separate a palette?
5. What are keyboard shortcuts?

Quiz Answers

1. Yes. You can change the screen itself by turning the menus, toolbox, and palettes off and on, and you can work in Full Screen mode. You can modify the different palettes as well.

2. You can switch between the various Screen modes by selecting one of the three icons at the bottom of the toolbox. You can also cycle through the modes by pressing the F key.

3. The small black arrows on a tool indicate that there are similar tools beneath the current tool. Holding the mouse over one of these tools brings out a flyout menu that displays, and enables you to select, the other tools.

4. You can separate the palettes by clicking and dragging a palette's tab.

5. Keyboard shortcuts are key combinations that enable you to use many of Photoshop's options and features. Using a shortcut bypasses having to wade through several levels of menus.

1

DAY 2

Customizing Photoshop Preferences

Although today will be a fairly short day, I suggest that you start to explore a little on your own once you have Photoshop installed and set up. This will help you become accustomed to the program and perhaps come up with some questions on your own that will likely be answered in the upcoming days. If you've played around a little and have some questions, when you get started on the following chapters, you'll probably be ahead of the game and find yourself going "Oh yeah!" rather than "Huh?" As each of your questions is answered, you'll find yourself building on your knowledge base of how Photoshop works and what can be accomplished with it. This chapter covers:

- Preferences for saving your images
- Setting up your display and cursors
- Working with rules, guides, and grids
- Working with the Memory options

Setting Your Preferences

Once Photoshop has been installed, the first thing you should do is check and set the preferences. You can find the Preferences menu under the File menu. You can also use the keyboard shortcut Ctrl-K (Cmd-K). This brings up another menu with the choices shown in Figure 2.1. Being able to set the different preferences enables you to customize Photoshop to the way you work, which can result in increased productivity.

FIGURE 2.1

The Preferences menu.

Aside from being able to set the General preferences, you can move through the other Preference setting dialog boxes as well. You can do this two ways (three really, if you count using the keyboard shortcuts). You can select a new Preference dialog box from the pulldown menu. By clicking the small black arrow to the right of the word General, you can select any of the other Preference settings. It's here that you'll also find the keyboard shortcut keys: Ctrl-1 (Cmd-1) for General, Ctrl-2 (Cmd-2) for saving files, and so on. You can also toggle through all the Preference dialog boxes by selecting either the Prev or the Next buttons. Doing so cycles through all the dialog boxes, one after another.

General Preferences

When you choose General from the Preferences menu, you'll get the dialog box you see in Figure 2.2. The following section describes each of the available options. One of the most important options is the Color Picker, so we'll start with that.

FIGURE 2.2

*The General
Preferences dialog
box.*

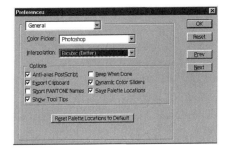

2

(Note) The Color Picker is the dialog box that enables you to select the foreground
and background colors (see Figure 2.3). To access the Color Picker, simply
click either the Foreground or Background Color swatches on your toolbox.

From the General Preferences dialog box, you can choose which Color Picker you wish
to use. The choices are Photoshop and Windows. I prefer the Photoshop Color Picker
because I like its flexibility and power. It gives you easier access to the colors and shows
you the values of the colors you're choosing in HSB (Hue, Saturation, and Brightness),
Lab, RGB (Red, Green, and Blue), and CYMK (Cyan, Yellow, Magenta, and Percentage
of blacK). I'll discuss color in depth on Day 16, "Correcting the Color." The Windows
Color Picker is more sparse, as you can see in Figure 2.4.

FIGURE 2.3

*The Photoshop Color
Picker dialog box.*

The Windows Color Picker gives you less control and even less information. Actually
there is no real information available in the standard Color Picker dialog box. There is
just a selection of 48 colors, a place for 16 custom colors, and a couple of buttons.
Selecting the Define Custom Colors button extends the standard dialog box as shown in
Figure 2.5.

FIGURE 2.4

*The Windows Color
Picker dialog box.*

FIGURE 2.5

*The extended Windows
Color Picker dialog
box.*

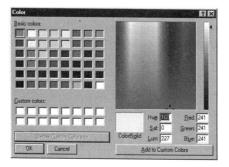

The extended Color Picker dialog box enables you to choose from millions of colors, as
does the Photoshop Color Picker, and gives you the HSB and RGB values for the color
you've selected. The reason that the dialog boxes differ is that Photoshop is geared
towards printing as well as onscreen display, while Windows is geared more for onscreen
display only. Either of the two settings is appropriate if you're working with images
meant for a computer screen. If, on the other hand, you need more flexibility, more information, or are working on images for print, you should stick with the Photoshop Color
Picker.

Aside from the Color Picker, you can decide which Interpolation method Photoshop
should use: Nearest Neighbor (Faster), Bilinear, or Bicubic (Better). This setting determines which method will be used to delete or add pixels when you use Photoshop to
resize, or resample, an image. The method you select determines the quality of the choices Photoshop makes. Although the Bicubic method is slower, it's not that much of a
problem on today's faster machines. I'd leave the default Bicubic method set.

The other options are somewhat less important and can pretty much be left at the default settings:

- **Export Clipboard option.** This allows information that you've cut or copied to the Clipboard to remain on the Clipboard after you've exited Photoshop. This information is then available to other applications.

  This option also enables the automatic conversion of the Clipboard contents to bitmap format when switching from Photoshop to another application. If you do not plan to copy and paste Clipboard information between Photoshop and other open applications, you won't have to wait for Photoshop to convert the Clipboard contents every time you access another application.

- **Short PANTONE Names.** This option is a way of ensuring compatibility when you'll be exporting Photoshop images to other imaging programs.

- **Show Tool Tips.** When checked, this option displays an extra bit of information when you move the cursor over different tools in the Tool palette. With the ToolTips active, you'll see a description of the tool that the mouse is over and its keyboard shortcut as well.

- **Beep When Done.** If you select this option, Photoshop sounds a beep whenever a task that uses a progress bar is completed.

- **Dynamic Color Sliders.** These enable and disable whether the color changes in the Color palette's sliders in real time as you move the arrows around to select a new color (see Figure 2.6). With the Dynamic Color Sliders option selected, the colors of the sliders, which are the three bars in the middle of Figure 2.6, change dynamically.

- **Save Palette Locations.** Selecting this option always ensures that Photoshop saves the location of the palettes that you've set during a session. If this option is not set, Photoshop starts with the palettes in the default positions.

FIGURE 2.6

The Photoshop Color palette.

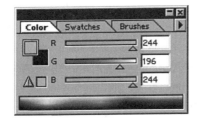

Note Settings such as Anti-alias Postscript are not something you'll come across often enough to matter that much. I'll discuss some of these settings as they come up. The anti-aliasing of Postscript, for example, is only important when you import an image from some other program. You might want to import an EPS file from CorelDRAW, for instance, and you can always decide at that time whether or not to anti-alias the Postscript file. Anti-aliasing, like bicubic interpolation, can take more time, but it results in a better image.

Saving Files

The Saving Files Preferences dialog box (see Figure 2.7) lets you set some of the options available when you save your work.

FIGURE 2.7

Saving Files Preferences.

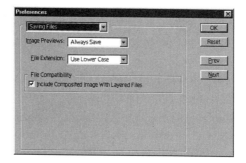

Your options in this dialog box include whether or not to save image previews, if Photoshop should use lowercase for the file extensions, and whether or not to use the File Compatibility option:

- **Never Save, Always Save, and Ask When Saving.** These are the choices for saving image previews. You can have Photoshop save a preview along with the image. I find this option a big help when searching through tons of files searching for something I created several weeks or months back. This option adds a little extra to the file size, but it can be a real time saver when you're searching for a file.

- **Lowercase Extension.** This option may not seem that important, but it has been a big issue in the Photoshop newsgroup on the Internet. To help with compatibility, Adobe has included this option with Photoshop 5, which is sure to make many Photoshop users happy. The problem lies in the way that UNIX machines handle filenames (most Web servers run on UNIX machines). UNIX is case sensitive, so most people are used to the default file extensions being in lowercase. Photoshop 4 chose to use uppercase as the default, which meant having to manually change the file extensions or risk having your images not come up on your Web pages.

- **File Compatibility.** This enables you to select whether or not Photoshop includes a composited image with layered files. Selecting this option means that a composite version of the file is saved along with the separate layers. Again, this increases the file size, but it assures compatibility of your Photoshop files with other programs. As well, it enables users of versions of Photoshop prior to version 3 to open files saved with the current version. This option saves a copy of the flattened, or composited, data.

Display & Cursors

The Display & Cursors Preferences dialog box (see Figure 2.8) enables you to set some options for the screen display and the cursors.

FIGURE 2.8

The Display & Cursors preferences.

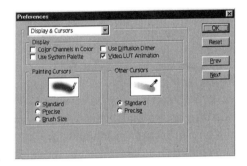

The Display Options

The first of the four radio buttons enables you to choose whether or not you'll see the Color channels in color or in grayscale. This is a matter of choice more than anything else. Because it's so easy to change, you can set it to color if, for example, you'll be doing some extensive work on an image within the Channels palette. This can help you keep track of which channel you're working on. I'll be discussing channels at length on Day 12, "Working with Channels."

The Use Diffusion Dither option is important if you work on a system with a limited color display. If your system is limited to 8-bit (256 colors), you should set this option to On to get a better quality display of your images.

You can set the Use System palette to use your system's palette instead of the Photoshop palette. Using the system palette makes the display of inactive images more accurate.

The Video LUT Animation determines whether or not Photoshop uses video LUT (look up tables). This option, when set, enables faster previewing of color adjustments. Normally this only works in 256-color mode.

Note On the Macintosh, you should turn off Video LUT Animation unless you have the proper video driver support for it. Otherwise, with Video LUT Animation enabled, the entire screen is controlled by any adjustment tool unless Preview is checked.

The Cursor Options

The two different Cursor preferences enable you to choose what the cursor will look like. You can set the Cursor preferences for the Painting cursors and for others as well. You can get an idea of what the choices are like because this dialog box shows you a preview of the different cursors.

For Painting cursors, you can choose Standard, which leaves the cursor looking like the tool you're using. When you're using the Paintbrush, for example, the cursor resembles a small paintbrush, and when you're using the Pencil, the cursor resembles a small pencil. The next choice enables you to set the cursor to Precise. This option turns the cursor into a small crosshair. This is great for precise, detailed work. The final option for the Paintbrush cursor is Brush size. With this option selected, the cursor adjusts its size depending on the Brush size you set for the Painting tool. This can help, for example, when you're painting color into different areas of an image. You should play with each of these options to get a feel for them and for when you might want to use one over another.

The Other Cursors option enables you to set either Standard or Precise for cursors other than the Painting tools. Again I encourage you to play with the settings, so you'll get a feeling for which choice is better under a given circumstance.

Setting the Cursor Options

To try out the different cursors, open a new file, set the cursor, select the Paintbrush, and draw something on the image. Then go back to the Preferences dialog box, change the Cursor setting, and draw on the image again. Change the Brush size (open the Brushes palette) and see how this affects the cursor if you've chosen the Brush Size option.

Transparency & Gamut

The Transparency & Gamut Preferences dialog box (see Figure 2.9) enables you to set up how the transparent background layer looks when you leave it as transparent. It also lets you set the Gamut Warning color.

FIGURE 2.9

*Transparency &
Gamut preferences.*

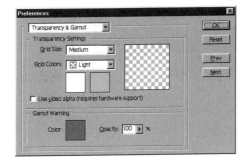

When you open a new Photoshop image, you have the option of leaving the background layer transparent. Because the image, or the background layer, is transparent, there is nothing to see, right? However, something must be displayed. The default setting uses a gray and white grid, as seen in Figure 2.10, to display the transparent layer.

FIGURE 2.10

The transparent layer.

In the Transparency & Gamut dialog box, you can set the size of the grid, whether it's darker or lighter, and even change the gray to a color. Play around to see which display suits you.

The Gamut option enables you to set which color is used to warn you of out-of-gamut range colors—that is, when you've selected a color that displays onscreen but has no printable counterpart. For more information on the Gamut option, see Day 16.

Units & Rulers

In the Units & Rulers Preferences dialog box (see Figure 2.11), you can set which units Photoshop uses for the rulers. If, for example, you do a lot of screen work, you might want to choose pixels as the default.

FIGURE 2.11

Units & Rulers preferences.

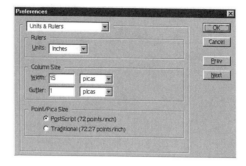

Figure 2.12 shows what an image looks like with the rulers visible. Here the rulers are set to pixels.

FIGURE 2.12

An image with rulers visible.

Using the options in this dialog box, you can also set the Column size of the grid. The Column Size and Gutter Size settings are used by the File, New command or by any command in which you can specify the units used. If you intend to use the image in a page layout program and know how many columns the image will span, you can enter the width of said column here, as well as the gutter width. Then when you adjust your image width in Photoshop using the "columns" unit for the width, Photoshop uses the values you entered in this preference box to correctly calculate the image's size.

Guides & Grid

You can use the Guides & Grid Preferences dialog box (see Figure 2.13) to set the various options for the guides and grids.

You can choose between lines, dashed lines, and dots for the grid, and you can also set the grid's color. This is helpful if you have trouble seeing one color over another when the grid is visible. Figure 2.14 shows an image with the grid turned on.

2

FIGURE 2.13

Guides & Grid preferences.

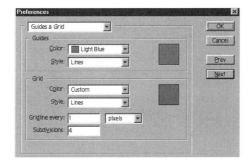

FIGURE 2.14

An image with the grid visible.

You can use the grids to help you with placing images precisely. You can choose to have objects snap to the grid as well. Choose View, Snap To Grid if you want to enable this option. You can toggle this option off and on via the View menu. The Snap To Grid option enables you to line up tools more easily. As you move toward a gridline, the tool snaps into place on the grid line or the subdivision line. The subdivisions are the number of spaces between the major gridlines.

Plug-Ins & Scratch Disks

From the Plug-Ins & Scratch Disks Preferences dialog box (see Figure 2.15), you can choose which directory your plug-ins are stored in and which disks to use for a scratch area. You could, for example, choose a second hard drive on your system that has more available space or is faster.

FIGURE 2.15

*Plug-Ins & Scratch
Disks preferences.*

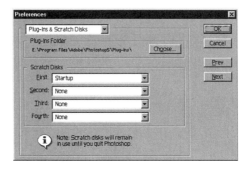

Plug-ins are built-in and third-party extensions to Photoshop. These plug-ins enable you to use special effects on images. For example, one of the built-in effects gives you the ability to render clouds. Using this filter, you can add a cloudy sky to a washed-out sky.

Note

When you change the directory in which Photoshop searches for the plug-ins, the change will only take effect once you've restarted Photoshop.

Scratch disks are used by Photoshop when it needs more memory than is available. You have the choice to set up to four scratch disks. If your start-up drive is quite full, you can set the scratch disk to another of your system's hard drives.

Memory & Image Cache

You have the option of setting how much memory Photoshop can use. You can set this option in the Memory & Image Cache Preferences dialog box (see Figure 2.16).

Note

This Memory setting is available only to Windows users. If you're using a Macintosh, you must close Photoshop in order to set your Memory preferences. After you've closed Photoshop, simply navigate to the directory where Photoshop is stored, click the name to highlight it, and choose Get Info from the File menu. In the Info dialog box that appears, you can set both the minimum and preferred memory sizes.

FIGURE 2.16

Memory & Image Cache preferences.

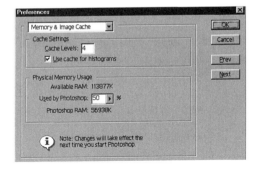

2

Playing with these settings can have an effect on the performance of not only Photoshop, but any other programs you are running as well. Unless you have a very slow system or a system with a small amount of RAM, you may want to leave these settings at their defaults.

Some users recommend that you set the physical memory used by Photoshop to 100% of the physical RAM, which allocates faster physical RAM to Photoshop. Photoshop performs faster if it has access to all the physical RAM before it must access the scratch disk, which is much slower.

Summary

As I stated earlier, this was a fairly short day. Even though it's difficult to know at this point exactly how to best set up all of your preferences, it will help you in the long run to try out some of them now. The more you play around with Photoshop, the more comfortable you'll become when working and playing with it.

Q&A

Q Are there any major differences between the Mac and the PC versions of Photoshop?

A Aside from the Command/Ctrl and Option/Alt keys, there are no significant differences in the interface. Some differences exist in the way that memory usage is set, because this is more OS dependent.

Q Which Color Picker should I use?

A You should try both the System Color Picker and Photoshop's Color Picker, and go with the one you feel most comfortable with.

Workshop

Here is a quick quiz. If you have any problems answering any of the questions in the quiz, see the section directly following it for all the answers.

Quiz

1. How do you access the General Preferences menu?

2. How do you save files with a lowercase extension?

3. Where do you set up the file-saving preferences?

4. How do you choose which unit of measurement to use as your default?

5. How do you turn your grids off and on?

Quiz Answers

1. You can access the General Preferences dialog box by choosing File, Preferences, General.

2. Yes. This is the option to set either uppercase or lowercase in the File, Preferences, Saving Files dialog box. As well, you can specify when saving the file.

3. Choose File Preferences, Saving Files.

4. You can choose the default unit of measurement by selecting File, Preferences, Units & Rulers and selecting the units you wish to use.

5. You can toggle the grids on and off by choosing View, Show Grid/Hide Grid.

DAY 3

Checking Out the
New 5.0 Features

This book covers the majority of Photoshop's features, including many of the features and options new to version 5. Instead of demonstrating all of the new features in this chapter, I'll briefly describe them, and point to the various places in the rest of the book where you can find out more information about them. There are a couple of features that I may cover here, though, as they don't really fit into the other chapters.

Photoshop 5 "feels" different. You can work smarter not harder. Adobe has taken an already excellent product and made it even more intuitive. The new tools, options, and features really do make a difference in the day-to-day running of the program. This chapter overviews the following new features:

- Improved color management
- The History palette (multiple levels of undo)
- Version 5's new tools
- Enhanced actions capabilities
- The new text editor

Color Management

Adobe has made great strides toward helping users make certain that their color images will display and print with some certainty that the final color will look like what they expect them to. Here's what Adobe's done to help with that process:

- All of the color settings dialog boxes have been upgraded and improved. The changes include being able to embed color settings with files. As well, users will be able to specify more settings for RGB, CMYK, and grayscale images.

- Users can now specify RGB and CMYK color spaces using ICC profiles.

- Images can be saved with ICC tags. This means that any system using Photoshop 5 can read these ICC tags when opening the image files.

- If the user is not using ICC for CMYK images, the Dot Gain Curves can be defined in the CMYK setup.

- Support for non-monitor RGB has been added. This means that the RGB color space used for editing images can be different than that set for the user's monitor. You can compensate for the differences in the RGB setup dialog.

- There's a new Gamma setup program included (see Day 7, "Calibrating Your System and Setting Color Modes," for instructions on setting up your monitor's gamma). This new setup program will enable you to save an ICC profile.

- The custom inks setup in the CMYK Setup dialog can allow Lab coordinates and includes two new color swatches for the white-and-black points.

- Users can now use Image, Mode, Profile-to-Profile to do on-the-fly conversions between different color spaces.

Note	For more information about color settings, see Day 7.

The History Palette

The History palette is an exciting new feature similar to, but far more powerful than, multiple undo. This palette enables you to step back through a series of steps that you've applied to your images. More than that, though, you can use this palette, and its features, in conjunction with the History Brush to perform tricks previously unavailable.

The History palette is a major addition to Photoshop. In previous versions there was only one undo available. If you made more than one change to an image, you were stuck with all but the most recent. Users can now "walk" backwards through the changes they've made.

To get acquainted with working with the new multiple-undo feature, let's try the following:

1. Open a new 400×200 RGB image at 72 dpi with the contents set to White.

2. Choose Window, Show History to turn on the History palette (see Figure 3.1). Notice that the only item currently visible is the "New" item. This is a result of your having opened a new file.

FIGURE 3.1

The History palette.

Click here to set the source for the History brush

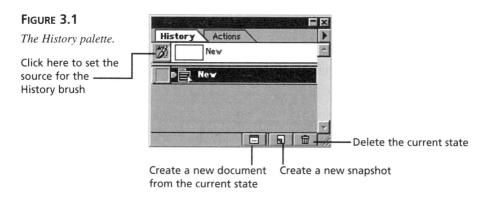

Create a new document from the current state · Create a new snapshot · Delete the current state

3. Click on the foreground color swatch in the toolbox and, using the Color picker dialog box, choose a bright red color.

4. Select the Airbrush tool and choose a wide brush from the Brushes palette (choose Window, Show Brushes if the Brushes palette is not currently visible).

5. Draw a vertical line down the left side of the image. You should see a new entry in the History palette signifying the use of the Airbrush tool.

6. Click the foreground color swatch and choose a bright green color.

7. Draw another line to the right of the first line. Again you'll notice an entry for the Airbrush tool is made in the History palette.

8. Set the foreground color to blue and draw a third line. You should now have three vertical lines drawn on your image (see Figure 3.2).

FIGURE **3.2**

*Three beautifully
airbrushed lines.*

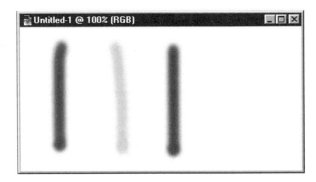

As well, you'll notice that there is a total of four entries in the History palette, one
for New (from creating the image) and one each for the three separate times you
used the Airbrush tool.

9. Click the title of the topmost Airbrush entry and you'll see the second and third
   lines disappear. To bring them back, select the bottom Airbrush entry.

What you just did in step 9 was step back to the point before you had added the second
and third lines. If you want, you could remove these steps all together. All you have to
do is drag and drop the entries, starting with the bottommost, onto the small trashcan
icon at the bottom right of the History palette.

If you start further up the chain, though, and drag and drop an entry onto the trashcan
icon, you'll delete the "states" and not the result of the states. This may be a little hard to
visualize at first, but it will become more clear to you as you start to understand the awesome power of this new feature.

One thing that would change if you deleted the states without removing the results of
creating the states would be that you'd be removing the ability to go back with the
History brush and affect changes with it.

The History Brush

The History Brush is almost magical in its abilities. To see what I mean, select the
History Brush tool from the toolbox and click on the blank icon to the left of the topmost
Airbrush entry. This will set the source for the History Brush.

Now click-and-drag across the image from the left of the lines over to the right (make
sure you go over the lines you drew). WOW! The first line remains intact, yet the second
and third lines disappear where you dragged the History brush through them (see
Figure 3.3).

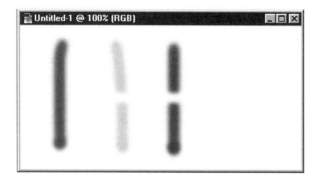

FIGURE 3.3

The History Brush has affected the second and third lines.

What's happening is that you're using the state where the second and third lines didn't exist as the source for the History Brush. Because of this the background appears under the areas where you drag the brush. Remember, at the time of the first airbrush entry the second and third lines did not exist.

Click the empty icon to the left of the second airbrush entry and drag the brush over the image again at a different position than in the last case. This time the first and second lines remain intact while the third line is affected.

The History palette is indeed a tool far more powerful than just a multiple undo and is far more advanced than I can demonstrate in this one chapter. I think whole lessons will appear around this new feature as digital artists explore the options and features this new tool presents.

Support for 16-Bit Channels

Photoshop now has support for 16-bit channels. 16-bit channels can hold more information than 8-bit channels and, in previous versions of Photoshop, you were restricted to less options with 16-bit channels than with 8-bit channels. Adobe has added the following options for images with 16-bit channels:

- Hue/Saturation, Brightness/Contrast, Color Balance, Equalize, Invert, and Channel Mixer options can be applied to 16-bit images.
- The Crop, Rubber Stamp, and History Brush tools can be used with 16-bit images.
- Image Size and Edit, Image, Rotate Canvas, Arbitrary can now be used with 16-bit images.

Layer Effects

Adobe has added a couple of new effects that can be used on different layers. These include Drop Shadow, Inner Shadow, Inner Glow, and Outer Glow. As well, there are effects for Bevel and Emboss, including Inner Bevel, Outer Bevel, Emboss, and Pillow Emboss.

 Note | I'll demonstrate some of these new features on Day 15, "Applying Filter Effects."

New Tools

Photoshop has a number of new tools that make your work easier. These include:

- **Color Sampler tool.** Enables you to sample four different colors from within your image.

- **Magnetic Lasso and Magnetic Pen tools.** Enable you to more easily create selections because these new tools snap the selection to the edges of your image.

- **Freeform Pen tool.** Enables you to draw freeform paths.

- **Measure tool.** Enables you to measure areas of your image. This tool can also measure angles.

- **Vertical Type tool.** Enables you to enter vertical type.

- **Vertical Type Mask tool.** Enables you to mask out vertical type.

- **Pattern Stamp tool.** Enables you to draw with predefined patterns.

- **Angle Gradient, Diamond Gradient, and Reflective Gradient tools.** Enable you to create special-effects gradients.

Type Layers

Adobe has completely changed how type works in Photoshop. Type is now kept on a different type (no pun intended) layer until you decide to render it. With the type on a type layer the text remains editable, and you can mix and match fonts and sizes. To edit your text, simply double-click on the type layer. As well, Adobe has added a Vertical Type tool and a Vertical Type Mask tool. You can now resize the type dialog box, too.

- The Horizontal and Vertical Type tools create type layers that can be re-edited by double-clicking the layer entry in the Layers palette.
- Users can adjust Kerning or use Auto Kerning.
- Users can set Tracking, Leading, and Baseline shift.
- Users can use multiple fonts, styles, and sizes for each type layer.
- There is full support for single- and double-byte characters.
- You have the ability to see a real-time preview of the text on the image as well as the ability to reposition the text.
- The dialog box is resizable and zoomable.
- There is a rotate option for vertical type.
- The type orientation can be set in the Type submenu in the Layer menu.
- Type layers can be transformed and can include layer effects.

Note

You will learn more about the new type features on Day 14, "Typing in Great Type Effects."

New Adjustments/Adjustment Layers

Version 5 has an improved Hue/Saturation dialog box, which enables the adjustment of any selected color. In previous versions you could not perform Hue/Saturation adjustments on separate colors with the same degree of precision as you can in version 5.

The Channel Mixer enables the color channels to be redefined using a custom mix of the existing channels.

Note

You can find more on channels in Day 12, "Working with Channels."

Spot Color Support

Spot color channels can now be added to an image using the new Spot Channel command in the Channels palette. The Merge Spot Channel will merge spot channels into the existing CMYK or RGB channels.

As well, duotones converted into Multichannel mode are now converted as spot channels.

Improved Actions Scripting

The Actions palette enables you to record and play back a series of steps. Using this option, you can perform a set of changes once and record the steps. This set of steps, or action, can then be saved and played back on other images. This is a great way to save time. You can also share your actions with others as well as download actions from the Internet.

The following commands, tools, and functions can now be recorded using the Actions palette:

- The Paths, Layers, and History palettes
- The Gradient, Marquee, Crop, Polygon, Lasso, Line, Move, Magic Wand, Paint Bucket, and Type tools
- The Apply, Image and the File, Info commands
- Lighting effects
- Calculations (which allow you to combine channels into new channels or new images)
- Switching and selecting documents
- Free Transform

As well, you'll find that more menus are "Insert Menu Item" savvy, meaning that you have the ability to insert more menu items into an action.

 Note   You can read more about actions on Day 18, "Saving Time with Actions."

3D Transform

By using the Filter, Render, 3D Transform command, you can select portions of an image and manipulate them as if they were 3D objects.

Figures 3.4 and 3.5 demonstrate this feature. Figure 3.4 is an illustration created with CorelDRAW and exported/imported into Photoshop; Figure 3.5 is the illustration 3D-transformed onto a sphere.

FIGURE 3.4

Yippee illustration.

FIGURE 3.5

Yippee illustration 3D-transformed onto a sphere.

File Format Additions

There are new file formats supported by version 5, as well as extended functionality for exisiting file formats. These include:

- Flashpix Import/Export.
- PDF support, including import and rasterization of PDF files, ability to control JPG and ZIP compression when saving PDF files, and ability to import multiple PDF files.
- DCS 2.0 support including saving separations and spot/alpha channels.

Transformation Improvements

The Free Transform option enables you to scale, add perspective, and more. In version 5 there are some additions and improvements to this feature. These new additions are

- The Free Transform now has a centerpoint for rotation.
- There is a new Repeat Last Transform command available from the menu.
- Selections can now be transformed.
- Paths can also be transformed.

All of the transform commands except for the Selection, Transform command are in the Edit menu instead of the Layer menu.

Other New Features

Along with all of the changes and additions described above, there is a collection of miscellaneous features that have been added to Photoshop 5. These include:

- The View, Preview submenu now includes separate preview modes for individual CMYK plates.
- Improved quality for 8-bit RGB-to-CMYK conversions.
- It's easier to align linked layers through the use of Layer, Align Linked and Layer, Distribute Linked menu choices.
- The Select, Re-select command will re-select the most recent selection.
- Improved quality for Indexed Color conversion.
- Postscript 3 support.
- Actions plug-ins, a new plug-in type that enables the control of complicated tasks.
- Option to save files with lowercase extension (default), which is available in the Save and Save As dialog boxes.
- Edition Manager no longer used in the Macintosh version of Photoshop.
- Faster saving of large files with thumbnails.
- Now saves Mac and PC thumbnails separately.
- Pressure-sensitive graphics tablets no longer need plug-ins.
- New options in Save a Copy make it easier to exclude certain information.
- Brush Size can now be as large as 32,000×32,000 pixels on the Mac.

User Interface Changes and Improvements

Along with the other changes that Adobe has made to Photoshop, it has also tweaked the interface to help you use it more effectivley. The changes they've made are

- New Status item for the currently active tool.
- More complete Windows help strings for tools.
- Tools show cancel sign when they can't be used. Double-clicking on the tool will tell why this is the case.

- All of the dragging-based selection tools get spacebar hand scrolling mode and -/+ zoom in and out behavior.
- Option key version of Apply Image dialog deleted.
- Target for Calculations restricted to: New Document, New Channel, and Selection
- New Edit, Purge, History command.
- New Edit, Purge All command.
- Files, Adobe Online command provides a new interface to Adobe on the Web.
- The clipping path controls are no longer available in the EPS format options dialog box. Instead you can access the clipping path in the Paths palette. This means access to clipping paths via actions.
- Small Calculations dialog is gone.
- Save Selection dialog allows naming of the new channel.

Summary

There will be some people who will argue that version 5 should be a point release. However, after having worked quite extensively with it over the last couple of months, I would argue that this new version contains enough small and large changes to warrant a new version number. I'm sure you'll find, as I do, that using Photoshop—and its new features—becomes almost second nature.

Q&A

Q Where else can I find more information about Photoshop 5's new features?

A A good place to start would be Adobe's Web site (`http://www.adobe.com`). You can also try some of the more popular Photoshop Web sites, such as GrafX Design at `http://www.grafx-design.com`, which includes links to other like-minded sites.

Workshop

The following section is a quick quiz about the chapter you have just read. If you have any problems answering any of the questions in the quiz, see the section directly following it for all of the answers.

Quiz

1. How do you access the new History palette?
2. What is the function of the History Brush?
3. What are the new layer effects?

4. Describe the major advantage that working with text in version 5 has over working with text in version 4?

5. How do you save files with a lowercase extension?

Quiz Answers

1. Choose Window, Show History.

2. The History Brush enables you to make changes to an image based on the history of changes you've made to the image.

3. They include Drop Shadow, Inner Shadow, Inner and Outer Bevel, and Inner and Outer Glow.

4. The major advantage of working with text in version 5 over older versions is that the text remains editable.

5. This option is on by default but it can be set within the Save and Save As dialog boxes.

DAY 4

Getting a Handle on File Types

Photoshop is capable of reading and writing many file formats. It can also use many different modes when operating on an image. This chapter is a primer on the different file types available to you as you use Photoshop to create and manipulate your images. More specifically, this chapter includes the following:

- Definition of file formats
- An explanation of Photoshop's native PSD format
- Comparison of the most often used file formats and how to use them to your advantage

File Formats

These days, many file formats are available—so many, in fact, that Photoshop alone has several different options for saving your work. Given so many options, making a decision about which format best suits a given need is difficult. Sometimes you have a choice and sometimes you don't. For example, you can choose to save your work in either the GIF or JPEG format because the Web recognizes both. If you're working in CorelDRAW, however, you can't choose to save your artwork in the native file format and then import it into Photoshop because Photoshop doesn't read CorelDRAW's native file format (in which case, you'd have to export your CorelDRAW art as an EPS file).

FIGURE 4.1

Just some of Photoshop's compatible file formats.

There are many reasons why you have to use one format instead of another, but, unfortunately, this chapter can't document all of them. What it can do, however, is provide you with an overview of the most common image file formats as well as guidance about the situations where one particular format is better suited than others. Of all the formats that Photoshop supports, you'll need to understand the formats covered in the following sections.

PSD

Saving a file in PSD format preserves all the layers, masks, channels, and selections you created (you'll learn about these in various sections throughout the book). You can also save caption and copyright information. If there's even a remote possibility that you'll need to rework, update, or change an image you've created with Photoshop, it's wise to keep a copy of the file in PSD format. The one drawback with PSD files is their size. Because they keep all of the layer, channel, and other information, they can be quite large. Other than that, though, there is no reason not to keep copies of your most important images in PSD format.

FIGURE 4.2

Choose File, File Info to save captions, credits, and copyright information.

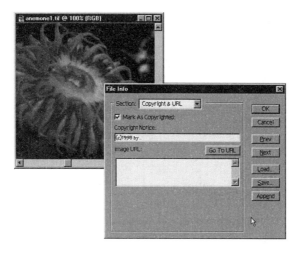

Note

In addition to saving captions, credits, and copyright information for your images (regardless of the file format), you can to choose to include keywords and categories for searching, as well as information about the origin of the image. All of this information is created and updated in the File Info dialog box, which can be accessed by choosing File, File Info.

4

BMP

BMP is the file format native to Windows and OS/2 machines. BMP (for bitmap) is an uncompressed file format that stores the pixels and their color information. This is a good format to use if you need to share files with other Windows users who may not have Photoshop.

PCX

The PCX file format is another PC format. PCX files are compressed, though, and are smaller than their BMP counterparts.

PICT

PICT is a file format that is native to the Mac system. If you need to exchange files with another Mac user that may not have Photoshop, PICT would be a good choice.

Photoshop 5 now makes it possible for users to save their images with low-ercase extensions. This is especially important when working with files for Web output because some programs and platforms are case sensitive when it comes to filenames. For example, image.tif and image.TIF are not read the same way. For more information about setting the preferences for file extensions, see Day 2, "Customizing Photoshop Preferences."

EPS

EPS (Encapsulated PostScript) is a good choice for transferring files between CorelDRAW and Photoshop. Photoshop can't read CDR (the native CorelDRAW file format), but it does a great job of reading EPS files. You can export a CDR file in EPS and read the resulting file into Photoshop. I often use this trick to export/import images from CorelDRAW into Photoshop. The EPS format works with both PC and Macintosh platforms.

TIFF

TIFF (Tagged Image File Format) is a good cross-platform format that uses LZW compression (LZW are the initials of the mathematicians who created the compression algorithm). This is a good choice if you need to save an Alpha channel with selection information; TIFF files can save one Alpha channel.

JPEG

JPEG images are 24-bit, or 16.7 million color images. Because of the color depth available in the JPEG format, JPEG is a good choice for photographs and images with smooth gradients or blends.

JPEG (Joint Photographic Experts Group) is a much misunderstood file format. This is due to its "lossy" nature. By losing, or throwing away actually, some of the information in a digital image, the JPEG format can achieve remarkable file compression. Compression rates of up to 100:1 are possible. As you raise the level of compression, though, you lose image quality. It's up to you to determine how small the compression can be versus how much quality loss you can put up with, as well as the circumstances under which you'll be displaying the image.

The other option to consider is the type of JPEG. You can choose from Baseline, Baseline Optimized, and Progressive. The difference between Baseline and Baseline Optimized is that the latter optimizes the color quality. Again, though, you may want to save a couple of images in both formats and inspect them to see what, if any, the differences in file size and image quality are. Figures 4.3 and 4.4 show you two copies of the same image; one was saved with Baseline Standard and the other was saved with Baseline Optimized. Notice the differences in the quality? Probably not.

There is a bit of savings in file size with the Baseline Optimized file, but not all browsers support the Optimized format. Both of these files were saved at a fairly low quality setting, as well, yet both are still acceptable in quality.

FIGURE 4.3

Image saved as Baseline Standard JPEG. File size: 93KB.

FIGURE 4.4

Image saved as Baseline Optimized JPEG. File size: 88KB.

Lossy refers to the compression method used by the JPEG file format. When compressing an image, the JPEG actually discards, or loses, some of the information in the graphic. Although some of the information is lost, this format can result in huge savings in file size. When this technique is used on photographic-type images, the missing information is not readily apparent to the human eye.

GIF

GIF (Graphical Interchange Format) is a file format that was developed initially for CompuServe members to be able to trade images back and forth online. This aging format is still around today and has enjoyed a new resurgence as a result of its capability to display animation. GIF files hold many frames that can be displayed one after the other. This capability has made GIF a popular choice for the Web.

Creating animations is a fairly simple process, especially if you create the frames in Photoshop. Once you've created an image with each layer holding a new frame, you can save the file in native PSD format and import it into an animation program, such as GIF Movie Gear from Gamani. Once you've imported the image, you can set the timing of each frame and perform the other steps necessary to change the file into an animation that can be viewed by virtually any Web browser. One of the drawbacks with the GIF format is that it can only display 8-bit, or 256-color, images.

One nice feature of the latest GIF specification, GIF89a, is the ability to choose a color that will not display—that is, a color that will be transparent when placed over another image. This is useful if you want your image to appear in a shape other than a square or rectangle. The GIF89a format is often used on the Web when a page has a background pattern the designer wants to be visible through parts of the graphic.

PDF

PDF, the Portable Document Format, is another file format from Adobe. Photoshop can export PDF files and, by using this format, you can create page layouts that can be read on any computer platform via a free reader, Adobe Acrobat Reader. This reader can even be run as a browser plug-in, making it possible to store and read PDF documents directly on the Web. Using Photoshop, you can create simple page layouts. You can use images, photos, text, and anything else that you require to create online documents.

The PDF format makes it possible to print files easily as well. You can put these documents on the Web or email them to someone who can then print the file.

Using PDF, it's also entirely possible to create online manuals and presentations. Another separate package available from Adobe, called Acrobat, makes it easy to create PDF files. With the Acrobat package and the utilities it contains, you can create PDF documents by simply choosing File, Print from most of your programs. You also have the option of password protecting any changes to your documents.

Comparing File Sizes

Whichever file format you choose, size will always be a concern. This is true if you'll be saving the file under several different formats for different purposes and even more so when creating Web graphics. Figure 4.5 shows an 8-inch×11-inch 72 dpi image.

FIGURE 4.5

8-inch×11-inch 72 dpi image.

The following table shows the file sizes of Figure 4.5 when the file is saved using different file formats.

File Format	File Size	Notes
PSD	435,836	Nine layers no extra channels
BMP	1,368,632	No compression
PCX	256,873	Lossless compression
PICT	214,812	32 bits/pixel
EPS	3,807,900	TIFF preview mode, ASCII encoding
TIFF	166,480	LZW lossless compression
JPEG	47,995	Medium quality (3) lossy compression, baseline standard
GIF	41,182	256 colors lossless compression, adaptive palette
PDF	60,635	Encoded as JPEG with Quality of 3 (Medium)

This example image has few colors, so it compressed well as a GIF. In fact, this particular image compressed better as a GIF than it did as a JPEG. This wouldn't be the case with a photo-quality image, though. Even with nine layers, the PSD file size wasn't too large. Again, you'll need to try this with different images that are more representative of the type that you work with. You may be surprised with the results.

Other File Formats

Many other file formats are available under File, Open; File, Save As; or File, Save a Copy. Many of these are there to facilitate moving your file between systems and other imaging software. If you have to move a PSD file from your system to another that may not have Photoshop, you can often save your file in another format that the other system is able to read. Even if the other system has an imaging program with a native file format that Photoshop doesn't write, chances are there is a format that the two programs have in common.

Summary

This chapter covered the basics of file types. File types, or file formats, describe the format in which files are saved to your hard disk. Many file formats are available to you when you use Photoshop. So many are available, in fact, that you may never use all of them. The ones I've described in this chapter, however, should be enough to get you started.

Q&A

Q **Are there any special concerns for saving PSD files that are being edited in both the Macintosh and Windows versions of Photoshop? Are the two platforms exactly the same?**

A You should be able to transport PSD files in both directions; there should be no difference in the files. You might want to add the PSD file extension if you're moving a file from the Mac to the PC, though.

Q **I created a text graphic in Illustrator. What do I need to do with it in Illustrator in order to open and edit it in Photoshop?**

A You could save the image as an AI (native Illustrator file) that Photoshop can recognize and open. Optionally, you could click and drag the image from Illustrator to Photoshop.

Q **Is it possible to save a Photoshop image in the GIF89a file format?**

A Yes and no. It is possible, but rather than "saving" the image, you must "export" it. Instead of choosing File, Save you must choose File, Export. It's preferable to change the image's mode to Indexed (choose Image, Mode, Indexed) before exporting it. This will enable you to use all of the GIF89a options. For more information about this topic, see Day 21, "Preparing Your Art for the Web."

Workshop

The section that follows is a quick quiz about this chapter. If you have any problems answering any of the questions in the quiz, see the section directly following it for all the answers.

Quiz

1. Which file type should you always save your images in to preserve the layers and channels?

2. What is the PDF format?

3. What's the difference between lossy compression and lossless compression?

4. What is the color limitation of a GIF image?

5. What are the native Windows and Macintosh file formats?

Quiz Answers

1. You should always save a copy of your file in Photoshop's native PSD format if you want to preserve the layers and channels.

2. The PSD format is the native Photoshop file format. It preserves all the layers and channels created with your image.

3. Lossy compression means that the algorithm used to compress the image discards some information to help achieve large compression ratios. Lossless compression keeps all the original information but doesn't achieve the same compression ratio.

4. A GIF image can only have up to 256 colors. Most other formats contain up to 16.7 million colors.

5. The native Mac file format is PICT and the native Windows format is BMP.

DAY 5

Importing Existing Images and Creating New Ones

Now that you've learned your way around the interface, set up your preferences, gotten a handle on some of the new features, and learned a little about file formats, it's time to get some images into Photoshop so you can start correcting and manipulating them.

There are many ways and places you can acquire images, and that's what this chapter is all about. You'll learn about the following:

- Taking photographs with a digital camera
- Scanning images into your computer
- Creating images from scratch

Digital Cameras

Digital cameras don't use film; rather, they store the photographic information digitally on memory chips in the camera. Once the information is in the camera, you can copy it to a computer and manipulate the photos there with your favorite bitmap program. You can manipulate the color, resize them, and add any effects you'd like.

The quality is not quite what you'd get from a 35mm camera, but, considering the state of the technology, the quality is quite acceptable. Figure 5.1 is a digital view of my workspace I took with my Casio QV-100. This particular model can store about 64 640×480, 24-bit images, or about 192 320×240 24-bit images.

FIGURE 5.1

I do get away from the computer every once and a while; it just feels like I live in front of it.

Note

For Windows users, most digital cameras come with TWAIN drivers that enable your TWAIN aware software, such as Photoshop and Paint Shop Pro, to import the image. TWAIN, in case you're interested, stands for Technology Without An Interesting Name. It's amazing the things you'll learn from a book on technology. This one's a real conversation stopper at parties.

If you're using a Macintosh, you don't have to worry about terms such as TWAIN. You can simply use existing SCSI-I external ports to connect most scanners.

Now that you've seen my digital workspace, let's take a step outside and take a look at some digital flowers (see Figure 5.2). Although the carnations are beautiful as a photograph, it might be fun to see what they look like as a watercolor. If you'd like to work through this exercise, you'll find the image on the accompanying CD.

The quality of the digital photo is okay, but it's not as good as the quality you might expect from scanning 8×10 prints from 35mm film. The quality is good enough, however, to play around with and learn a little about the filters that come with Photoshop.

FIGURE 5.2

Carnations photographed with a Casio QV-100 digital camera.

Opening an Existing Image and Applying a Filter

1. In Photoshop, choose File, Open and browse to the folder that contains the image Carnations.psd.

2. Double-click the image name or click the image name and then click Open.

3. Now choose Filter, Artistic, Underpainting, to instantly turn the digital carnations into an image that resembles a watercolor painting (see Figure 5.3).

I'll bet you didn't know that art had suddenly become that easy. Okay, okay, I'll admit it's not high-end art, but as an example of what someone artistically challenged can do with a couple of mouse clicks it's pretty good.

4. If you'd like, you can continue to explore the filters, choose Edit, Undo to get back to the original digital photo. Then you can try some of other filters, including Artistic, Brush Strokes, Sketch, Stylize, and Texture. Simply navigate to the Filter menu and select the filter effect you want to try. After you apply each filter, you can start over by choosing Edit, Undo.

5

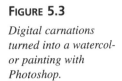

FIGURE 5.3

Digital carnations turned into a watercolor painting with Photoshop.

5. When you've finished playing with the various filters, select File, Close. You'll get a small dialog box asking you if you want to save the changes. Answer no to leave the image in its original state.

Digital Camera Pros and Cons

Digital cameras have, like most other computer hardware, dropped drastically in price. Although they're still more expensive than regular pocket cameras, you can probably save a fair bit in film and processing costs. As with all technology, digital cameras have good points and bad points.

Some of the advantages to using a digital camera are

- Windows users don't have to open up their computers to install any cards. The Casio, for example, comes with a cable that plugs into a free serial port. All you need to do is install the TWAIN drivers.

  The Mac installation process is just as easy. For most input devices, you simply drag a copy of the device's extension into the System's Extension folder or the Photoshop plug-in.

- You can also view the images from the camera on a television and copy them to your VCR. You can then output the images on a video cassette.

- You don't have to know a lot about the technology. Picture taking is as easy as point-and-shoot. You view the subject in a small LCD color screen.
- Your pictures don't have to be digitized because the camera is digital to begin with.
- Because the images are digital, there's very little work involved in emailing copies to friends and relatives or placing your photos on your Web site.

Some disadvantages of a digital camera are

- Although you can delete images, you can only store so many images, unlike a film camera where you just change rolls.
- Although the picture quality is almost as good as any snapshot pocket camera, the results won't even come close to a really good 35mm SLR.
- Printing hard copies of your photos can be expensive.

For a look at and comparison of several digital cameras, visit Norman Camera Online at http://www.normancamera.com. There you'll find comparison color photos taken with about 15 models of digital cameras. This is an interesting site for anyone interested in purchasing a digital camera.

Scanning

Only a few short years ago, scanning was much too expensive a proposition for the average computer user. At that time, the only options were flatbed or drum scanners. Drum scanners still cost upwards of $10,000, but flatbeds, which connect to your PC with relative ease, have come down in price considerably. This may be due in part to the presence of hand scanners. Of course, scanning technology itself, like other computer technology, has come down in price. The following sections take a look at two of today's more popular options: hand scanners and flatbed scanners.

5

Hand Scanners

Hand scanners, like the Logitech Scanman, cost only a couple of hundred dollars, and the prices are constantly dropping. These scanners can produce good results and have more than enough power to scan photos that you might want to use for your Web pages. Unlike the digital camera, you'll have to open up your computer and install a SCSI card to get the scanner to work. Of course, you may be able to get the technician where you bought the scanner to install it for you.

A couple of disadvantages to hand scanners is that you must have a steady hand. They are fairly narrow, so scanning a larger image requires several passes, and you can't really scan anything other than flat images, such as photos and printed text.

Flatbed Scanners

Aside from the difference in resolution that's possible with flatbeds versus hand scanners, there is one big difference. With a flatbed scanner you can scan objects as well as photos and text. Figure 5.4, showing a couple of more traditional art tools, is a result of placing the pencils on the glass of an HP 4C.

FIGURE 5.4

Traditional art tools scanned with an HP 4C flatbed scanner.

Just as a quick, inventive idea, Figure 5.5, a scan of a cellophane wrapped candy, could be used as a Web button. This "button" comes complete with its own drop shadow effect. All you need to do is add a little text.

FIGURE 5.5

Scan of a candy.

Tip

You can also get some interesting textures such as wood, water, and denim into your computer using a scanner. With the wood or denim, you can simply place the object on the glass of your scanner. Of course, if you want an authentic water texture, you'll need to take a picture with your 35mm camera and then scan the photo. Flatbed scanners do a nice job either way.

Scanning an Image

To scan an image into Photoshop, simply choose File, Import. Once the image has been scanned into the computer, you can adjust the brightness/contrast, colors, and so on, and you can add any effects you'd like. But before you get to that, you first need some information about scanning resolution.

I'm not going to get too in-depth into the technical details of resolution and lines per inch here. (I'll tell you more about the resolutions needed for printing on Day 6, "Saving, Exporting, and Printing Images.") If you're scanning images for use online, such as for your Web pages, you'll only need to scan at resolutions under 100 ppi (pixels per inch). This is because monitors are fixed at 72 to 96 dpi. Scanning at a higher resolution just makes your image appear larger. Scanning for print is much trickier, though, and is dependent on the printer to which you'll be outputting the image. Take a look at Figures 5.6 and 5.7.

FIGURE 5.6

Scan of Marianne at 100%.

5

FIGURE 5.7

Scan of Marianne at
300%.

Figure 5.6, an 8×10 black and white photo, is scanned with an HP 4C at 100 ppi with a
100% scale setting, and the file size is under 1.5 megabytes. Figure 5.7, the same image
scanned at 300% (a higher resolution), is over 10 megabytes. I've cropped it down so
that its physical dimensions are the same as Figure 5.6. Note that there is much less of
the portrait showing in Figure 5.7.

To get more predictable results from your scanner, you can set the resolution to the best
optical resolution for your scanner. In DeskScan, for example, choose Print Preferences
and set the resolution to 600 ppi. Save the setting as "Photoshop." Afterwards you can
choose this setting and adjust the scale to get the size of image that you're after.

Importing Images from Other Programs

Another way to get images into Photoshop is to export/import them from other imaging
programs. Illustrations created in Illustrator or CorelDRAW, for example, can be copied
into Photoshop for further processing.

You may be wondering why you'd want to use other programs in conjunction with Photoshop. As good as Photoshop is, it isn't a vector program and it can't do some of the things that can be done in an illustration program. You can't lay text along a path in Photoshop, for example, at least not without a great deal of time and effort, yet this process is quite easy in CorelDRAW or Illustrator. You can, therefore, create certain effects in a vector program and import the image into Photoshop for further manipulation.

With Illustrator you can simply drag and drop an image right into Photoshop. If you, like me, are more of a CorelDRAW user, you can export your CorelDRAW images as EPS files. When you import these files into Photoshop, you can choose whether or not they should be anti-aliased and at what size they should be imported.

I often use CorelDRAW to design interface templates (see Figure 5.8). Once the basic shapes are drawn, I'll export the file and import it into Photoshop. Once it's in Photoshop, the sky is pretty much the limit.

FIGURE 5.8

Illustration for Web page interface created in CorelDRAW.

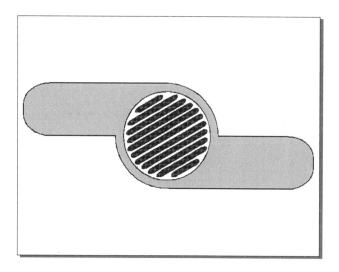

5

Figure 5.9 is the finished interface image. I added some gradients to give the interface some depth and also added a metallic texture and some text. For more information about adding textures, see Day 10; for more information about adding text, see Day 14.

FIGURE 5.9

Interface finished up in Photoshop.

Here's how this image was created. First I created a new image in CorelDRAW and built the main shape by "welding" a circle together with a couple of round-cornered rectangles (see Figures 5.10 and 5.11).

FIGURE 5.10

A circle and two round-cornered rectangles in CorelDRAW.

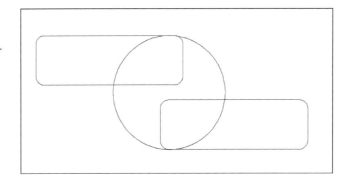

FIGURE 5.11

All three shapes welded into one.

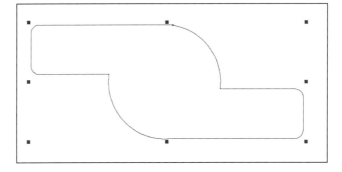

Next I added another circle and "combined" the circle with the existing shape, which cut the new circle out of the template (see Figure 5.12). The front screen is simply a series of round-cornered rectangles combined with (cut out of) a circle that fits into the template (see Figure 5.13); the back screen is a series of black dots over a gray background (see Figure 5.14).

FIGURE 5.12

A circle cut out of the middle.

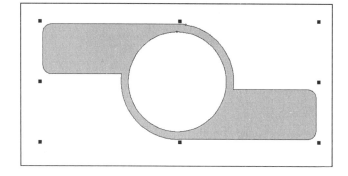

FIGURE 5.13

The front screen.

5

FIGURE 5.14

The back screen.

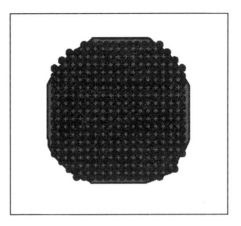

When all the pieces are assembled you end up with something like the illustration, or template, in Figure 5.8.

After importing the image into Photoshop, I applied several textures and a couple of filters to arrive at the final image that you see in Figure 5.9. This image is being used as the title image on the Web page that enables readers to send me email comments and questions. If you'd like to see it in action, visit `http://www.grafx-design.com` and select the email button on any of the pages.

Using a combination of programs, if you can, is a great way to create artwork. Although it's true that imaging software is becoming more powerful with each revision, it is also true that no one program can do everything.

Creating New Images

Although it's much easier to create templates and illustrations in programs like Illustrator and CorelDRAW, it's possible to create some pretty cool stuff just using Photoshop's built-in tools too. Some of the art on some of my favorite Web sites is created strictly with Photoshop. In fact, the button bar you see in Figure 5.15 was created in a matter of minutes just using the Marquee tools and the built-in gradients.

FIGURE 5.15

Button bar created completely in Photoshop.

Creating a New Image

To get a feel for what it's like to create something original in Photoshop, try the following:

1. Open a new image by choosing File, New.

2. In the New file dialog box, give the file a name and set both the Height and Width to 400 pixels, the Resolution to 72 pixels per inch, and the Contents to White (see Figure 5.16). This gives you a good size canvas to work on.

FIGURE 5.16

The New file dialog box.

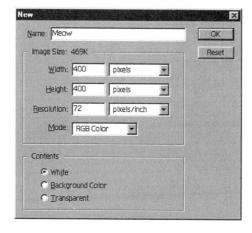

3. Select the Paintbrush tool from the toolbox.

4. Open the Brushes palette by choosing F5 and then clicking the Brushes tab. Choose a medium-size soft brush (see Figure 5.17).

FIGURE 5.17

Choose a brush from the Brushes palette.

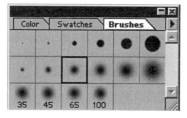

5

5. Now move the cursor onto the image and doodle. You'll get a feel for how easy this is. If you have a graphic tablet, it's almost as easy as sketching on a pad with a pencil. Figure 5.18 is a stylized cat that I drew using just the one brush and the default black color.

FIGURE 5.18

Stylized cat drawn in Photoshop.

Remember this is your first Photoshop creation, so it may not seem too exciting or too advanced. But don't worry, you'll get there soon enough. In later days, I'll demonstrate how you can create collages and your own original Web graphics.

Although this isn't haute-art, you can start to see the possibilities. If you'd like to see what can really be done using Photoshop as an artistic tool, take a look at Figures 5.1, 5.2, and 5.3 in the color section of this book. Laren Leonard, a digital artist and regular reader of my online tutorials, scanned a photo she took of some fall leaves (see Figure 5.19 below and Figure 5.1 from the color section.)

Starting with the photo, Laren applied an Impressionist filter to the entire image. The result is what you see in Figure 5.20 (Figure 5.2 in the color section).

At this point, Laren selected a portion of the image that she believed showed the most promise. She then added some color to the image and applied some other filters, including AlienSkin's Eye Candy—Fire. You can see the final result, "Fireman," in Figure 5.21 (Figure 5.3 in the color section).

FIGURE 5.19

Scan of fall leaves.

FIGURE 5.20

Scan of fall leaves with the first filter applied.

5

FIGURE 5.21

Laren's final image.

Note

One item you may wish to look into if you'll be creating or retouching lots of images is a graphics tablet, which enables you to draw on your computer with a pen and tablet. The tablet plugs in to a serial port on your computer. By drawing on the tablet with the pen that comes with it, you're actually able to draw on the screen. With programs such as Metacreation's Painter, this is almost like drawing and painting with pens, pencils, and brushes. With programs like Photoshop, a tablet and pen can help you be more exacting with retouching. Photoshop supports all of the latest functions on today's tablets. For example, a pen and tablet can be pressure sensitive. As you apply more pressure with the pen, you can get thicker lines, apply more color, and vary the opacity of the stroke.

Working with Digital Stock

If you don't have access to a digital camera or a scanner, how can you get images to use for your digital needs? One way is to buy digital stock. Digital stock is available from a wide variety of sources. Some of the companies and their Web addresses are shown in the following list:

Adobe Systems, Inc.	www.adobe.com
Corel Corporation	www.corel.com
PhotoDisc	www.photodisc.com
Digital Stock	www.digitalstock.com
Metacreations	www.metacreations.com

This list should get you started, but many more are out there. Doing an Internet search using the keywords "digital," "stock," "images," and "photographs" turns up a large list, and then you can pick and choose to search from there.

Some of the companies listed above also provide images on CD-ROM. In fact, CorelDRAW comes with a collection of royalty-free images, as does Adobe Photoshop. Pop in the CDs that came with Photoshop and do a little exploring.

There should also be a couple of images tucked away in the Photoshop folder on your hard drive. Figure 5.22 is a sample image from the Goodies folder.

FIGURE 5.22

Sample stock image from the Photoshop Goodies folder.

5

You can sometimes find CD-ROM collections of digital stock images at your local computer store. These collections, often containing as many as five discs or more, can sometimes be had at bargain prices.

If you need a specific image, though, you should probably visit one of the Web sites shown in the previous list. Web sites, such as the one at PhotoDisc, offer different ways to search through their large catalogs.

You can usually search by category or even by keyword. At one site I narrowed down the search for a goldfish bowl by first searching for "goldfish," which yielded a fairly large number of hits, and then searching for "goldfish" and "bowl." This more specific search gave me about a dozen or so images to choose from. Because the site provided thumbnails, I was able to quickly home in on the exact image I needed. All that was left to do was order the image in the resolution I needed.

The companies that sell digital art often have the images available in different sizes or resolutions and offer these in a range of prices. You might be able to find that one particular image you need for a Web page layout at a very reasonable price.

Some of the companies also offer starter kits on CD-ROM that give you a number of images. You can use these not only to familiarize yourself with digital stock, but you can use these images to try your hand at collages and montages.

Some images come in varying formats, also. You can often get images in TIFF format that have built-in masks in alpha channels. This makes it easy to use the images in montages, and so on.

Whatever method you choose to search for and buy digital stock, you're sure to be surprised by the choices available in file format, image quality (and quantity), and availability.

What to Consider when Setting Up an Image for the First Time

Before you even get started with an image, whether it's coming from a digital camera, a scanner, some digital stock, or another source, you should have already decided on what the intended purpose of the image will be. Knowing what the image will ultimately be used for helps you decide a number of things necessary to the success of the final image.

For example, the resolution of the image can make a big difference if the image is intended for print rather than the Web or some multimedia purpose. Most screens are fixed at 72 dpi to 96 dpi, and having a 300 dpi image means that the image might be much larger than necessary. This can have consequences that bear upon the cost of the image. Most digital stock companies charge a lot more for high-resolution images than their lower-resolution counterparts.

Buying an image that's in a lower resolution than needed can have consequences as well. Resizing an image to make it larger is extremely detrimental to the image's quality, as you'll see in the next section.

You might want to consider the color depth of an image before you decide to use it. Taking a 256-color GIF file and changing its mode is possible, but this has an effect on the image's quality as well.

Lowering the color depth of an image also affects the image's quality. Taking full-color photographs and changing them into GIFs for a Web page may not only reduce the number of colors in the image, but it reduces the quality and may also make the image unnecessarily large. You'll be better prepared to work on an image if you know ahead of time exactly what you want to do with the final image.

Resizing an Image

It is, of course, possible to resize an image in Photoshop. This is even warranted under certain conditions, such as softening up jagged edges from aliasing. You should be aware, though, of the effects that resizing has on images.

Reducing Images

Reducing an image means that some of the information that makes up your image is discarded. This can have an effect on an image. How adverse this effect is depends largely on how big the reduction is and it partly depends on the original image. Taking an image that contains a lot of text and reducing it heavily may make the text unreadable. The image in Figure 5.23 contains text at 120 points. The image is 500×200×72 dpi.

FIGURE 5.23

Text at 120 points in a 500×200×72 dpi image.

FIGURE 5.24

Figure 5.23 reduced to 50×20×72 dpi.

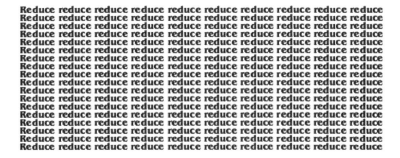

The text in Figure 5.24 is still readable, but this is because it was quite large and very legible to begin with. Figure 5.25 shows the same text starting out at 12 points, which is what the text in Figure 5.24 ended up at.

FIGURE 5.25

Text at 12 points in a 500×200×72 dpi image.

Reduce reduce reduce reduce reduce reduce reduce reduce reduce reduce
Reduce reduce reduce reduce reduce reduce reduce reduce reduce reduce
Reduce reduce reduce reduce reduce reduce reduce reduce reduce reduce
Reduce reduce reduce reduce reduce reduce reduce reduce reduce reduce
Reduce reduce reduce reduce reduce reduce reduce reduce reduce reduce
Reduce reduce reduce reduce reduce reduce reduce reduce reduce reduce
Reduce reduce reduce reduce reduce reduce reduce reduce reduce reduce
Reduce reduce reduce reduce reduce reduce reduce reduce reduce reduce
Reduce reduce reduce reduce reduce reduce reduce reduce reduce reduce
Reduce reduce reduce reduce reduce reduce reduce reduce reduce reduce
Reduce reduce reduce reduce reduce reduce reduce reduce reduce reduce
Reduce reduce reduce reduce reduce reduce reduce reduce reduce reduce
Reduce reduce reduce reduce reduce reduce reduce reduce reduce reduce
Reduce reduce reduce reduce reduce reduce reduce reduce reduce reduce
Reduce reduce reduce reduce reduce reduce reduce reduce reduce reduce
Reduce reduce reduce reduce reduce reduce reduce reduce reduce reduce
Reduce reduce reduce reduce reduce reduce reduce reduce reduce reduce
Reduce reduce reduce reduce reduce reduce reduce reduce reduce reduce

Figure 5.26 shows the image in Figure 5.25 reduced to 50×20.

FIGURE 5.26

Figure 5.25 reduced to 50×20×72 dpi.

Pretty cool. It looks like a bar code, but readable it's not.

This is extreme, of course, but I've had people ask if they should reduce an image by almost the same percentage. I've also had people ask how they could retain an image's integrity even though they planned on making a large reduction in an image's size. This is just not possible. When you discard that much information, you're bound to lose a lot of the quality with it. There's no way around it, except to plan ahead before you get stuck having to make this large a change to an image.

Enlarging Images

Going the other way and enlarging an image is even worse. Don't believe those television shows or movies where they take a photograph with a face or a license plate one-quarter the size of a postage stamp and blow it up so that it's recognizable. Figure 5.27 is the image from Figure 5.26 blown back up to its original 500×200 pixels. Can you read the original words? Of course not.

FIGURE 5.27

Figure 5.26 enlarged back to its original 500×200 pixels.

5

Figure 5.28 is a blown-up image of an everyday object. Because Photoshop does a really good job, when you use the bicubic method, you should be able to tell that it's a wristwatch face, but I doubt that you can tell what time the watch says, though.

Figure 5.29 shows the effects of the same enlargement using the nearest neighbor method. Not only can you not tell the time, you probably can't even be sure that it's a wristwatch.

Again, this shows that you should plan ahead, whether choosing an image or creating one from scratch. It's better to be sure of your needs at the beginning than to have to go back and redo an entire image or set of images.

FIGURE 5.28

Wristwatch enlarged 20 times using the bicubic method.

FIGURE 5.29

Wristwatch enlarged 20 times using the nearest neighbor method.

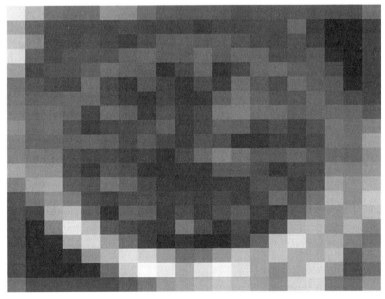

Summary

Today you've seen how images can be imported into Photoshop from digital cameras and scanners. You've also seen that you can export/import images from other programs.

Q&A

Q I saw an image on the Web that I'd like to tinker with. How can I download it for personal use?

A First, you might want to make sure that the creator of the art work won't mind if you use the image. After that, it's a simple matter of right-clicking the image in your browser and following the instructions in the dialog box to save the image. You can then load it into Photoshop and play around with it.

Q How do I import an image from Illustrator?

A There are a couple of methods: You can choose File, Open and open an existing AI or EPS file created in Illustrator. You can also drag-and-drop files directly from Illustrator into Photoshop.

Q Is it possible to have a digital camera, scanner, and other hardware hooked up to a computer at the same time?

A Yes, it is possible. That's the short answer though. Any computer has fairly limited resources. Many peripherals require IRQs, which are kind of like addresses where the computer can find and communicate with the hardware. When you run out of these addresses, adding more hardware becomes difficult, if not impossible. However, I currently have a mouse, a graphics tablet, a scanner, a digital camera, two CDs (one that is recordable), a printer, and a network card on my main machine. This in addition to the keyboard, monitor, two hard drives, and a floppy. I doubt that even one more piece of hardware would fit.

5

Workshop

The next section is a quick chapter quiz. If you have any problems answering any of the questions in the quiz, see the section directly following it for all of the answers.

Quiz

1. What are some of the various ways to acquire images?
2. How do you open an existing image?
3. Are hand-held scanners or flatbed scanners better? Why?

4. How do you create a new image?

5. What is a graphics tablet?

Quiz Answers

1. You can get images on the Web, buy images on CD-ROM, scan photos and slides, and shoot pictures with a digital camera.

2. Choose File, Open from the menu.

3. Flatbed scanners are a better choice because of the size of the image you can scan; hand-held scanners are limited to about four inches across and you need to "stitch" smaller pieces together to get larger images into your computer. As well, you need a pretty steady hand to get good results from a hand-held.

4. Choose File, New. In the dialog box, name the file and set the height, width, resolution, mode, and contents.

5. A graphics tablet is a piece of computer hardware that enables you to draw on your computer as you would with a pencil and paper.

WEEK 1

DAY 6

Saving, Exporting, and Printing Images

Of course, as when using many other types of programs, there'll come a time when you will want to save or print your work. With Photoshop though, you have many choices available to you. Photoshop is capable of saving files to many different formats including its own native format, PSD. As well as being able to save your images, you'll also need to be able to export and print them. Whether you'll be exporting images for Web output or printing images to an inkjet printer connected to your personal computer, Photoshop is up for the challenge and this chapter is ready to explain it to you. This chapter covers

- Saving images as well as copies of images
- Exporting images for Web output
- Printing to your local printer

Saving Your Artwork

As you learned in Day 4, "Getting a Handle on File Types," Photoshop is capable of saving your images in 20 separate file formats. Many imaging programs,

Photoshop included, have a native file format that allows them to save extra types of information along with the file. Some formats are compressed and others may save color information differently than their counterparts.

Photoshop's Save and Save As Options

Saving a Photoshop file is often as simple as choosing File, Save or File, Save As. Whether you are working with the Macintosh or PC version, choosing either of these options brings up a dialog box asking you to give the file a name, to choose a file format, and to choose a directory or folder where the file will be saved. With the Windows version, however, you have two additional dialog box options: Save Thumbnail and Use Lower Case Extension (see Figure 6.1). (For more information about Save options, refer back to Day 2, "Customizing Photoshop Preferences.")

FIGURE 6.1

The Save As dialog box.

You may notice, however, if you have any sort of Photoshop-specific information in the image, such as layers or channels, the only choice available is PSD. As I stated earlier, this is because these options are native to Photoshop. Before you can save in a non-PSD format, you must go back to your image and flatten it. This can be accomplished from the Layers palette. I'll describe the exact process on Day 13, "Layering Your Images."

Some other imaging programs can read the Photoshop format. The latest version of Jasc Software's Paint Shop Pro (version 5), for example, can read the layer information in a PSD file. As well, some animated GIF programs, like Gamani's GIF Movie Gear, read Photoshop layers and translate the layers into separate frames of an animation file.

One other option in the Save As dialog box that's new to version 5 is the Use Lower Case extension. With this option selected, Photoshop uses lower case letters for the file extension. One of the major complaints with the previous version is that it defaulted to upper case letters. This caused problems with Web servers and HTML files not serving up image files due to the discrepancy in file extensions. This has been fixed in version 5 and you now have the choice.

In the Save As dialog box, you'll notice that the Thumbnail option is grayed out. To set this option, choose File, Preferences, Saving Files, and set the Image Previews to Always Save. This saves a smaller version of your file, which will be visible in folders when you explore your hard drive (see Figure 6.2).

FIGURE 6.2

PSD thumbnails visible in a Windows 95 folder.

If you're accustomed to saving files in other programs, you'll notice that Photoshop is not that different. For those of you who want to practice, however, I've included the quick practice tutorial below.

Saving a File in the PSD Format

1. Create a new image by selecting File, New.

2. In the dialog box that appears, choose an image size of 400×400. Leave all other options at the default. Choose OK.

3. With the Paintbrush tool, draw a simple picture of a sailboat.

4. Now choose File, Save.

5. In the dialog box that appears, name the image boat. In the Save As dropdown box, choose Photoshop (*.PSD, *PDD) to save your file in Photoshop's native format.

6

6. If you want to create a thumbnail icon to accompany your image, set the Image Previews to Always Save in the Saving Files preference dialog box (File, Preferences, Saving Files). If you want the PSD extension to appear in lowercase, select the Use Lower Case Extension option.

7. Click the Save button.

The Photoshop format, as I said earlier, really is the best way to save your images, but there will come a time when you need to use different formats. If you'll be creating images for the Web, for example, you'll need to save them as JPEG or GIF. But what if you're working on a file and want to save an intermediate version without flattening it? What should you do? That's where Save a Copy comes in.

The Save a Copy Option

The Save a Copy option enables you to choose a file format other than PSD that you can save your image in while still working on it, thus preserving the layers, channels, and so on. All you have to do is choose File, Save a Copy. The Save a Copy dialog box that appears is quite similar to the Save As dialog box (see Figure 6.3).

FIGURE 6.3

The Save a Copy dialog box.

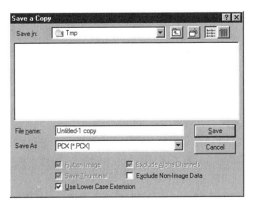

The main difference you'll notice is the presence of some extra options, including Flatten Image, Exclude Alpha Channels, Save Thumbnail, Exclude Non-Image Data, and Use Lower Case Extension. Some of these options may be grayed-out depending on which file type you're choosing to save your image as. The main benefit of the Save a Copy option is that you can retain all of your work in the current session while saving an intermediate copy of your image in the chosen file format.

This can be handy if you want a copy of the current image, you don't necessarily need the channel and layer information, and you want to keep working on the layered image. The following walks you through how the Save a Copy option works.

Saving a Copy

1. Open a PSD file by choosing File, Open. Browse through your hard drive or through the folders on the accompanying CD-ROM until you find and image with the PSD extension.

2. Note the filename in the title bar of the image.

3. Choose File, Save a Copy.

4. Name the file, select JPG from the Save As pulldown menu, and click Save.

Note that the filename in the image's title bar remains the same and doesn't take on the name of the copy that you saved. This is because the file you saved is a copy of the image you're working on and is not really related to the current image that still retains its Photoshop qualities.

Once you've selected the file format, chances are that you'll encounter another dialog box. For example, if you choose to save your work as a JPEG or BMP file you'll see the dialog boxes in Figure 6.4.

FIGURE 6.4

Even after you choose OK, you may be presented with a dialog box that offers Save options particular to that file format.

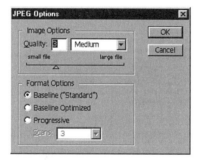

I'm not going to cover all the file formats and options that Photoshop can save a file with because that's a bit beyond the scope of this book. In fact, whole tomes have been written that contain nothing more than information on different file formats. If you have the need to find out more about a particular file format, I suggest you look up one of those fine volumes. You can also check out Day 4 of this book or try an `amazon.com` search with the keywords "Graphics," "File," and "Formats."

Exporting Files

Aside from saving copies, there are other means to convert your Photoshop images to other file formats. You'll find a couple of these options under File, Export. One option is to save your images in the GIF format; the other is to export paths to Illustrator.

6

Exporting to the GIF Format

If you looked over the available file formats in the Save As and Save a Copy dialog boxes, you may have noticed that the GIF format is conspicuously absent. This is because the GIF file format is handled through an external export filter. To save a file as a GIF, you should choose File, Export. Doing so brings up the GIF89a Export Options dialog box (see Figure 6.5).

Note

If you've flattened an image and changed its mode to Indexed Color, it is possible to access the GIF format through the File, Save or Save a Copy menu choices. However, you'll still be unable to use GIF89a specific options, such as transparency.

FIGURE 6.5

The GIF89a Export Options dialog box.

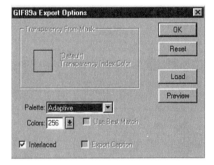

The dialog box you see in Figure 6.5 doesn't have many options available and is not really the dialog box you need to use if you want to save a GIF file. There's nothing wrong with using this export method, but if you want to be able to use all the GIF89a options, you should change the image mode to Indexed Color before saving a GIF file.

Exporting a GIF Image

1. Open the file GreenWood.psd from the Day06 folder of the accompanying CD.

2. Choose Image, Mode, Indexed Color. You'll get a warning dialog box that asks if you want to flatten the image. Choose OK only if you've saved your work as a PSD or are absolutely certain that you don't need the layers and channels information.

3. Once you've clicked OK, you'll get the Indexed Color dialog box (see Figure 6.6).

4. From the Indexed Color dialog box, you can choose a palette, the color depth, the number of colors, the Diffusion method, and the Color Matching options. (More information about palettes and diffusion can found on Day 21, "Preparing Your Art for the Web.") For the purposes of this example, leave the options at their defaults. Then choose OK.

FIGURE 6.6

The Indexed Color dialog box.

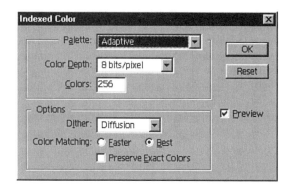

5. Now you need to go back to the File menu and choose Export and then GIF89a Export. When you do, you'll get the "real" GIF89a dialog box (see Figure 6.7).

FIGURE 6.7

The GIF89a Export Options dialog box.

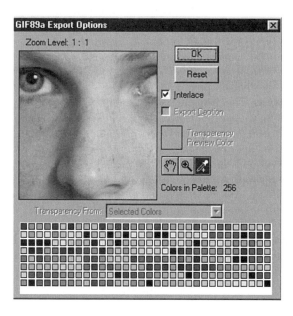

6

I call the dialog box shown in Figure 6.7 the "real" GIF89a dialog box because you can select a transparent color from it. This option is not available until you've changed the image to Indexed Color mode.

Note

> The reason you need to set a color to transparent is so that you can display an image on a Web page that has a textured or patterned background. Without the Transparency option, any image you display will be rectangular in nature. With the Transparency option you can choose to have odd or irregularly shaped images, which in effect allows the background to show through portions of your image.

Note

> Unless you've loaded any new export plug-ins, the only other option available when you choose File, Export will be Paths to Illustrator. We'll cover this in more detail in Day 11, "Masking with Layer Masks and Quick Masks."

You can select a color that will be transparent by clicking the Eyedropper icon and then moving over the image in the Preview window. When you're over the color you want, simply click the mouse. (See Day 21 for a demonstration of GIF transparencies.)

Export Plug-ins

If you have any export type plug-ins available, they will be found under the File, Export menu as well. One that I use daily in my work as a Web graphics designer is the Ulead SmartSaver plug-in. This plug-in enables you to save your Photoshop images as GIF, JPG, and PNG files.

This plug-in, which works with any imaging program that supports Photoshop export plug-ins, is meant for exporting Web-ready images. It has a ton of built-in features, such as real-time preview, that make it easy to save your images (see Figure 6.8).

In Figure 6.8, you can see the real-time preview image. The current Photoshop image is on the left and the preview is on the right. I'm saving the file as a JPEG and you can see the horizontal slider that runs across the middle of the tabbed palette. As you move the slider, the real-time preview changes to show you what the results of saving the file at this compression level would be. If you were saving the file as a GIF, you'd be able to see the colors and the results of any dithering.

FIGURE 6.8

The Ulead SmartSaver.

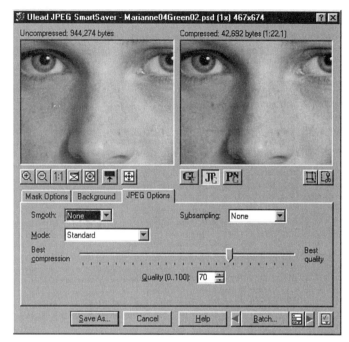

If you create images for the Web, this is a product that you absolutely need to look into. Once it's installed, it is accessible from File, Export, Ulead SmartSaver.

Printing

Aside from saving and saving copies of your files, another way to output them is to print them. Printing image files can be quite a process even if all you'll be doing is printing them to your inkjet printer. It can be quite a process, that is, compared to outputting from, say, your word processor. The reason is that Photoshop offers you many more choices for printing.

Printing to a Personal Printer

Today there is a huge choice of printer types available, most of them affordable even to mere mortals. Even color printing is available to those with a small budget. You can choose from laser printers, inkjet printers, and more.

Generally speaking, to print your image in Photoshop, all you'll need to do is choose File, Print. Doing so brings up the Print dialog box (see Figure 6.9).

6

FIGURE 6.9

The Print dialog box.

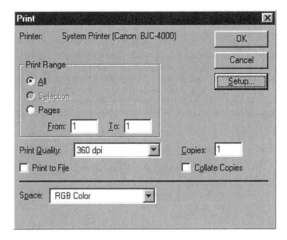

This dialog box should be similar to what you'd see in any other application. You can set the Print Range and the Print Quality (which depends on your particular printer). As well, you can select the Space.

The Space refers to the color space you'll be using. You can choose from Grayscale, RGB, or CMYK. You can also set the Gamma or choose to print using the color space of your monitor or your particular printer. Check through the list to see if your printer and/or monitor are listed. If not, stick with RGB for color and Grayscale for black and white images.

 Note   For information about gamma, see Day 7, "Calibrating Your System and Setting the Color Modes."

Printing in Black and White

Printing your images in black and white is a fairly simple process. At least it's much simpler than printing in color. With your printer set up and available to the system, you really should be able to just choose File, Print and achieve good results with the default settings. Printing in color, on the other hand, can be a little trickier.

Printing in Color

The quality of today's color inkjets is amazing. For the price, usually only a couple of hundred dollars, you can print all your Photoshop images in color. The results may be somewhat disappointing, though. Your images may have a different color shift from what you see onscreen, but this may simply be because you haven't calibrated your system.

So many monitors and printers are available that it's darn near impossible for the system to match one to the other. Even with different models from one manufacturer there may be differences. Part of the difference can be as simple as user preference. Some people like to run the brightness quite high, while others prefer the display a little darker. Some monitors may display colors a little warmer (tending to the red), while others display them a little cooler (tending towards blue). If you're familiar with photography, you may have heard of lens being referred to as "warm." It's the same idea.

In the next chapter, I'll show you how you can set up your monitor so that you'll get more predictable results when you print your images.

Preparing Images for a Service Bureau

If you work with Photoshop, you can have your images printed professionally. This usually means taking them to a service bureau. Service bureaus typically have all the high-end printers, such as dye-sublimation or color laser, that we'd like to own ourselves but simply can't afford.

Service bureaus can make four-color separations and prepare the plates that are required for printing. They can also print single or multiple images for you on color laser printers. The resulting prints are not all that different in quality from a professional print from a negative.

To find out how your local service bureau handles files, you should give them a call.

Note

If you send your files to a service bureau, one thing you need to be conscious of is file size. How do you get that file from your hard drive to the printer? Does anything fit on a floppy anymore? If you're going to do any serious image creation and/or image manipulation with Photoshop, you'll find that new, extremely large Giga-drive getting small very quickly.

Removable media to the rescue. Today you can get zip drives and recordable CDs at a pretty reasonable price. Something like this will come in handy for archiving your Photoshop images. You may want to check with your service bureau, though, as the format they accept will surely play an important part in your purchasing choice.

As well, with the rising popularity of the Internet, you may find that your service bureau has a way that you can send them your images electronically.

6

Four-Color Separations

If you'll be needing four-color separations, you'll need to convert your images to CMYK. Note, though, that converting an existing image in Photoshop requires that you flatten it first. If you know that you'll be requiring four-color separations, you should start your images out as CMYK. You might want to visit your local service bureau to see if you can get some advice on how to prepare your images. Because they'll be working with you and printing your work, they may give you some advice that'll save both you and them some time when it comes down to the actual printing.

Summary

Today you've seen how you can save your file in a number of formats and how to preserve the layers and channels in a Photoshop image. You've also had a look at how to print your work with various printers. Tomorrow I'll discuss calibrating your system, so that the results you get from your printer will be more predictable.

Q&A

Q Is it possible to save Photoshop image layers in formats besides PSD?

A No. To save the layer and channel information, you must save a copy of your image in PSD format.

Q What's the difference between the GIF format and the GIF89a format?

A The GIF89a format has new features, such as the capability to save transparency information in a file.

Q How do I set up my files for color separations?

A Choose File, Color Settings, CMYK and set the following options based on your service bureau's recommendations:

- **The Separation Type**, which enables you to choose between GCR (gray component replacement) and UCR (undercolor removal). These are different techniques for translating RGB to CMYK.

- **The Black Generation**, which specifies how much the black printing plate is used.

- **The Black Ink Limit**, which defines the maximum percentage of black ink used.

- **The Total Ink Limit**, which defines the maximum combined percentage of all four inks (cyan, magenta, yellow, and black).

- **The UCA Amount**, which specifies how much cyan, magenta, and yellow is added to the black in the darker parts of the image. This can result in richer blacks than with just the black ink.

Workshop

Here is a quick quiz about the chapter you have just read. If you have any problems answering any of the questions in the quiz, see the section directly following it for all of the answers.

Quiz

1. How do you save a file?
2. How do you save a copy of an image?
3. What's the best method for exporting a GIF?
4. How do you determine whether you have export plug-ins?
5. Where do you set up the print range and print quality?

Quiz Answers

1. Choose File, Save; File, Save As; or File, Save a Copy—depending on how you'd like to save the image.
2. Choose File, Save a Copy.
3. Choose Image, Mode, Indexed Color and then choose File, Export, GIF89a.
4. Choose File, Export. If you have any export type plug-ins available, they will be found here.
5. In the Print dialog box (found by choosing File, Print).

6

DAY 7

Calibrating Your System and Setting the Color Modes

Different people see colors in different ways, and I don't just mean how individuals see colors. Artists see colors and how they relate to other colors. They also have an understanding of how to mix certain colors to arrive at another completely different color. Photographers, however, see colors in terms of light and temperature. Daylight is cooler (bluer), while indoor lighting is warmer (redder). They also see how colors relate to one another. Psychologists see colors and how they relate to people's moods. Given all of the above, it's already easy to see how important color is. In relation to digital graphics, in general, and to Photoshop, more specifically, color is extremely important.

When taken all together, color is also one of the hardest digital graphics topics to understand. There are a lot of new buzzwords and some really geeky computer stuff involved. In this chapter, we'll cover the following:

- Understanding the various color models
- Working with color depth

- Selecting and building Color palettes
- Calibrating your monitor

Color Models

For our discussion of color, there are a few models that you need to know about. Some of these, such as CMYK, which stands for cyan, magenta, yellow, and percentage of black (yes, K equals black and that isn't a typo!), are intended more for printing, while modes such as RGB and Indexed Color are more applicable to online images, such as Web graphics. These various models are really just different ways of looking at the same thing, similar to the way a word in a foreign language has a counterpart in English. The words sound different and look different, but they mean the same thing.

To access the various color modes, choose Image, Mode. When you do, you get the options discussed in the following list. In the following sections, we'll discuss those modes you'll use most often.

- **Bitmap.** Unlike the bitmap you talk about when you discuss Windows BMP files, bitmap images are only black and white. I don't mean black and white in the same sense as black and white photographs. In digital terms, black and white photos would be referred to as grayscale.
- **Grayscale.** This is the term used to describe black and white photographs when you're discussing digital images.
- **Duotone.** Duotones are similar to grayscale except that another color or shade is added. This is done to expand the depth of the colors used to print grayscale images. Many printers, when printing grayscale, can print significantly less shades of gray than can be seen on a computer screen. To make up for this, you can change the image's mode from grayscale to duotone and add more shades. This mode can be used to create sepia tone images from black and white photos.
- **Indexed Color.** Indexed Color is a subset of RGB. Normally an indexed image contains 256, or fewer, colors.
- **RGB Color.** Used primarily for onscreen and Web work, this color model is composed of colors red, green, and blue.
- **CMYK Color.** Mostly used for print output. This particular model is composed of the colors cyan, magenta, yellow, and black.
- **Lab Color.** Lab color is a color mode native to Photoshop.

RGB

RGB, which stands for red, green, and blue, is the most common computer graphics color model. There are 256 possible values for each of the three colors. Without getting into the higher math, what this means is that you have a possible 256*256*256 colors. A quick glance at a calculator will show that there are 16.7 million colors available with this model. You may or may not have access to all of these colors, depending on a number of software- and hardware-related factors. We'll look at the issue of color depth more closely a little later in this chapter. If you're working on images intended for onscreen use, RGB is the mode you should use. After all, all monitors, like all television sets, are RGB.

CMYK

As mentioned earlier, CMYK is the color model associated with color printing. Even if you don't intend to do much printing from Photoshop, you may still come across the CMYK color mode. If, for example, you sometimes import graphics from predominantly print-type graphics programs, such as CorelDRAW or Adobe's Illustrator, into a program like Photoshop, you may have a problem with the default mode being reset from RGB to CMYK. The first clue that this has happened may come when you go to apply a plug-in filter only to find the entire menu is grayed out. If this happens, don't panic. Check to see if the color mode has been reset and, if it has, set it back to RGB.

If you intend to output your images to print, especially if you'll be sending them to a service bureau for printing, or if you'll need color separations, you'll need to either work in CMYK mode or convert the image to CMYK before printing.

Indexed

Indexed color is similar to RGB and might be considered a subset of it. I say similar because this is still an RGB mode intended for onscreen images. With indexed color, you are limited to 256 colors. These 256 colors, though, can be any 256 colors from the 16.7 possible colors. Indexed color is important with GIF images. GIF is one of the two possible image types available for Web graphics.

Grayscale

Grayscale is the mode you should use when working with black-and-white photos. Grayscale gives you 256 shades of gray, from white straight through to black. Of, course, you might want to convert a grayscale image to RGB or CMYK to add color to it.

Note

HSL or HSB (hue, saturation, and luminance or brightness) is just another way of looking at the RGB model. Hue means the same as color, saturation is the amount of color, and luminance, or brightness, is self evident. Usually in cases where you can adjust the color within your software program, both the HSL and RGB models share a common dialog box. This is true in Photoshop, for example.

If you become more familiar with one color model over the other, use whichever you please. During the course of this book, I'll use mostly the RGB model.

7

How the Color Models Work

Because computers start counting at 0 rather than 1, the possible values for red, green, and blue go from 0 to 255. If all three values are 0, the resulting color is black, and when all three values are 255, the resulting color is white. As expected, then, a value of 0, 0, 255 (no red, no green, and all blue) yields a vivid blue. A value of 0, 255, 0 gives you a bright green and 255, 0, 0 is bright red. Mixing these values gives you one of 16.7 million colors.

CMYK works a little differently. Each of the three colors (and the black) can have percentages ranging from 0% to 100%. You have fewer colors available in this mode than in RGB. This is the reason that you'll get the Out of Gamut warning when selecting colors based on RGB. Many of the RGB colors do not yield printable colors. Photoshop warns you when this is the case so that you don't choose colors that won't print.

Note

> Your color television uses the same method of displaying colors as your computer monitor. When all three of the colors are fired at full strength, the result is bright white. If you could get close enough to your television, although I don't recommend this, you might be able to see that what appears to be a white dot is actually a collection of very small red, green, and blue dots.
>
> On the computer these dots are called pixels, which stands for picture elements. Your computer screen displays an array of these dots in a fixed set of numbers like 640×480, 800×600 and 1024×768. The more dots or pixels displayed, the better, or higher, the resolution is. This higher resolution, though, requires more video memory.

Your Computer Screen

How many colors does your screen display? Chances are good that, if you bought your computer recently, it was sold to you as a multimedia machine capable of great wonders. When you bought the machine was it set up correctly, though? How do you know how many colors it's displaying? If you're running Windows 95, it's fairly easy to find out. Right-click anywhere on the desktop and you'll find the pop-up menu. At the bottom of this menu is the Properties selection. Clicking this choice brings up the Display Properties dialog box as seen in Figure 7.1.

FIGURE 7.1

The Display Properties dialog box.

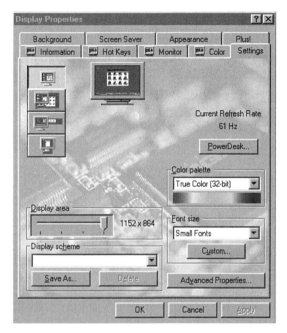

Your dialog box may appear a little different than this one. The dialog box seen in Figure 7.1 is enhanced by the software that came with my video card. In any event, you should have a tab labeled Settings. Clicking this tab allows you to view the current color depth and resolution of your computer's monitor. You can see that mine is currently set to 1,152×864 at 32-bit color depth. You should be able to change the resolution and color depth to something higher than the standard 640×480 with 256 colors.

Experimenting with the settings shouldn't prove troublesome because the drivers normally won't allow you to select higher resolutions or color depth than your machine can handle. Even on today's 14-inch monitors and with a 1 MB video card, you should be capable of seeing 640×480 with 64,000 colors or even 800×600 with 64,000 colors. Some people find that text on a 800×600 setting is too small to read. However, you should also be able to choose large fonts from the same dialog box. In any event, you should play around until you find a setting that gives you an acceptable picture with the highest resolution and color depth that your system can give you.

Color Depth

Color depth is a way of describing how many colors your hardware and software are capable of displaying. The buzzwords most often used are 8-bit, 16-bit, and 24-bit. Of

7

course, color depth is sometimes described by the actual number of colors being displayed, such as 256 colors or 16.7 million colors.

Hardware is the real determining factor. Your Web browser, for example, displays as many colors as your system can use. The next limiting factor is the type of image being displayed. GIFs are capable of displaying only 256 separate colors. These colors can, however, be chosen from all 16.7 million available colors. JPEGs can display up to 16.7 million colors. This makes the JPEG format a popular choice for photographs and other real-world images that will ultimately be displayed on a Web page.

8-bit

Eight-bit or 256 colors is what many systems use, although they are often capable of displaying more. Sometimes referred to as VGA (Video Gate Array), 8-bit is somewhat limited. With your system set to 8-bit, you're at the mercy of your browser software, as we'll see later in the section on palettes.

16-bit

Sixteen-bit color, often referred to as hi-color, is a good choice if your system's video memory is limited. Using 16-bit color is a great compromise between speed and color. With 16-bit color, up to 64,000 colors are possible (65,536 actually).

Note

Where does the number 65,536 come from? The number 65,536 is the number you'd get if you raised 2 to the power of 16; in other words, 16 bits equals 2 possibilities (on and off or 0 and 1). Likewise 2 raised to the power of 8 yields 256; 256 colors equals 8 bits. Finally, 24-bit equals 2 raised to the power of 24 or 16.7 million colors.

With 64,000 colors, your Web-viewing experience will be much more enriched. Using this color depth reduces the need for dithering.

24-bit

Twenty-four-bit is the best color depth to use when creating and viewing computer images. To use this color depth, though, your video card must have at least 1MB of memory. The reason for this is that for each pixel you must have 24 bits (or three bytes) of memory available. With a little simple arithmetic, you can see that a 640×480 screen, which means 307,200 (640 times 480) pixels, requires 307,200 times 3 (or 307,200 pixels times 3 bytes per pixel) equals 921,600 bytes.

32-bit

Thirty-two-bit is specific to certain video card adapters used under Windows 95. This color depth is labeled True Color by the operating system. In addition to supporting three 8-bit color channels, this mode adds an 8-bit alpha channel for system use. If your adapter supports this bit depth for your preferred screen size, you may want to use it. With some older S3-chip video cards, 32-bit True Color may be the only option higher than 16-bit.

Note for Windows 95 Users: Since Photoshop 5 includes a new system-wide gamma and color calibration utility, keep any additional color calibration tools set to their defaults. Many video adapters add a proprietary Color or Calibration tab to the Windows 95 Display Properties dialog box. The example in Figure 7.2 shows such a tab with the ATI driver set. Changing values in these areas is not recommended, and if you decide to experiment with the values, you need to re-run the Adobe Gamma control.

FIGURE 7.2

The Color tab of the ATI display settings in Windows 95. If you are using the Adobe Gamma control panel, it is best to leave these settings alone or reset to their defaults before running the Adobe Gamma Step-by-Step Wizard.

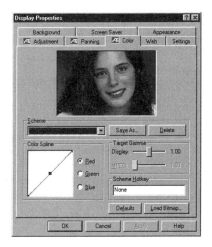

Note for Macintosh Users: Third-party Macintosh video cards usually install their own control panels and/or extension for specific gamma settings. Also, previous versions of Photoshop installed the Knoll Gamma correction utility. Since Photoshop 5 automatically installs the Adobe Gamma control panel on startup, you will want to disable any other gamma controls in the Extensions Manager (usually under Startup Items in Mac OS 8.0). However, you will want to keep the following extensions or control panels active to maintain control over bit-depth and screen size: Monitors & Sound, Control Strip, and any third-party video accelerators that are not gamma related. If it's gamma related, it will usually say Gamma in the name.

7

Tip

Photoshop gives you a built-in indication of the color depth your monitor is using. Every time you start Photoshop, you will see a splash screen with the Photoshop logo, the registered user, and serial number. At each screen bit-depth, this splash screen will appear quite differently. If you notice extreme banding in the splash screen image, you'll most likely be using an 8- or 16-bit color depth. If the gradations in the image are smooth and continuous, your monitor's color depth is 24-bit or higher.

Now that you have an understanding of color depth, it's time to look at palettes.

Color Palettes (or Color Lookup Tables)

Traditionally, a palette was a surface where an artist would mix his colors before applying them to the canvas. With computer graphics, a palette is somewhat similar. Most graphics programs have some window available that you can pick your colors from. In certain circumstances, your color choices are limited. Those limited sets of colors are also referred to as palettes.

Note

Many software programs refer to indexed color palettes as palettes. Photoshop, however, chose to use the term color lookup table, or CLUT for short. I'll use the term palette because it's in fairly common use due to the popularity of the Web and Web browsers. The two most common Web browsers, Netscape and Microsoft's Internet Explorer, have palettes they use as do the two most common systems, Windows and Macintosh.

Palettes will be of more importance when working with GIF images. Because of their limited color depth, GIF images can only use a specialized palette. This palette, though, can contain a different selection of colors. Sometimes you will have control over the selection of the colors and, unfortunately, sometimes you won't.

Problems with Limited Palettes

There are problems associated with limited palettes. One of these is that if you choose to work with a limited palette while creating your images, many of the features of your graphics programs will not be available to you. Options such as drop shadows and blurring need to have access to the full range of colors to do their magic. The option here is to create your image using the higher color depth and then reduce the depth or, in the case of Photoshop, change the mode to Indexed Color once your image is finished.

You should always keep a copy of the image with its color depth set at the higher resolution, which makes applying subsequent changes much easier. However, saving your image as a BMP, a TIF, or a PCX, for example, is probably going to cost you in terms of larger file sizes. Don't forget to always save a copy of your most important images in Photoshop's native PSD format.

Exact Palette

The Exact palette is built from the colors currently being used in an image. The number of colors in the image must be equal to, or less than, 256 before you can select the Exact palette option.

Adaptive Palette

An Adaptive palette is built from the colors currently used in the image. Photoshop uses the most often used colors to build this palette. Any other colors are changed to one of the 256 or are dithered so that there will be 256 colors or less left.

The problem is that while you're working on your images you're probably only working on them one at a time, right? So you create one image and save it and go on to create the next one. You get this great idea for a different set of colors and create the second image with a completely new color scheme from the first. You then save the image after adjusting the mode appropriately. Still no problem. You sign on to the Internet and load your Web page, but the colors on both images look really bad. What happened? Well, what happened is that if the browser is running on an 8-bit setup, it can't show you the 256 colors from one image and another 256 from the next. It can, after all, only display 256 different colors at one time. This brings us to the dreaded Netscape, or Web, palette.

Web Palette

The Web palette is the scourge of Web graphics artists the world over. This palette consists of 216 colors that, if used when constructing your images, display your images exactly the same no matter what the platform is that they're being displayed on.

Why 216 colors and not 256? Because both the operating system, Windows for example, and the browser, Netscape let's say, use up 40 colors between them. This leaves 216 colors. This palette is sometimes called the cube, which refers to it being a 6×6×6 (6 times 6 times 6 equals 216) cube. Six colors wide, six colors high, and six sides.

Due to the popularity of Web graphics, many graphics programs are now shipping with a version of the Web palette built in. In fact, if you change an image's mode to Indexed

7

Color in Photoshop, one choice for the palette is Web. Although this makes the process of creating images that use this set of colors easier, it doesn't change the fact that you are limited to this particular color set.

So what can you do about this? One answer is to use your own set of colors, being careful that all of your images use the same restricted palette. The other is you can hope that many of the readers of your pages are using machines capable of displaying more than 256 colors. I wouldn't bet on the second being the case for a little while yet. Many people are out there surfing the Web with older 386s. Of course, you could build your graphics with these limitations in mind and take them into account when the images are really important for navigation around your site.

Custom Palettes

In Photoshop, you also have the option of choosing a custom palette. Many third-party plug-ins offer additional palettes to optimize your images for specific Web usage, usually producing better results than Photoshop's built-in Web palette. BoxTop's ColorSafe offers specific sub-sets of the 216 Web palette to use for image mode changes. You can download a demo version of ColorSafe from the BoxTop Web site at `http://www.boxtopsoft.com`. Refer to the next section for tips on building your own palettes.

How to Build or Select a Palette

Building a palette can be done in a number of ways. You can load an indexed (or GIF) image into your graphics program as one alternative. Having done so, the palette associated with that image is available to you. You can also open up a palette and add, edit, or remove colors from it. Figure 7.3 shows the Color Table dialog box.

FIGURE 7.3

Photoshop's Color Table dialog box.

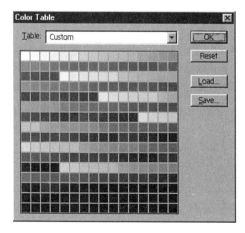

Selecting a Palette

To access the Color Table dialog box, choose Image, Mode, Color Table. (Note that this mode is unavailable to you unless you're working on an Indexed mode image.) To give this a try, load an image and change its mode to Indexed by choosing Image, Mode, Indexed Color. You can view the Color table that Photoshop created for this indexed Color image now by choosing Image, Mode, Color Table.

Clicking one of the colors in the Color Table dialog box brings up the Color Picker dialog box (see Figure 7.4). Using the Color dialog box, you can change the color you clicked to any one of 16.7 million other colors.

FIGURE 7.4

The Color Picker dialog box.

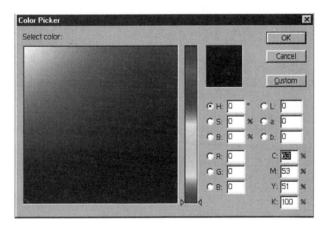

The Importance of Palette Consistency

The Web isn't the only place where you'll have to pay attention to 256 color limitations. If you are creating or optimizing graphics for any multimedia production to be distributed to the general public (such as CD-ROM titles), you need to use identical palettes (referred to as global palettes) with any images appearing on the screen simultaneously. To ensure that all the images on any given screen match one another, follow this simple exercise:

1. For a given screen in the multimedia production, open each graphic individually in Photoshop. Ideally, you'll want to use screen-size (72 ppi), 24-bit versions of the images. In Figure 7.5, you can see three photographic images opened in Photoshop.

7

FIGURE 7.5

Three 24-bit photo-graphic images opened in Photoshop.

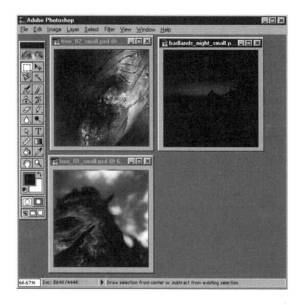

2. Create a new Photoshop document (File, New) with a width and height that will accommodate the combined width and height of every graphic (see Figure 7.6). For example, if you have three 300 pixel×300 pixel images, you'll want to make a new 900 pixel×300 pixel document. You may want to add more pixels to either dimension to give you some room to place the images easily. Use either a transparent or white background for the new image.

FIGURE 7.6

The New dialog box with settings for the example images.

3. Click on one of the previously opened images, and use the Move tool to click and drag the image into the newly created empty image. If the image is in Photoshop format with more than one layer, use the Select, All and Edit, Copy Merged commands to copy the layered image. Then, use the Edit, Paste command in the new image to place the copied material. Repeat this step for each image you have opened.

4. Once all the images are in the new image, make sure each individual image is showing completely (see Figure 7.7). Check to make sure that the edge of one image isn't overlapping another. For more precise control with image placement, use the arrow keys (with the Move tool active). If you need more room to move the images around, increase the canvas size by using the Image, Canvas Size command.

FIGURE 7.7

The new image with all three photographic images.

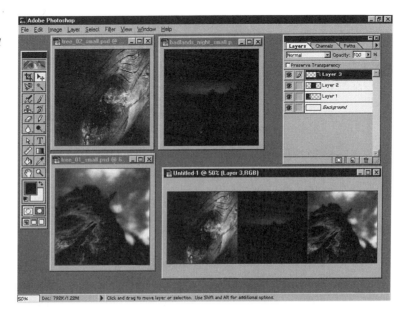

5. Close the original image files, and leave the new image open. If you made any changes to the original image files, do not save the changes.

6. Choose Image, Mode, Indexed Color. You may receive a confirmation box asking if you want to flatten layers. Click OK. Choose Adaptive for the Palette, 8 bits/pixel for the Color Depth, and Diffusion for the dithering method (see Figure 7.8).

FIGURE 7.8

The Indexed Color dialog box with appropriate settings.

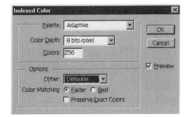

7

7. Choose Image, Mode, Color Table to view the Custom palette (see Figure 7.9), and press the Save button. Give an appropriate name to the color palette, like the name of the scene where this global palette will be used.

FIGURE 7.9

The Color Table dialog box can be accessed by using the Image, Mode, Color Table command.

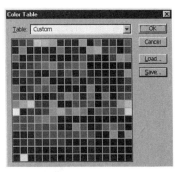

8. Close the new image. There is no need to save this image because you only needed it to build a color palette. You already have each image saved individually.

9. Now, re-open one of the original 24-bit images and choose Image, Mode, Indexed Color. Under Palette, choose Custom and click Load to find the palette you just created. If you're performing this exercise in one sitting, you may also use the Previous option in the Palette drop-down list because the last palette created was the one you want to use with this image.

10. Save the image in the format that your multimedia authoring application can use. If you are using Macromedia Director, you may want to use the PICT or TIFF format.

11. Repeat steps 9 and 10 with the other images you used to create the palette.

Congratulations! You now have your images ready to be imported into your authoring application. Make sure that you import the color palette with each new screen image; don't let the authoring program remap the colors to a system palette.

Do You Really Need to Calibrate Your System?

You won't really miss anything by not calibrating your system right away. In fact, if you're happy with the way your printed images correspond to what you see onscreen, you can probably skip this section altogether. If, on the other hand, you're experiencing major discrepancies between what you see onscreen and what your printouts look like, then this section will help.

Calibrating Your Screen

Calibrating your screen is much easier in Photoshop 5 than in previous versions. For those of you who want to calibrate your monitor, the following exercise will show you the way.

If you are using a Macintosh, see the Note at the end of this section to find steps for calibrating your screen.

Note

> The final release of Photoshop 5 for Windows 95 may have automatically performed the following installation steps. If your Control Panels folder already has an Adobe Gamma listing, then you do not need to follow these steps.

Before you begin, locate Adobe Gamma.cpl and copy it to your Windows/System folder if you're on a Windows system. You should be able to locate this file in the folder where you installed Photoshop. It will be in a folder named Calibrate. After copying it, you can access this applet from the Control Panel dialog box under Windows. To do so, click Start, Settings, Control Panel. Find the Adobe Gamma icon and double-click it. This runs the Gamma setup application and walks you through setting up your monitor.

You should also copy the file NewGammaWinLoad.exe onto your hard drive. That way, you can create an alias for apmload.exe to your Startup group. Here's what you need to do:

1. Click the Start menu and select Settings.
2. Select Taskbar.
3. Select the Start Menu Programs tab.
4. Click the Add button.
5. In the Create Shortcut Wizard, browse for where you put apmload.exe. Click Next.
6. Select the Startup folder and click Next.
7. Give it a name and click the Finish button.
8. Click the OK button in the Taskbar Properties dialog box.

This applet will now load every time you boot. Once it runs, it loads any custom Gamma Ramp you may have created.

7

Even though Photoshop 5 will automatically add the Adobe Gamma loader to the StartUp program group, other monitor utilities may unload the Adobe Gamma settings and replace the color settings with their own. If you find that the screen changes color more than once during startup, the Adobe Gamma settings may no longer be active. To be sure, re-run the Adobe Gamma Loader from the Start, Programs, StartUp, Adobe Gamma Loader shortcut. If the settings unload everytime you load Windows 95, try changing the name of the shortcut in the StartUp program group to X_Adobe Gamma Loader so that it is the last program in the group to load.

Note

> On a Macintosh, Photoshop 5 automatically installs the Adobe Gamma Loader control panel to the System folder. Go to the Apple menu and choose Adobe Gamma from the Control Panel sub-menu. Choose the Step-by-Step assistant to create a custom ICC profile for your monitor. Apple's ColorSync software is automatically installed with Mac OS 8.0. Check the profile that ColorSync is using by accessing the ColorSync System Profile in the Control Panel sub-menu or folder. The current version of ColorSync is 2.5. If you don't have it, you can download it for free at http://www.color-sync.apple.com. Apple has ColorSync Photoshop plug-in modules that can be used by any application that accepts the Photoshop plug-in standard.

Calibrating Your Printer

Now that you've set up your monitor, all you should need to do when printing is to select the printer's space from the Print dialog box (see Figure 7.10).

FIGURE 7.10

The Print dialog box.

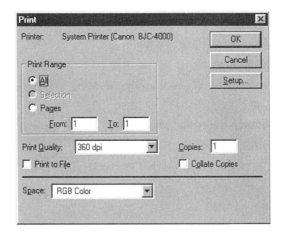

You might want to test the difference between how your printer's drivers convert the image and how Photoshop converts it, and then choose the best of the two. Try converting your image to CMYK in Photoshop and sending it to your inkjet printer to see how the Photoshop conversion does. Then send the same RGB image to your printer and compare the output.

If you own a newer printer, it should be listed under the Space pull-down menu. Any output you send to a printer should now match up quite well with what you see onscreen.

Controlling Color Profiles in Photoshop 5

By default, Photoshop 5 will automatically convert any images that you open to the color profile that you have set up in the Photoshop Preferences. This will generally increase the amount of time it takes for the image to open, and it may unnecessarily change the actual color values of the image. If you don't want to concern yourself with exact color matching, then you may want to perform step 5 and leave the rest for later. For both Windows and Macintosh platforms, follow the steps below to configure the profile setup:

1. Choose File, Color Settings, Profile Setup.

2. If you want to always embed your color profile in each image you save in Photoshop, check all the color modes at the top of the Profile Setup dialog box: RGB, CMYK, Grayscale, and Lab (see Figure 7.11). This will add some file space to your images, but it will ensure that any other output device using ICM profiles will see the image the way you saw it on your monitor.

FIGURE 7.11

The Profile Setup dialog box.

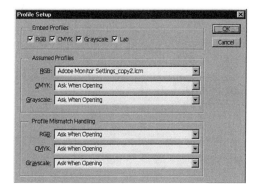

7

3. In the RGB drop-down list under Assumed Profiles, find the name of the profile you created with the Adobe Gamma control panel. If you have created multiple profiles, choose the one that you want to use most of the time. For example, if most of the images you use in Photoshop are acquired through your own scanner, it may be best to create or obtain a profile for it.

4. For CMYK and Grayscale, choose either None or Ask When Opening. If you frequently exchange Mac and PC grayscale images, you may want to choose Ask When Opening for the Grayscale category.

5. Under the Profile Mismatch Handling heading, choose Ask When Opening for all three categories. If you do not want to concern yourself with color profiles at all, then choose the Ignore option. If you want it to automatically convert images to your preferred profiles, then choose the Convert To option under each category.

Okay, we're almost done. Go back to the File, Color Settings menu. Notice that there are three other setup choices: RGB, CMYK, and Grayscale. Although we have already told Photoshop which profiles to use for each of these modes when opening an image, Photoshop still needs to know how it should handle conversions after the image has been loaded and edited using the Mode command.

6. Choose the RGB Setup menu choice from File, Color Settings (see Figure 7.12). For each option in the RGB Setup dialog box, choose the same setting that you used when creating your monitor profile with the Adobe Gamma control panel. Place a check mark in the Display Using Monitor Compensation box.

FIGURE 7.12

The RGB Setup dialog box. Make sure your settings here match the ones you used in the Adobe Gamma Step-by-Step Wizard or Assistant.

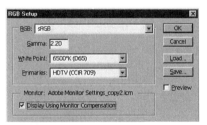

7. If you know what settings your service bureau recommends for CMYK files, choose File, Color Settings, CMYK Setup and enter the appropriate ink colors and dot gain, as well as separation options. Only change these values if you are certain that your preferred CMYK output device will benefit.

8. For the Grayscale setup, leave the Grayscale behavior setting at the default RGB option.

For the most part, Photoshop's color settings are now optimized for your particular needs. See the following Note to find out what else you can do to get the best color-matching results out of Photoshop.

Note

> If you have mid- to high-end input and output devices and truly want to get the best color results from your equipment, you may want to create ICM profiles for your scanner and printer. Creating profiles, these devices can be vary in difficulty and importance. There are many third-party applications that can produce ICM profiles for any device. For a general listing of cross-platform applications, see
> `http://www.colorsync.apple.com/Products/Findproduct.fqry?fn=profile`.

Summary

Today was a bit tough, but this ends the first week, and we'll be moving on to the fun stuff next. This chapter showed you a little about color and how Photoshop handles it. You also learned that calibrating your system, while not absolutely necessary, isn't as difficult as it used to be.

Color is the hardest part of digital graphics and is a subject you'd be wise to spend some time on. Don't worry if you don't become an instant expert, though. Some people spend a great part of their lifetime studying color.

Q&A

Q Why are there so many color modes?

A The only modes you really need to be concerned with are RGB for computer images, grayscale for black-and-white images, and CMYK if you'll be printing to high-end printers. The rest are more for special techniques and circumstances, which I'll discuss as necessary throughout this book.

Q Do I really have to calibrate my system?

A It's not absolutely necessary unless you're finding a big difference between what you see on your screen and what you see on the screens of others, or big differences between your screen and any printouts you make. If you consistently use the same service bureau for output services, you may need to calibrate your system to the devices the service uses.

7

Q What if I only have an 8-bit system? What do I do about using 24-bit mode when creating my images?

A Although the program will be set internally to 24-bit, you'll still only see 8-bit images on your screen. As long as the software is set to high color resolution, there should be no problem. Even though your hardware may only be capable of 8-bit color, you'll have to set the software to the higher color resolution to work with all the possible options.

Workshop

This section is a quick quiz about the chapter you just finished. If you have any problems answering any of the questions in the quiz, see the section directly following it for all the answers.

Quiz

1. What does RGB stand for? What does CMYK stand for?

2. How do I change the color depth of an image?

3. What is a Color palette?

4. What is a Limited palette?

5. How do you select a Color palette?

6. What is a global palette?

7. What are color profiles? Is it necessary to use them?

Quiz Answers

1. Red, Green and Blue; Cyan, Magenta, Yellow, and Black.

2. You don't really change the color depth on an image with Photoshop; rather, you choose a mode that has a different color depth associated with it.

3. A Color palette is a limited set of colors, normally 256 colors or less.

4. A palette that is restricted to a set of specific colors, such as a System palette or a Web palette.

5. You can open an image that was built with a certain palette or you can convert an image to Indexed Color mode and specify the palette.

6. A global palette is a color palette that is referenced by many images. Creating global palettes is essential for optimized 8-bit multimedia playback.

7. A color profile is a platform-independent description of input and output imaging devices. Their necessity is entirely up to you and your digital work-flow. Reliable color profiles can reduce the number of inconsistent and costly high-resolution hard copies on film or paper.

WEEK 2

At a Glance

During the first week, you learned the basics behind creating Photoshop images. Now comes the really fun part: manipulating them. This week, we'll cover the following:

- Using the editing tools
- Using with the selection tools
- Defining and editing selections and paths
- Working with the Paint Bucket and Gradient tools
- Understanding aliasing and anti-aliasing
- Using and customizing the various brushes
- Working with layer masks, quick masks, and Adjustment layers
- Editing with channels
- Using channels for lighting effects
- Creating, selecting, and editing text

WEEK 2

DAY 8

Understanding the Editing Tools

Now that you've got some of the technical stuff out of the way, it's time to roll up your sleeves, open a photo or two, and get down to some fun with Photoshop. The first thing I'll cover is the editing tools and, of those, I'll look at the Dodge and Burn tools first. Specifically, this chapter covers:

- Using the Dodge, Burn, and Sponge tools
- Applying the Blur, Sharpen, and Smudge tools
- Working with Rubber Stamp and Pattern Stamp

The Toning Tools

The Dodge, Burn, and Sponge tools make up the Tone group. Together these tools can affect an image's tonality. Using these tools, you can lighten, darken, and change the saturation of any area of the image you're working on.

In many ways, you can look at Photoshop as a digital darkroom. In fact, the Dodge and Burn tools work just as you'd expect if you ever did any darkroom work. The Dodge tool lightens portions of an image and the Burn tool darkens portions of an image. You can see both the Dodge and the Burn tools, along with the Sponge tool, in the flyout menu in Figure 8.1.

The Tone tools flyout.

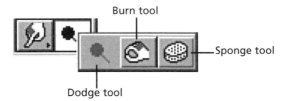

Burn tool

Sponge tool

Dodge tool

The Dodge Tool

The really nice thing about the digital versions of these tools is the control you have. To see an example of the power these tools have, open a photo image. If you'd like to follow along with the steps I'm using, you can open the PAM.PSD image from the CD-ROM (see Figure 8.2).

This photo of one of my favorite models, and coincidentally, my wife, was taken oddly enough for a darkroom class. As it happens, Pamela has really blue eyes. Of course, they don't look quite as remarkable in black and white. Let's see if we can add a little drama back into the photo.

Using the Dodge Tool to Lighten a Selection

1. Select the Zoom tool.
2. Now click near the eyes in the image to zoom in to a level that you think you'll feel comfortable working in. Remember you'll be working just on the eyes for now so you might want to blow up the image to the point where the eyes fill the screen. In fact, that's what I've done. In Figure 8.3, you can see that I've blown the image up to 500%.

FIGURE 8.2

Pamela.

FIGURE 8.3

Pamela at 500%.

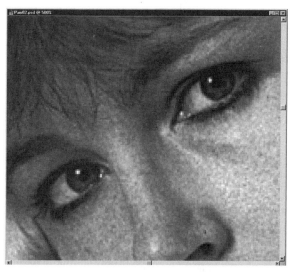

3. Now select the Dodge tool. With the Dodge tool selected you can view and change the tool's settings in the Dodge Options palette (see Figure 8.4).

FIGURE 8.4

The Dodge Options palette.

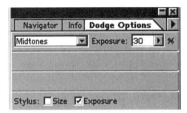

The default settings are for Midtones with an Exposure of 50%. You can change these to Highlights and Shadows and choose any Exposure from 1% to 100%. The lower the exposure, the less the effect. Set this value to about 30% and leave the Midtones selected. With the Midtones selected, you'll only affect the color of Pam's eye, not the pupil, which is black, or the specular highlight.

At the bottom of the palette, you'll see Stylus settings. If you have a pen and tablet, you can set these to change how the pressure of the pen affects the tool.

There's only one thing left to do before you apply the tool. You have to select a brush size. This is where the digital tool shows its power over the darkroom tool. To select a brush size, open the Brushes palette by clicking its tab or by choosing Window, Show Brushes and clicking the brush icon that you want to use.

4. I selected the smallest soft-edged brush (see Figure 8.5). I selected the smallest brush because of the small area and I decided to use the soft edge to make any small errors harder to see in the final image.

FIGURE 8.5

The Brushes palette with small soft-edged brush selected.

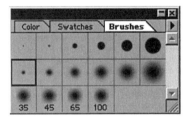

Oops. There's one more quick change needed before you begin. Because of the delicate nature of the work, you might want to set the Cursor preferences so that you see the brush size.

5. Choose File, Preferences, Display & Cursors, and set the Painting Cursors option to Brush size. That's it; you're ready to begin.

6. Click and drag the cursor around the iris of one eye and then the other. As you move the cursor, you'll see how the areas you move over lighten. I chose to stay away from the outer edges for a more dramatic effect. I also didn't overdo the dodging. You can see the changes I made in Figure 8.6.

FIGURE 8.6

Before (left) and after (right) comparison of Pamela's portrait.

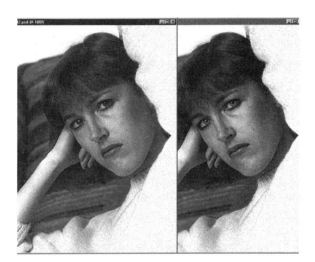

7. If you'd like to save the changes you made to the file, choose File, Save. You can save the file under another name with File, Save As to keep a copy of the original and a new copy of the changed image.

8. You can now close the image with File, Close unless you want to continue working on it, which we pick up with in the following section.

You can see that the changes are subtle enough to remain believable yet are strong enough to add some drama to the portrait. This same tool can be used with color photographs. In fact, you could use it to remove freckles, for example, by lightening them until they match the skin shade surrounding them. You can also use the Rubber Stamp tool, which I'll demonstrate later in this chapter, to do small corrections for dust and scratches on photos.

I recommend you play around with this tool and try the different settings until you're comfortable with how this tool works. Just make sure that you're not working on an original photograph.

The Burn Tool

The Burn tool works exactly the same as the Dodge tool except that it darkens an area. To complete the dramatic changes to the portrait, I decided to darken Pam's lips. In the original photograph, Pam was wearing a pinkish color on her lips, which didn't show up very well on the print: Photoshop to the rescue.

Darkening a selection with the Burn tool

To follow along, you use the PAM.PSD image you were working on in the last exercise, or you can start fresh by opening the PAM.PSD image from the accompanying CD-ROM.

1. Zoom in on the area you wish to work on. This time, with the same portrait, it's Pam's lips. Select the Burn tool and choose a brush size. I decided to use a bit larger brush, one size up from the smallest.

2. Move the Burn tool over the area you want to darken, by clicking and dragging the mouse, until you're satisfied with the change (see Figure 8.7). As with the Dodge tool, you can set the Shadows, Midtones, or Highlights, and you can select the opacity of the tool in the Burn Options palette.

FIGURE **8.7**

Before and after comparison of Pamela's portrait.

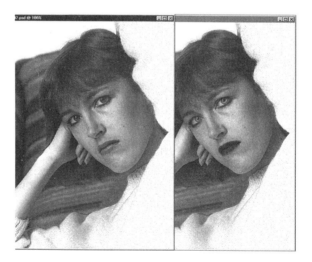

There are many things that still could be done to this photo, but I think that you should be getting an idea of how powerful the Photoshop tools are. The third tool in the Dodge, Burn, and Sponge flyout menu is the Sponge tool, which we cover in the next section.

The Sponge Tool

The Sponge tool saturates/desaturates areas of an image. Of course, this won't be very evident with a black-and-white image, so I'd like you to do the following exercise with a color image and see for yourself exactly what happens to the image as you apply the tool.

Saturating an image with the Sponge tool

1. Create a 300×100 new image by choosing File, New (Ctrl+N or Cmd+N). Set the width to 300, the height to 100, the resolution to 72, the mode to RGB, and the contents to white.

2. Choose the Rectangular Marquee tool and select a square area in the middle of the image.

3. Click the foreground color swatch in the toolbox to bring up the Color Picker. Enter 160, 221, and 221 for the RGB values. It will be a pale grayish-blue.

4. Select the Paint Bucket tool and then click somewhere in the selected area to fill it with the blue color.

5. Click the default Foreground and Background colors to set the default black foreground and white background.

6. Select the Magic Wand tool and click the white area to the right of the blue area.

7. Select the Paint Bucket tool and click in the selected area.

You should now have an image similar to Figure 8.8. You're ready to see how the Sponge tool works.

FIGURE 8.8

White, blue, and black bars.

8. Select the Sponge tool from the toolbox and take a look at the available options in the Sponge Options palette.

9. You'll notice that you can't choose Highlights, Midtones, or Shadows for this tool. Instead you can only choose Desaturate or Saturate. You can still set the Pressure, though. In fact, set the pressure to 100% and set the tool to desaturate.

10. Choose a fairly large brush size and then click and drag the brush back and forth across the top half of the image.

What do you see happening? The white and black areas remain unchanged while the blue area starts to lose color, which is, in effect, desaturating. In fact, if you apply the Sponge tool several times, the blue color becomes totally desaturated until it is a shade of gray (see Figure 8.9).

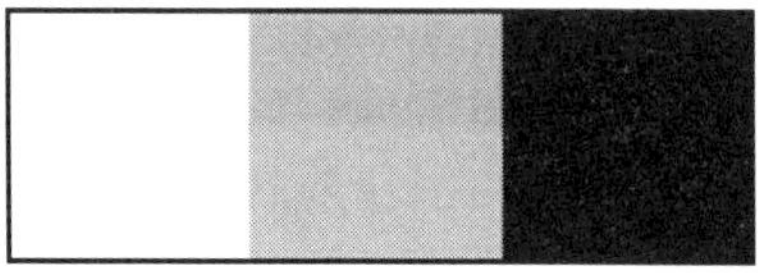

FIGURE 8.9

White, blue, and black bars with the top half of blue desaturated.

11. Now select the Saturate option and move the tool over the bottom half of the image. Again, the white and black areas remain unchanged. The blue area, on the other hand, becomes more saturated, picking up more and more color. If you apply the tool several times, the blue becomes quite bright (see Figure 8.10).

12. Save your image at this point so that you can use it again in the following section.

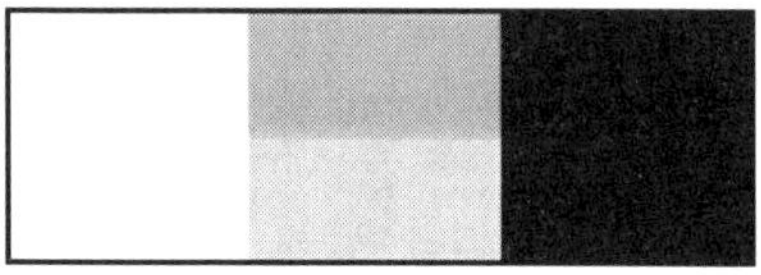

FIGURE 8.10

White, blue, and black bars with the bottom half of blue saturated.

Of course, it's not readily evident in the black and white images in the book. However, if you followed along, you can see the changes yourself.

The new RGB values clearly show the difference as well. The original RGB values for the blue were 160, 221, and 221. The top half of the center square now contains the color 198, 206, 206. Almost totally without color, the bottom half of the center square now holds the color 81, 255, 255.

Viewing Color Values

You can see these values by using the Eyedropper tool to select the color of the image and then clicking the foreground color swatch in the toolbox to bring up the Color

Picker. Optionally, you can open the Info palette by clicking its tab or by choosing Window, Show Info. As you move the mouse over your image, the color values are displayed in the Info palette.

As well as seeing the numerical values for the new colors, you can see where these colors lie in respect to other colors in the same shade. You'll notice that the top, desaturated color lies near the left of the color swatch towards the grays, and that the bottom, saturated, color lies closer to the right half of the color swatch. If you looked at the position of the original blue, you'd see that it lay somewhere between the two new colors.

The Focus Tools

The next group of tools comprises the Blur tool, the Sharpen tool, and the Smudge tool. These tools are accessible from a flyout menu that is hidden under the current tool, (whichever of the three is current) just to the left of the Tone tools group. Holding the mouse over the current tool causes the flyout to appear (see Figure 8.11).

FIGURE 8.11

The Focus tools flyout.

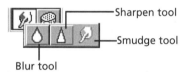

Sharpen tool

Smudge tool

Blur tool

The Smudge Tool

The Smudge tool works as you'd expect it to. It smudges the colors into one another, much like finger painting. You can use the image you created in the last exercise to get a feel for how the Smudge tool works. Before you begin, though, I'll describe the available options.

To begin, select the Smudge tool and take a look at the Smudge Options palette. You'll notice that the first option is the mode. Figure 8.12 shows the modes that are available for this tool.

Note

> I'll discuss the different modes in depth on Day 13, "Layering Your Images," where I demonstrate layers. For now, just leave the mode set to Normal to get a feel for the Smudge tool.

Once you set the mode, you have several remaining options. You can set the pressure for the Smudge tool to determine how much change takes place as you use the tool. As well, you can choose Use All Layers or Finger Painting.

FIGURE 8.12

The Smudge Options palette showing the available modes.

If you choose Use All Layers, the tool uses the color that you see in the composite image. If you leave this option unchecked, the tool uses only the colors from the active layer.

The Finger Painting option causes the tool to use the current foreground color at the beginning of the Smudge. With this option unchecked, the tool uses the color below the cursor as it starts to smudge.

Applying a smudge

1. Using the image you saved in the last exercise, set the mode to Normal and the Pressure to 50%, and leave Use All Layers and Finger Painting unchecked.

2. Move the cursor over the white square and click and drag the cursor into the blue area. See how the white gets smudged into the blue (see Figure 8.13).

FIGURE 8.13

White pixels smudged into the blue area.

3. Set the foreground color to black.

4. Now check, or turn on, the Finger Painting option and click and drag from the white area into the blue area again. Notice that this time the smudge starts out with black instead of the white from the area you started in (see Figure 8.14).

FIGURE 8.14

Black and white pixels smudged into the blue area.

Although this exercise doesn't look at a real-world application, you can see how this might be useful in doing small touch-ups. You could, for example, use this technique to cover up blemishes on a photo.

The Blur Tool

The Blur tool does exactly that; it blurs an area of your image. To see this tool in action, I'll go back to the portrait of Pam. I did some corrections to this image that left a few sharp edges visible, which you can see along the sleeve. They appear as dark lines where I made my selection for the corrections (see Figure 8.15).

FIGURE 8.15

Sharp areas from corrections.

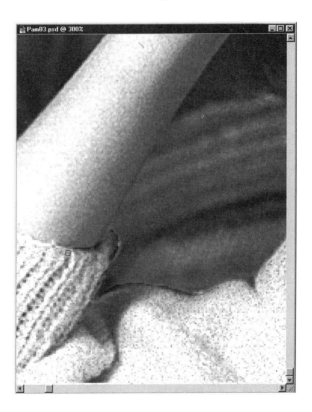

The Blur tool helps soften the edges and hides the fact that corrections were made to this portion of the image. If you want to follow along, load the image into Photoshop and zoom in to about 300%.

Softening an edge with the Blur tool

1. Select the Blur tool and in the Blur Options palette (see Figure 8.16) set the mode to Normal and the Pressure to 50%. Because this is a single layer image, you can leave the Use All Layers option unchecked.

FIGURE 8.16

Blur Options palette.

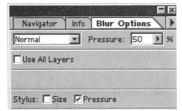

2. Move the cursor to the dark lines along the sleeve, hold down the mouse button, and drag the mouse over the area you want to blur.

You'll want to keep a light hand with this tool because the blurring process can quickly get out of hand, leaving you with a blobby mess. Done properly, the result is quite subtle and not very noticeable. To see the difference, though, take a look at Figure 8.17, which compares the blurred area with the original sharp edge.

FIGURE 8.17

Comparison of the sharp areas and blurred correction.

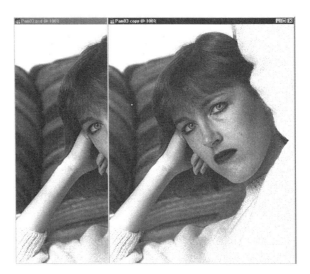

8

The opposite of the Blur tool is the Sharpen tool.

The Sharpen Tool

The Sharpen tool, while it brings out detail in an area, won't repair an out-of-focus image. There's only so much that even Photoshop can do.

In fact, I recommend using an even lighter hand with the Sharpen tool than with the Blur tool. To get a feel for this tool, select and use it to sharpen the blurred edges you just created in the last exercise.

If you were to compare this to the original portrait, you'd see that it doesn't really reverse the blurring. It's much easier to soften and blur an area than it is to add detail where none exists.

The next, and last, tools I'll demonstrate today are the Rubber Stamp and the Pattern Stamp tools.

The Stamp Tools

The Stamp tools are very powerful yet misunderstood and probably quite underused. The Pattern Stamp tool, which is new to version 5, and the Stamp tool can be very effective in correcting and manipulating images. The Rubber Stamp and the Pattern Stamp tools are under the same flyout (see Figure 8.18).

FIGURE 8.18

The Rubber Stamp and Pattern Stamp flyout.

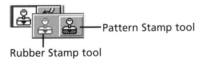

Pattern Stamp tool

Rubber Stamp tool

The Rubber Stamp

Do you have any photographs that you've found, after shooting and developing, were ruined by telephone wires? Do you have an image that you'd like to remove a portion (or person) from? Well, this is where the Rubber Stamp tool comes in.

You can use this tool to copy one portion of an image over another, essentially removing a portion of an image. The Rubber Stamp tool has similar options available as the other tools you've seen today. It has more blending modes, though, and another option called Aligned (see Figure 8.19).

FIGURE 8.19

The Rubber Stamp Options palette.

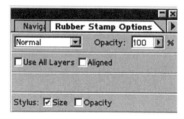

The Aligned option keeps the cursor and the crosshairs relative to each other. The Aligned option unchecked means the Rubber Stamp repeats the cloning from the original area you selected to start the process.

To see how this tool works, load an image into Photoshop. I'll be using a portrait of a dog, whose leash is hanging off to one side.

Editing out a section of an image with the Rubber Stamp

1. Select the Rubber Stamp tool and click anywhere on the image.
2. Oops, this results in an error (see Figure 8.20). You need to select an area for the tool to clone. I'll be removing the leash that runs across the left side of Figure 8.21.

FIGURE 8.20

You have to select an area to clone first.

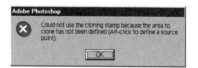

3. To get started, Alt-click (Option-click on a Mac) the leash. Now that the Rubber Stamp tool knows the area you want to clone, you're ready to get started.
4. Click the Rubber Stamp tool and then simply click and drag over the area you want to replace. This can take a little getting used to.

As you work you'll notice that you have two cursors, the one where you're painting and another in the shape of crosshairs. The crosshairs show you which part of the image you're cloning from (see Figure 8.22).

FIGURE 8.21

This picture would look a lot better without the dog's leash.

8

FIGURE 8.22

The Rubber Stamp brush and crosshairs cursor.

Note

At any time you can change the placement of the crosshairs by resampling another area of the image. Simply Alt-click again to grab another cloning area.

Done correctly, this tool can remove any portion of an image by replacing it with another portion of the same image.

You can see in Figure 8.23 that the leash has been removed from the background. What really happened is that I painted over the leash using different parts of the background so that the leash would disappear and be replaced with existing portions of the original image.

FIGURE 8.23

The dog's leash is gone.

This same technique can be used to remove the leash completely. However, this tool really shines at replacing complex portions of an image. Where the image is more monotone, such as just a blue sky, it's a much easier challenge. I'll demonstrate this when I talk about selections.

The Pattern Stamp Tool

8

As I mentioned earlier, the Pattern Stamp tool is new to Photoshop 5. It's a really cool addition, too.

To use the Pattern Stamp, you need to first define a pattern. To define a pattern, you need to make either a rectangular or square selection. This tool won't work with elliptical or circular selections.

To demonstrate the Pattern Stamp, I'll use a scan of a photograph taken of the side of a barn (see Figure 8.24).

FIGURE 8.24

A scan of some wood.

Working with the Pattern Stamp

1. Choose Select, All and then choose Edit, Define Pattern. Again you may notice that if you try to do this with a circular, elliptical, or odd-shaped selection, the Define Pattern option is grayed out.

2. Now that you've defined a pattern, it's time to paint with it. Open a new file with File, New.

3. Select the Pattern Stamp tool and select a brush size.

4. Click and drag anywhere in the image. Presto! You're painting the image with a brush that contains the pattern. Cool! You can see the results in Figure 8.25.

FIGURE 8.25

A wood pattern stamped onto an image.

Summary

Well, that's it for today and for the editing tools. Now you should load some images of your own (make sure you have backups) and play around with all the tools you learned about today. These are some of the more powerful tools available from the toolbox, and you should be able to choose a tool based on the image and the editing you need to do. With Photoshop, as with many other things, there is always more than one way to accomplish a particular task. If you play around with these tools enough, though, you'll usually be able to choose the proper tool for the job. This can save time as well as giving you the best results.

Q&A

Q What are some of the other options I have for changing how an editing tool performs?

A You can set the pressure or opacity of the different editing tools. As well, you can set the Blending modes. I'll explain the modes on Day 13.

Q When opening two images, is there an easy way to size them so that they appear side by side and have the same height and width?

A Yes, you can resize the image's window by clicking and dragging its sides. You can move an image around the workspace by clicking and dragging its title bar.

Workshop

The section that follows is a quick quiz about the chapter. If you have any problems answering any of the questions in the quiz, see the section directly following it for all the answers.

8

Quiz

1. Briefly describe the function of the Dodge, Burn, and Sponge tools.
2. How do you access color information values and percentages?
3. What effect does the Exposure option have on a tool?
4. What's the difference between the Rubber Stamp tool and the Pattern Stamp tool?
5. How do you create a rectangular selection?

Quiz Answers

1. The Dodge tool lightens an area, the Burn tool darkens an area, and the Sponge tool softens an area.
2. You can view color information by opening the Info palette and moving the mouse over your image.
3. It determines how drastic the changes the tool makes will be.
4. The Rubber Stamp tool copies a defined area of the image, while the Pattern Stamp replaces areas with a predefined pattern.
5. You can select the Rectangular Marquee tool and click and drag it to define a rectangular area.

DAY 9

Creating Selections and Defining Paths

Some of the real power of Photoshop lies in how you can manipulate images. The effects you can apply are even more powerful, however, when you can limit where you apply the effect, which you can do by first selecting an area of your image. Selections can be made in a number of ways with Photoshop and the selection tools available are quite powerful. The basic operations of the selection tools are easy to understand, but you can do some amazing things with selections as you come to understand the process. This chapter covers the following topics:

- Working with the selection tools
- Defining and editing selections
- Creating paths

The Marquee Tools

The first thing you'll notice is that there seems to be two ways to create or manipulate selections. There are the Marquee tools at the top of the toolbox and there is also a menu called, oddly enough, Select.

Available at the top of the toolbox are the Marquee Selection tools, including the Elliptical Marquee, Lasso, Move, and Magic Wand tools (see Figure 9.1). But these aren't all the selection tools. Both the Elliptical Marquee and Lasso tools have flyouts that house even more selection tools (see Figures 9.2 and 9.9).

FIGURE 9.1

The Marquee tools.

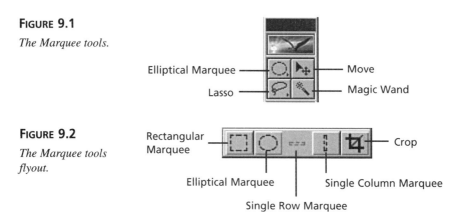

Elliptical Marquee — Move
Lasso — Magic Wand

FIGURE 9.2

The Marquee tools flyout.

Rectangular Marquee — Crop
Elliptical Marquee
Single Column Marquee
Single Row Marquee

Each of these selections tools has an associated Marquee Options palette. To access the Marquee Options palette, first choose one of the Marquee tools. Then click F8 to bring up the Info palette and choose the Options tab. Within the Marquee Options palette, you can set the feathering, the anti-aliasing, and the style of the tool:

- **Feathering** softens the edges of a selection.
- **Anti-aliasing** smoothes the transition of the edges.
- **Style** enables you to set either Normal, Constrained (in other words, a circle instead of an ellipse), or Fixed, where you define the size of the selection.

For example, if you select the Rectangular Marquee tool, you can choose Normal, Constrained Aspect Ratio, or Fixed Size from the Style options. The Normal option enables you to select rectangular areas, the Constrained Aspect Ratio option enables you to select square areas, and the Fixed Size option enables you to enter numerical values for the selection. In the case of the Rectangular Marquee tool, you can also set the width and height. We'll learn more about these options in the following sections.

Defining a New Selection

All selections on an image are denoted by broken lines that appear to march around the selected area (see Figure 9.3). Of course, the lines won't be marching on the book page, but if you select the Rectangular Marquee tool and draw a shape on a new image, you'll see the movement I'm describing. Because of this movement, the Marquee is often referred to as "marching ants." Everything inside the Marquee is selected.

FIGURE 9.3

*Dandelions with
Rectangular Marquee.*

In the following steps, you'll practice making simple selections and then deselecting them. To begin, you'll need to open the image dandelions.psd from Chap09 of the accompanying CD-ROM.

1. Choose the Rectangular Marquee tool by clicking it.

2. Draw a selection around the bottom dandelion in the image by clicking and dragging the mouse. When you let go of the mouse, the marching ants should be dancing around the bottom dandelion.

   As you can see, a Rectangular Marquee doesn't fit too nicely around the flower. Instead you'd be much better off using an Elliptical Marquee.

3. Choose Select, Deselect to deselect the Rectangular Marquee.

 4. Select the Elliptical Marquee tool and then repeat step 2.

Now the selection fits much more closely around the dandelion (see Figure 9.4), but the selection doesn't look too great on the left side of the image. Let's move the selection, or the Marquee, so that it fits around the flower a little better.

FIGURE 9.4

Dandelion with the Elliptical Marquee.

5. With the dandelion still selected, move the cursor into the selected area.

6. Click the selection and drag it to the right and down a little (see Figure 9.5).

FIGURE 9.5

The Elliptical Marquee repositioned.

7. Deselect the selection by choosing Select, Deselect.

8. If you want, you can save your image at this point, but it's not really necessary.

Editing a Selection

Once a selection has been made, you can do all sorts of wondrous things to it. You can stroke it, fill it, change its brightness and contrast, change its color, you name it.

Stroking, for example, is a great and easy way to create new shapes. Stroking a selection applies an outline to a selected area. To see this in action, follow along below:

1. Create a new file of about 400×400 pixels. Set the resolution to 72 dpi and the contents to White.

2. Select the Rectangular Marquee tool and draw a selection somewhere in the middle of the image by clicking and dragging the mouse in the image.

3. Choose Edit, Stroke. This brings up the Stroke dialog box.

4. Enter the same values you see in Figure 9.6. Click OK. The value you enter for the stroke width determines the width of the outline.

FIGURE 9.6

The Stroke dialog box.

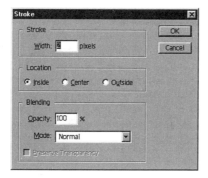

5. Choose Select, Deselect and you should have a rectangle drawn on your image as in Figure 9.7. If you want, you can save this image or you can close it without saving.

FIGURE **9.7**

*Rectangular shape
drawn in Photoshop.*

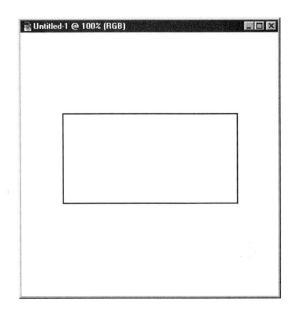

Note   You can draw circles, ellipses, and squares the same way using the
Rectangular and Elliptical Marquee tools. You already know how to create
rectangles and ellipses, but you may be wondering how to go about creating perfect circles and squares. The answer lies in the Shift key. As long as
you press the Shift key while you drag, your selection is automatically constrained to a circle or square. Also, pressing the Alt+Shift (Option+Shift) keys
draws your square or circle at the place where the cursor is when you begin
the selection at the center (it draws the selection from the center out).

Cropping an Image

The Crop tool, included with the Marquee tools, enables you to crop an image quickly.
Once you've selected an area with the Crop tool, you can manipulate the area. You can
resize it and rotate it, for example.

In the following steps, you'll learn to crop an image. To begin, you'll need to open the
image cangoose.psd from Chap09 on the accompanying CD-ROM.

1. Select the Crop tool by clicking it (it's in the flyout menu with the Marquee tools).
2. Click somewhere above and to the left of the Canada Goose in the image, and drag
   to make a selection around the goose. When you let go of the mouse, the marching
   ants and bounding boxes should surround the goose, as shown in Figure 9.8.

FIGURE 9.8

Canada Goose with crop marks visible.

3. You can adjust the selection by dragging any of the bounding boxes around the selection's perimeter. As well, you can drag the center of rotation and then rotate the cropped area. Try this now until you get an image that you like.

4. Double-click, or press the Enter key, to perform the final crop.

5. If you want, you can save your image at this point, but it's not really necessary.

The Lasso Tools

Just as there are times when a rectangular selection won't work, there are times when a circular selection won't work any better either. Sometimes you'll need to draw polygon-shaped selections, and that's when you need to use the Lasso tools (shown in the Lasso tool flyout in Figure 9.9).

FIGURE 9.9

Lasso tool flyout.

Lasso ——— 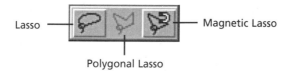 ——— Magnetic Lasso

Polygonal Lasso

The Lasso enables you to draw freehand selections, and the Polygonal Lasso enables you to draw polygon-shaped selections, but of interest in Photoshop 5 is the new Magnetic Lasso tool.

The Magnetic Lasso helps you draw freehand selections by staying within the lines as you drag it around. This can be a little hard to get used to but is also very powerful. It works by measuring the contrast between areas.

Say, for example, you want to change the color of the lipstick on a portrait. The first thing you'd want to do is select the model's lips, right? How you should go about this is another matter. You could just draw a freehand selection around the lips, but this can be hit-and-miss. What if the tool followed the outline between the model's lips and her face? This would be a big help.

To show you how this works, I selected the Magnetic Lasso tool and set the options as you see in Figure 9.10. (If the Magnetic Lasso Options palette isn't visible, you can access it by choosing Window, Show Options.) This enabled me to make the selection around the lips in the portrait by simply dragging the mouse loosely around the lips (see Figure 9.11).

FIGURE 9.10

The Magnetic Lasso Options palette.

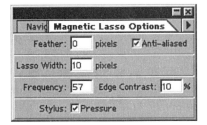

FIGURE 9.11

The model's lips select-ed using the Magnetic Lasso tool.

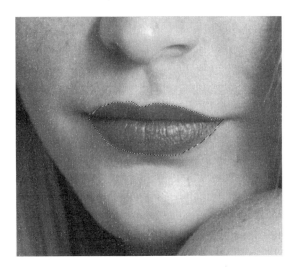

With the lips selected, it is a simple matter to change their color, brighten them up, or even invert the selection (choose Select, Inverse) and desaturate the rest of the portrait, leaving only the lips with any color on them.

Modifying Selections

In a perfect world, all your selections would be, well, perfect. However, this isn't a perfect world and it's unlikely that you'll create the perfect selection every time. In Photoshop, though, it's a relatively simple matter to modify a selected area.

Adding to a Selection

After you've made a selection, you can add to it by using the Marquee or Lasso tools and holding down the Shift key while using the tool. If, for example, you select the Lasso tool and hold down the Shift key, you'll notice that a small plus sign appears next to the cursor. This means that the tool will add to the current selection. The new area you select can be an adjoining area, but it doesn't have to be. By adding selections you can build up an area and actually draw some quite complex shapes. I sometimes use this method to rough-out shapes for interfaces for Web pages. If the shape is too complex, I'll turn to my vector drawing program, CorelDRAW, but if the shape isn't too hard to draw with circles, squares, ellipses, and rectangles, I'll just rough it out in Photoshop. Figure 9.15 is a shape I created as a template for an interface idea.

To get an idea of how this is done, try the following:

1. Open a new 400×400 image at 72 dpi and with the content set to white.

2. Select the Rectangular Marquee tool and draw a rectangular selection in the middle of the image (see Figure 9.12).

3. Now select the Elliptical Marquee tool and set the Style to Constrained Aspect Ratio in the Options palette.

4. Place the cursor along the top of the rectangle at about the same distance from the top-left corner as half the vertical depth of your rectangle. Then draw a circular selection while holding down the Shift key to add this selection to the rectangular selection. This may seem a little difficult, but you'll see what I'm talking about as soon as you try it. If you're too close or too far, the circular selection won't quite fit with the circle. If you get it right, you'll see something like Figure 9.13.

5. Now do the same to the right side. Don't forget to hold down the Shift key. You should now have a pill-shaped selection, as seen in Figure 9.14.

6. Save your figure to your hard drive so that you can use it in the next exercise.

FIGURE 9.12

Rectangular selection.

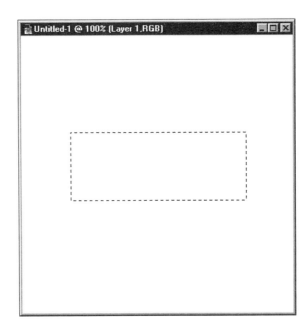

FIGURE 9.13

The circular selection added to the left side of the rectangular selection.

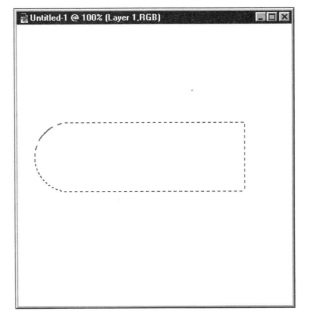

FIGURE 9.14

A pill-shaped selection created from a rectangular and two circular selections added together.

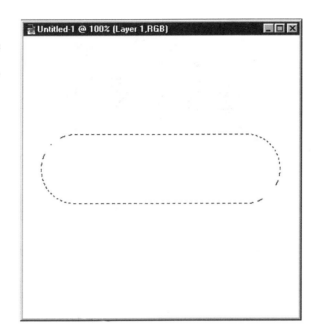

Some Photoshop users may argue that this can be accomplished more easily by choosing Select, Modify, Smooth. It's true that you can do this by Smoothing the selection, but I don't think that the resulting shape is as good. Also, because you're limited to a maximum value of 16 pixels, you must run the Smooth option several times to get the same effect. In any event, this is merely an exercise to show you how to add selections. Once you've seen how this works, you can use it to create many shapes that could not be created by smoothing.

The shape was put together with a couple of circles and several rectangles (see Figure 9.15). After adding some textures and a couple of rounded buttons, the final image is shown in Figure 9.16.

FIGURE 9.15

The template drawn using selection tools.

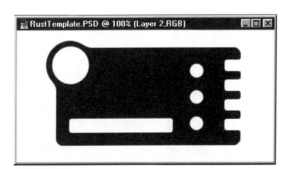

FIGURE 9.16

*The final interface cre-
ated completely in
Photoshop.*

Subtracting from Selections

Subtracting circular areas from the main selection created the circles that you see in the template. You can subtract an area using any of the Marquee or Lasso tools by holding down the Alt key (the Option key on a Mac).

Being able to add to or subtract from a selected area is a very powerful feature. There are other ways to modify a selection as well.

To see how this works, use the selection you created in the previous exercise.

1. Select the Elliptical Marquee tool and place the cursor above and to the left of center of the existing selection.

2. Hold down the Alt (Option) key and draw an oval selection over the middle of the pill-shaped selection. This cuts the pill-shaped selection into two pieces (see Figure 9.17).

FIGURE 9.17

*A pill-shaped selection
cut in two by having
an elliptical selection
subtracted from it.*

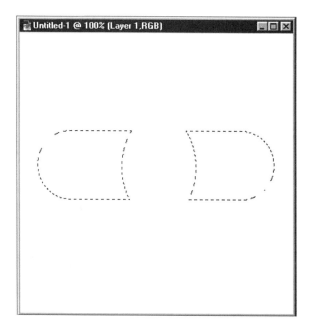

You can keep adding to and subtracting from a selection. Figure 9.18 shows the pill shape with several rectangular pieces cut out from it. Although there is quite a bit of work involved, you can actually create some complex shapes using these methods.

FIGURE 9.18

A pill-shaped selection with several rectangular selections cut out.

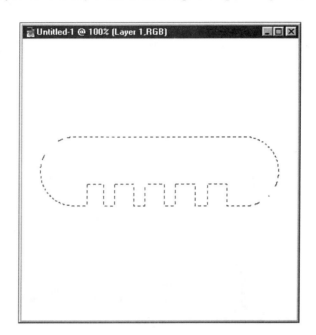

9

Selection Menu Modifications

As I mentioned earlier, you can also manipulate selections from the Select menu, where a number of choices are available (see Figure 9.19). You can select all of an image, deselect the selection, reselect a selection that you've deselected, or invert the selection so that the selected area becomes unselected and the rest of the image becomes the selected portion. This can be a great way to select an area of an image that might be difficult to select any other way.

If, for example, you have some textured text surrounded by a solid background and you wanted to select the text, you would simply select the background using the Magic Wand tool, and then choose Select, Similar to select any of the holes in letters such as a, b, d, and so on, then choose Select, Inverse. Believe me, this is easier to do than to explain. To see how this works, open the CoolText.psd file from folder Day09 (see Figure 9.20).

You can see how it would be difficult to select the text because it's textured and filled with several colors. What you can do, though, is select the background and invert the selection so that you end up with the text being selected.

FIGURE **9.19**

The Select menu.

FIGURE **9.20**

CoolText.psd.

1. Select the Magic Wand tool and click somewhere on the background to select it (see Figure 9.21).

FIGURE **9.21**

Cool text with the background selected.

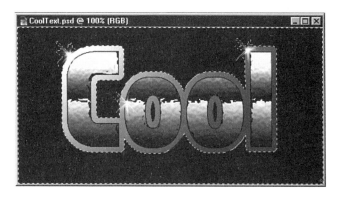

2. At this point, you can choose Select, Similar to select the holes in the "o's". However, this may end up selecting the black areas within the letters because the color is the same in these areas as it is in the holes. Try it and see. You can choose Edit, Undo once you see that more of the image is selected than you intended. The best option in this case might be to add to the selection by holding down the Shift key and clicking in the holes with the Magic Wand.

3. With the entire background selected (see Figure 9.22), it's a simple matter to inverse the selection. Choose Select, Inverse. You'll then have only the textured text selected (see Figure 9.23).

9

FIGURE 9.22

Cool Text with the entire background selected.

FIGURE 9.23

Cool Text selected.

There are a couple of ways that the selection can be modified from the Select menu. Choosing Select, Modify brings out another menu that enables you to Border, Smooth, Expand, or Contract a selection (see Figure 9.24).

FIGURE 9.24

*The Select, Modify
menu.*

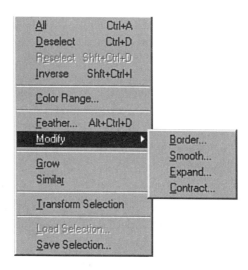

Feathering a Selection

Even though you can specify the feathering value for a selection tool via its Options
palette, you can change the feather value from the Select menu. Choosing Select, Feather
brings up the Feather Selection dialog box (see Figure 9.25).

FIGURE 9.25

*The Feather Selection
dialog box.*

You can enter a value here to lower or raise the feathering effect of the selection.
Feathering a selection softens its edges. For example, Figure 9.26 is a simple black and
white portrait. Figure 9.27 is the same portrait, but I made an oval selection, inverted it,
and pressed the Delete key.

FIGURE 9.26

Black-and-white portrait.

9

FIGURE 9.27

Black-and-white portrait with oval vignette.

Note the hard edge of the selection. The overall vignette effect might be better with soft edges, right? No problem. By making the selection and choosing Select, Feather, you can soften the edges of the selection. I entered a value of 10 and ended up with Figure 9.28 after inverting the selection and pressing the Delete key. Notice the softer edge.

Figure 9.28

Black-and-white portrait with "feathered" oval vignette.

9

Adding Borders to a Selection

Choosing Select, Modify, Border draws a border around your selection. This is easier to see than to explain, so I'll walk you through the steps involved and you can see for yourself how this works.

1. Create a new 400×400 image by choosing Ctrl+N (Cmd+N).

2. Select the Rectangular Marquee tool and make a rectangular selection. (see Figure 9.29). If you fill, this selection you'll have a filled rectangle, and if you stroke it—as I demonstrated earlier—you'll have a lined rectangle.

3. Now choose Select, Border, enter 40 for the Width, and click OK. You've just drawn a 40-pixel border around your selection (see Figure 9.30).

FIGURE 9.29

Rectangular selection.

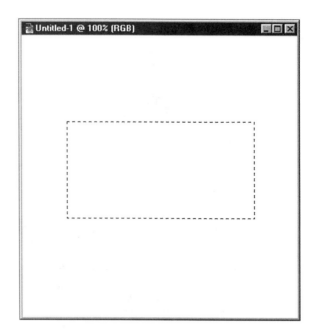

FIGURE 9.30

Forty-pixel border drawn around the rectangular selection.

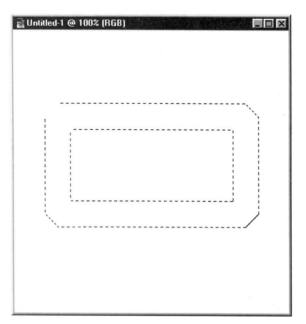

4. If you choose Edit, Stroke, you'll see that this selection is quite different from the original rectangular area. Try it. You can use Edit, Undo to undo the effect.

5. You can save your image at this point if you want, but it's not necessary.

Smoothing a Selection

You can also smooth a selection by choosing Select, Modify, Smooth. This option smoothes out corners, effectively rounding them. If you apply the Smooth option (with a sample radius of 10 pixels) to the rectangular selection in Figure 9.30, you'll end up with a selection that resembles Figure 9.31.

FIGURE 9.31

Smoothed rectangular selection.

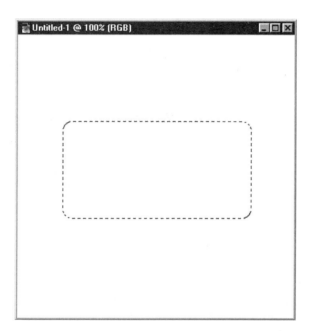

Expanding and Contracting a Selection

Expanding and contracting a selection enables you to expand or shrink a selection by a given number of pixels. When you choose one of these options, you get a small dialog box where you can enter the value you'd like to have the selection modified by. This shrinks or expands the marquee, effectively enabling you to select less or more of the image.

Grow and Similar Selection Options

Growing a selection adds to the area that you've selected. When you choose Grow from the Select menu, Photoshop expands the selected area by matching pixels with the same attributes as those pixels already selected. Growing is restricted, however, to areas that are adjacent to the selected area. It's different from expanding, in that expanding grows outward evenly by the amount that you specify in the dialog box, while grow encompasses pixels of similar color. To see what I mean, take a look at Figure 9.32. I've selected one of the gray squares. Now I can expand the selection as I've done in Figure 9.33.

FIGURE 9.32

A selected gray square.

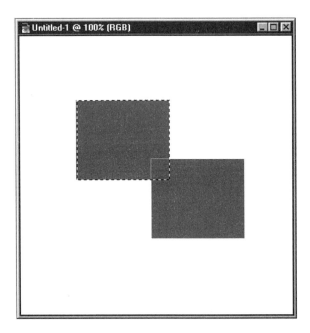

Instead of expanding the selection, though, I could use the Grow option (Select, Grow), which grows the selection to include all the adjacent gray areas (see Figure 9.34).

You can also select similar areas of the image by choosing Select Similar. Similar acts much like Grow except that the selection is not restricted to adjacent areas. It selects all areas in an image that are similar to the area(s) that is already selected.

FIGURE 9.33

A selected gray square with the selection expanded.

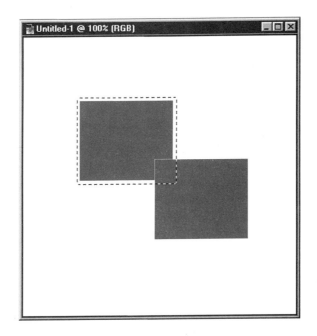

FIGURE 9.34

Both gray squares selected with the Grow option.

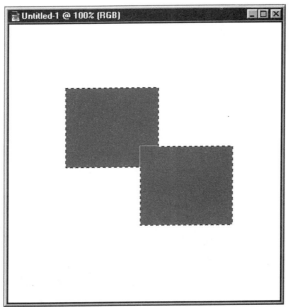

Transforming a Selection

Transforming a selection enables you to perform all kinds of neat tricks with a selection. To see what I mean, try the following with the rectangular selection that you created a few moments ago in the previous section, or you can quickly re-create it by following step one:

1. Create a new 400×400 image at 72 dpi and with the contents set to white.

2. Select the Rectangular Marquee tool and draw a rectangular selection (see Figure 9.29 from the preceding exercise).

3. Choose Select, Transform Selection. You'll see the marching ants change into a bounding box with small squares at each corner, small squares between each corner, and a small center of rotation icon (see Figure 9.35).

FIGURE 9.35

The Transform bounding box around a selection.

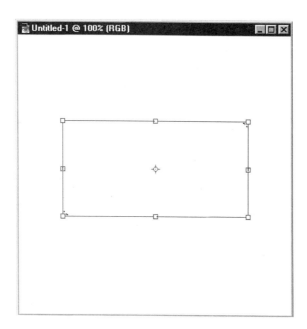

4. Click and drag the selection (place the cursor inside the bounding box). You'll see that it moves about freely.

5. Expand the selection by dragging outward on one of the small squares.

6. Now move the mouse near one of the corner squares outside of the selection until the cursor turns into a small curve. You can now rotate the selection as I've done (see Figure 9.36) by dragging the cursor.

FIGURE 9.36

Rotated rectangular selection.

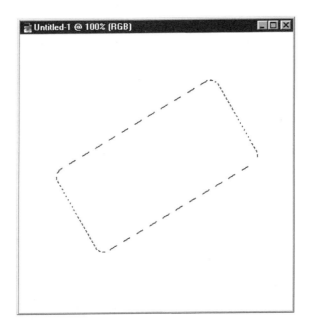

7. Double-click within the bounding box to get the marching ants back or, in other words, turn the transformed area back into a selection.

8. If you want, you can save your image at this point, but it's not necessary.

Loading and Saving Selections

Before you can load a selection you must save one. Using the image with the rectangular selection that you created earlier active, choose Select, Save Selection. This brings up the Save Selection dialog box (see Figure 9.37).

FIGURE 9.37

The Save Selection dialog box.

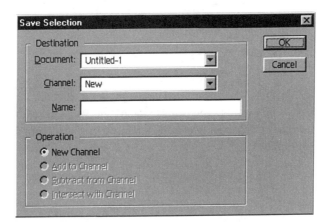

You can set the destination for your selection. You can use the current image or a new image as the document. As well, you can choose the channel and select a name. If this is the second or subsequent selection, you can choose to add it to another already-saved selection, subtract it from another previously saved selection, or intersect it with a previous selection.

The selection(s) you save become channels and are subsequently saved if you save your images in the PSD file format. This is a great way to save complex selections. For example, when I made the selection around the model's lips earlier, I could have saved that selection and then made further modifications to the selected area without having to redo the selection.

Note   Selections are saved as alpha channels. I'll describe these channels along with other channels on Day 12, "Working with Channels."

Once a selection has been saved, it can be loaded. You can even load selections that were saved along with other images. Quite powerful, I'm sure you'll agree. Figure 9.38 shows some of the Load Selection options.

FIGURE 9.38

The Load Selection dialog box.

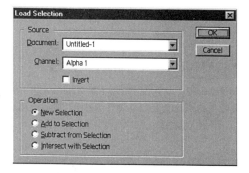

The Magic Wand Tool

Ahh, the Magic Wand... The Magic Wand tool is the last selection tool in the toolbox, but it's certainly not the least powerful. The Magic Wand is, well, magic. Okay, so it's not magic, but it is pretty cool. You can use the Magic Wand to select large similar areas. Just how similar is dependent upon the tolerance that you set in the Magic Wand Options palette (see Figure 9.39).

FIGURE 9.39

The Magic Wand Options palette.

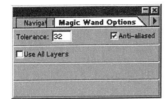

A lower Tolerance setting decreases how much of the image surrounding the Wand is selected. What gets selected is dependent on the color of the pixels. An extremely low Tolerance value selects only a few pixels on a portion of the image with many subtle changes. A high setting will end up selecting the entire image. You can see how powerful this tool is and how hard it can be to get it to cooperate. It's well worth the time spent playing around with it, though. As you go through some of the tutorials later in the book, you'll see that the Magic Wand can be very helpful.

Selecting by Color Range

Now that you've had a glimpse at the Magic Wand and how it works, you might see the reason why I grouped the Magic Wand with the Color Range menu selection, or you will after seeing how the Color Range option works.

I can't remember seeing this option discussed in other beginner's Photoshop books. It's kind of hard to get a handle on, but I'm going to walk you through it step-by-step. I've created an image that you can use with this exercise, too. By opening the image CLR.GRAD.PSD (see Figure 9.40) from Day09 on the accompanying CD-ROM and following along on the computer, you'll get a good idea on how the Color Range Selection option works.

FIGURE 9.40

The Colors and Gradient image from the CD-ROM.

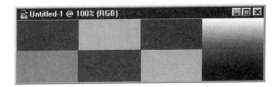

Part of the reason you need to open this image to see what's going on is that the pages you're reading are in black and white, which doesn't really help when you're trying to grasp a concept that works with color.

The image is composed of seven parts. Along the top, you have red, green, and blue rectangles. Along the bottom, you have cyan, magenta, and yellow rectangles. At the right is a white to black linear gradient.

All of the colors are pure. That is to say, the red is 255, 0, 0 in the RGB palette. The green is 0, 255, 0, and so on. The same is true for the cyan, magenta, and yellow except that their values are in the CMYK space.

With the image open and visible, choose Select, Color Range to bring up the Color Range dialog box (see Figure 9.41). What you see is the result of selecting the red area of the image. The selected area shows up as white, while the rest of the image, the part that hasn't been selected, shows as black.

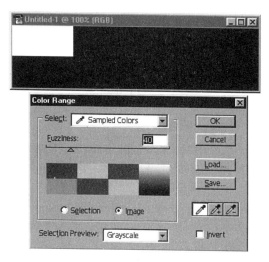

I chose Select Sampled and used the Eyedropper with the plus sign to "sample" the red rectangle. As well as sampling areas of the image, you can select using different colors. You can choose from red, green, blue, cyan, magenta, and yellow. You can select highlights, midtones, and shadows as well. Figure 9.42 shows what the result of selecting the highlights of the image would be.

In Figure 9.42, I've chosen to view the preview using a Quick Mask. Although this isn't really visible in black and white, if you select the same option (Selection Preview), you'll see that the non-selected area is a dark-reddish color, while the selected area is pale red.

If you click OK at this point, you'll see that the areas you chose based on colors or brightness do indeed translate to selections. Again, this is a very powerful feature, and one that is worth examining in some depth when you have a few moments to play around with Photoshop.

FIGURE 9.42

The Color Range dialog box with Highlights selected.

Creating Paths

Although paths are a bit beyond the scope of this book, I'd like to at least introduce you to them so that you have an idea of what they're all about.

Paths are vector in nature, that is, they have nodes that can be manipulated, and they are much more flexible than selections. With this flexibility, though, comes a steeper learning curve. If you've ever worked with a drawing program such as Illustrator or CorelDRAW, then you have an idea of what paths are. In a drawing program, virtually everything is a path.

If you create a selection as you did earlier with the Rectangular Marquee tool, I'll show you what paths are all about.

1. Create a selection. I'll use the transformed one from Figure 9.19 for this exercise.

2. With an area selected, click the Paths tab in the Layers, Channels, and Paths palette.

3. Click the small black arrow to the left of the Paths tab in the Paths palette and choose Make Work Path (see Figure 9.43). Leave the Tolerance set at the default and click OK.

The dialog box disappears and not much else seems to happen, right? Well, your selection is now a path and can be manipulated in ways that a selection never could.

FIGURE **9.43**

The Paths palette.

4. Select the Direct Selection tool from the toolbox and click somewhere on the selection/path.

5. Whoa! There ya go! Notice all those small circles around the path (see Figure 9.44). These are nodes and they can be used to shape the path. This is not something that you could do to a selection.

FIGURE **9.44**

The path with nodes visible.

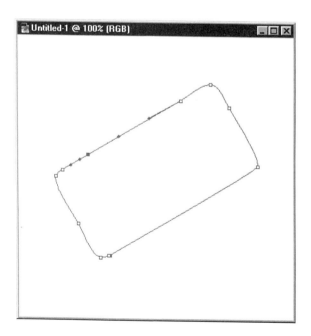

6. Using the Direct Selection tool, again click and drag the node at the lower-right corner towards the center of the rectangle (see Figure 9.45).

FIGURE 9.45

Node manipulation in a bitmap program. Incredible!

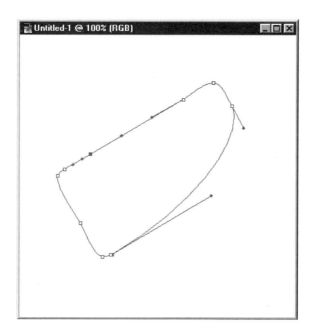

9

Once you've manipulated the path into the exact shape you want, you can turn it back into a selection.

7. To do so, click the small black arrow again. Choose Make Selection and click OK in the dialog box. Click the arrow again and choose Turn Off Path. Once again, you now have a selection.

As I said, I won't go to deeply into paths here, but I think you've just had a glimpse of the power of paths. There's much, much more though.

Summary

You probably feel that this was a rather long day, and I don't blame you. You've covered a lot of ground today. However, having a good idea of how the selection tools and options work is an essential step on the road to becoming proficient in the use of Photoshop. This may well be one chapter that you come back to again and again. Being able to make good selections is something that you'll find yourself relying on just about every time you want to make an adjustment to an image in Photoshop. All the tools are here; it's just a matter of patience and practice. As you move through the rest of this book, you'll plenty of chances to practice your new selection skills.

Q&A

Q Why are selections necessary in Photoshop?

A Selections that you make in Photoshop let the program know what areas of the image you wish to change or work with. Remember, Photoshop is mostly about selecting groups of pixels and making changes to those groups.

Q You mentioned viewing the selection through the Quick Mask in the Color Range section of this chapter. What is a Quick Mask?

A A Quick Mask is a way of making selections that wasn't covered in this chapter. I'll demonstrate that technique later on Day 11, "Masking with Layer Masks and Quick Masks."

Q Is it possible to save a path?

A Yes. Click the small black arrow to the right of the Paths tab and choose Save Path. This creates a path much as a layer or a channel is created. The resulting path is saved along with your image.

Workshop

The next section is a quick quiz about the chapter you have just read. If you have any problems answering any of the questions in the quiz, see the section directly following it for all the answers.

Quiz

1. How do create a selection in the shape of a perfect circle?
2. How do you move a selection?
3. How do set the tolerance for the Magnetic Lasso tool?
4. How do you invert a selection?
5. What's the difference between a selection and a path?

Quiz Answers

1. You can constrain the selection via the Options palette or you can hold down the Shift key to constrain the ellipse to a circle.

2. You simply click and drag it.

3. You can set it with the Magnetic Lasso Options palette by changing the Edge Contrast value.

4. Choose Select, Inverse.

5. Although they are similar in some ways, paths are more powerful in that you can manipulate their shapes more easily and to a greater extent. Paths can also be exported to Illustrator.

9

WEEK 2

DAY 10

Painting with Fills, Patterns, and Gradients

Even though Photoshop was intended to be, and still is, a photo enhancement and manipulation tool, it has capabilities that allow it to be used to draw and paint. In fact, Photoshop has a pretty impressive collection of drawing and painting tools. You can draw with an airbrush, a paintbrush, or a pencil. You can paint with solid colors, patterns, and gradients, and you can define your own patterns and brushes. All these options make Photoshop a very versatile paint program as well as a superb photo-manipulation program. In this chapter, we'll cover the following:

- Working with the Paint Bucket and Gradient tools
- Understanding aliasing and anti-aliasing
- Using and customizing the various brushes

Using the Paint Bucket Tool

The Paint Bucket is very easy to use. With it you can fill selected areas or the entire image with either a solid color or a predefined pattern. Although the Paint Bucket tool has few options, it's still quite powerful (see Figure 10.1).

To use the Paint Bucket tool, simply select it and click where you'd like to apply the fill. You can fill an entire layer, restrict the fill to an area with a certain color, or restrict the fill to a selected area. You can also set the fill to be anti-aliased (I'll describe aliasing in a moment), vary its Opacity, and set the Tolerance.

FIGURE **10.1**

The Paint Bucket Options palette.

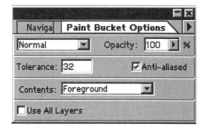

The Tolerance setting determines how the fill moves into areas of different colors. The Fill tool fills from where you click the mouse outward. It stops when it comes across a different color, the edge of a selection, or the edge of the image. The following steps walk you through the Tolerance options.

1. Begin by creating an image that's half white and half black (see Figure 10.2).

FIGURE **10.2**

Half-white, half-black test image.

 2. Set the foreground color to a light gray, select the Paint Bucket tool, and then click in the white area (see Figure 10.3). Only the white area is filled with light gray because the Tolerance setting is at the default 32.

FIGURE **10.3**

White area filled with light gray.

3. Now repeat step 2, but bump up the Tolerance from the default 32 to the maximum setting of 255. When you click in the white area this time, the entire image is filled with light gray (see Figure 10.4).

FIGURE 10.4

FIGURE 10.4

White and black areas filled with light gray.

Depending on how you want the tool to work in any given situation, you'll need to play with the Tolerance settings. Most of the time the default will be okay, but you may need to adjust it to get a certain effect.

One other Paint Bucket option you need to know about is the Use All Layers option. With this option unchecked (the default), the Paint Bucket tool acts as expected when you fill an area on one layer that's above another.

For example, if you fill a layer with gray and that layer is above another layer with a black circle on it, the black circle is covered by the gray that fills the entire area of the top layer. However, if you check the Use All Layers option, the Paint Bucket tool fills only the area on the top layer that's not occupied by a different color on the layers below it. To see what I mean, look at Figure 10.5.

FIGURE 10.5

Black circle on Layer 1.

Note

Some of the information described in this day requires that you understand layers. Layers, described in their simplest form, are like multiple sheets of tracing paper placed one on top of another. For now, all you really need to know is that whatever information you need to have in order to understand what's going on here is included. Day 13, "Layering Your Images," is where you'll find the in-depth information.

10

Now I'll create another layer on top of Layer 1 and fill the layer with gray by clicking in the white area (it really doesn't matter where you click because the whole layer will be filled with gray) (see Figure 10.6).

Note

Again, a more in-depth look at layers appears on Day 13, but if you're following along with this example and would like to know how to add a new layer, it's simple. At the bottom of the Layers palette is a collection of small icons. Locate the one that resembles a small sheet of paper with one corner bent over. Clicking this icon (the Create New Layer icon) creates a new layer and places it above the current layer. Optionally, you can choose Layer, New, Layer. The current layer is highlighted in the Layers palette.

FIGURE 10.6

The entire top layer filled with gray, covering the circle on the layer below.

If I try that again starting with the image in Figure 10.5 but check the Use All Layers box, the fill works much differently. This time the fill covers only the area on Layer 2 that has no changes on Layer 1 (see Figure 10.7).

FIGURE 10.7

Gray doesn't cover the circle on the layer below.

This time the Paint Bucket acts as if the black circle is on the same layer. Because of this, it won't cross the boundary into the circle, even though the actual circle is on a separate layer. You can see how the top layer fills in the gray everywhere but the area occupied by the black circle in the layer below by looking at the Layers palette (see Figure 10.8).

FIGURE 10.8

The Layers palette, showing how Use All Layers affects a fill.

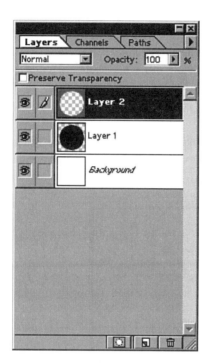

Painting with a Pattern

The Paint Bucket tool can also be used to fill areas with patterns. You must define a pattern—via a selection—before using it, though.

To recap, you can define a pattern by selecting any rectangular or square area of an image. With the selection made, you choose Edit, Define Pattern, and the pattern you define stays valid throughout the current session.

Once the pattern is defined, you simply choose Pattern, instead of Foreground, from the Paint Bucket Options palette under Contents. Then it is simply a matter of clicking within the area you want to fill with the pattern.

Note The Tolerance, Opacity, and Anti-aliased options for the pattern fills work the same as the options for the solid fills.

Anti-aliasing

Before I get into the other tools, I think I should explain what anti-aliasing is all about. All of Photoshop's tools have the ability to anti-alias. Before I explain what anti-aliasing is, though, I'll cover aliasing. These two subjects are, of course, closely related. People almost never discuss aliasing, though.

Aliasing

Aliasing is what happens when analog data is represented in a digital system. A curved line drawn on a grid is a good example of analog data in a digital system (see Figure 10.9).

FIGURE **10.9**

Line on grid represent-ing analog data in digital system.

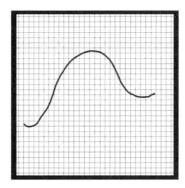

When the analog data is converted to digital, some problems arise. The digital system in this example is the grid. To convert the analog line to a digital line, each point in the grid can either represent a point in the line by being filled in, or represent an area where the line does not exist by remaining white. There can't be a square that is only partly filled. Each square must be either filled in or not. That's all part of it being digital.

Okay, no problem, right? The line goes through the different squares, so we'll fill in each square that the line goes through. This isn't a problem with some portions of the line, as in the portion circled in Figure 10.10.

But what about sections like the one circled in Figure 10.11?

FIGURE 10.10

A portion of the line easily converted to digital.

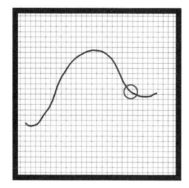

FIGURE 10.11

A portion of line NOT easily converted to digital.

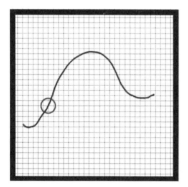

10

That portion cuts right across the intersection between four points. That's where aliasing comes in. An algorithm decides where all the portions fit in the digital system. Figure 10.12 demonstrates what the resulting digital line might look like.

See how the line in Figure 10.12 looks kind of choppy? The same thing happens to any aliased text, for example, that you display on your Web pages.

FIGURE 10.12

A digital version of a line.

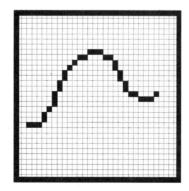

Is There a Solution to Chunky Edges?

Yep! It comes in the form of ta-da…anti-aliasing. What anti-aliasing attempts to do is, using mathematics again, fill in some of the digital system with colors that are in between the two adjoining colors. In this case, a medium gray would be between the black and the white. Some gray squares placed in the grid might help soften up the "jaggies" (see Figure 10.13).

FIGURE 10.13

An anti-aliased line.

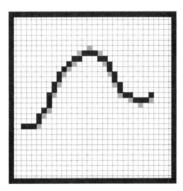

Keeping in mind both that this example was hand drawn and the low resolution of the final printing in this book may make this seem like it's not really an improvement. To give you a better idea of aliased versus anti-aliased, here are a couple of lines drawn with Photoshop. The first, Figure 10.14, is aliased.

FIGURE 10.14

An aliased line drawn with Photoshop.

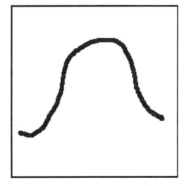

Figure 10.15 is an anti-aliased line drawn in Photoshop.

So there'll be no mistaking the difference, Figures 10.16 and 10.17 are the aliased and the anti-aliased lines blown up 500%.

Notice the jagged appearance of the line in Figure 10.16, while the line in Figure 10.17 is smooth. Of course, at this resolution, the line in Figure 10.17 seems a little blurry. This is something else to consider when using the anti-aliasing option for your graphics. The fuzziness can be especially problematic with text. Because text, as well as the rest of an image, is generally anti-aliased whenever it is resized, you may want to add text only after you have decided on the final size of your image. This helps keep your text more readable.

FIGURE 10.15

An anti-aliased line drawn with Photoshop.

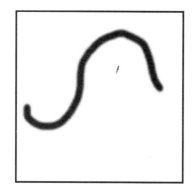

10

FIGURE 10.16

Aliased line at 500%.

FIGURE 10.17

Anti-aliased line at 500%.

Painting with Gradients

The Gradient tool is similar to the Paint Bucket tool, except that instead of using a solid color to fill an area, it uses a gradient. The gradient can be selected from a series of presets or you can build your own. As well, the gradient can be applied with a couple of different shapes. The shapes you can use are selected from the Gradient tool flyout (see Figure 10.18).

FIGURE **10.18**

Gradient tool flyout.

They say a picture is worth a thousand words; well, in this case, it's worth at least five. Instead of just telling you which gradient shapes you can choose, I'll show you. Figure 10.19 shows an example of all five types of gradient fills you can use (along with their names for good measure).

1. To follow along, create a new 400×100 72 dpi image with the contents set to white.

2. To use the Gradient tool, you select the shape you want from the flyout and apply it to the image. You can, optionally, select an area first, of course.

3. Now place the mouse where you want the gradient to begin and drag the mouse to where you want it to end.

FIGURE **10.19**

The types of gradients available in Photoshop.

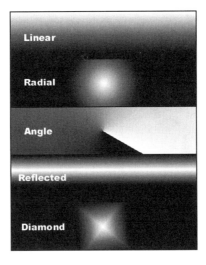

To create a gradient that goes from black to white and from the left of an image to the right, for example, the steps below show you what you need to do.

4. Set the default black/white foreground and background colors (this is easily accomplished by clicking the really small black and white squares icon below the foreground/background color swatches).

5. Select the Linear Gradient tool from the toolbox.

6. In the Linear Gradient Options palette, set the Blend mode to Normal and the Opacity to 100%. For the gradient, choose Foreground to Background. Also, you need to select the Transparency and Dither options. Leave the Reverse option unchecked.

7. Place the mouse near the middle of the left side of the image and click and drag the mouse to the right side of the image. You can hold down the Shift key to keep the line from straying from the horizontal (actually this limits the line to angle increments of 45 degrees). The result should resemble Figure 10.20.

8. If you want, you can save your image, but it's not necessary.

FIGURE 10.20

The Linear gradient.

Editing (or Creating Your Own) Gradients

As well as different shapes, you can control the colors and where they're placed in the gradient. To begin, simply click the Edit button in the Linear Gradient Options palette. This will bring up the Gradient Editor dialog box (see Figure 10.21).

FIGURE 10.21

The Gradient Editor dialog box.

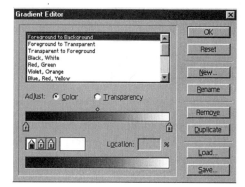

By clicking just below the first gradient (near the middle of the dialog box), you can add points. With a point selected, you can change its color by clicking the small swatch below the gradient. In Figure 10.22, I've added a red point to the gradient.

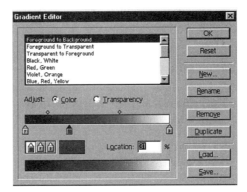

From this dialog box, you can create and save new gradients. You can also load gradients that others have created. In fact, you'll find a number of gradients available on your hard drive after Photoshop is installed or on the CD-ROM in the Goodies folder.

Using the Brushes

Aside from painting, you can also draw using Photoshop. There is an Airbrush, a Paintbrush, a Pencil, an Eraser, and a Line tool available (see Figure 10.23).

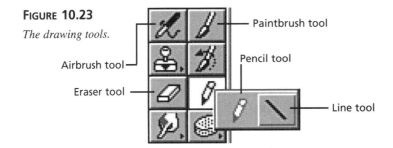

All these brushes can have the opacity/pressure and the Blend mode varied. Some can also have the Fade changed, use Wet Edges, and more. If that isn't enough, you can even create custom brushes.

Using the Airbrush Tool

The Airbrush enables you to paint soft strokes on your image. You can set the Blend mode, Pressure, Fade steps, and, if you own a tablet/pen, the Pressure and Color. Figure 10.24 shows how the Fade and Pressure work.

FIGURE 10.24

Airbrush strokes.

10

The vertical lines were created with the Fade option set at 10, 20, and 80 steps respectively. The horizontal lines cover the vertical lines at 50% (the top horizontal line) and 20% (the bottom line). Notice how you can see more of the vertical lines through the bottom horizontal line. This was created with lower pressure (20% compared to 50%). This tool works much like a real airbrush, only it's digital.

Using the Paintbrush Tool

The Paintbrush tool is similar to the Airbrush except that you can set Wet Edges and use Opacity instead of Pressure. You have the same choice of brushes as well.

Once selected, you can click and drag the cursor to draw with the selected brush. You can vary the colors by changing the foreground color, changing the Opacity in the Options palette, and choosing Wet Edges. Wet Edges applies more paint (digital, of course) towards the edges, leaving the center of the stroke more transparent. The line on the left in Figure 10.25 was created without Wet Edges, while the line on the right was done with them.

FIGURE 10.25

Non-Wet Edges versus Wet Edges.

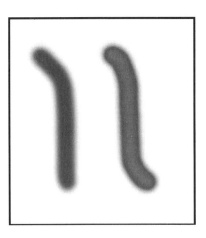

Using the Pencil Tool

The Pencil tool is similar to the Airbrush and the Paintbrush except that you can use only hard-edged brushes (this is really just aliased brushes).

Another option available with the Pencil tool is Auto Erase. With this option checked, you can erase to the current background color, but this works only if you draw over lines made previously. If you start the stroke on a surface where you haven't drawn before, the Pencil tool works normally.

Using the Line Tool

The Line tool, which is accessible from the flyout beneath the Pencil tool, draws (surprise, surprise) lines. As well as setting the Blend modes and the opacity, you can vary the line's width and set the anti-aliasing option. Figure 10.26 shows aliased and anti-aliased lines. Notice how the aliased line is quite jagged, as you read about earlier in today's chapter.

In the Line Options palette, you can choose to have arrowheads at the beginning, the end, or both the beginning and the end of your lines (see Figure 10.27).

The arrowheads can be customized as well. From the Line Options palette, click the Shape button to bring up the Arrowhead Shape dialog box (see Figure 10.28).

You can set the width, the height, and the concavity. Figure 10.29 demonstrates arrowheads with no concavity and with 50% concavity.

FIGURE 10.26

Aliased and anti-aliased lines.

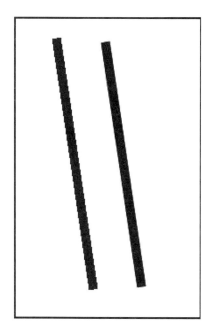

10

FIGURE 10.27

Lines with arrow-heads.

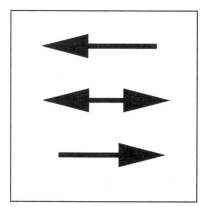

FIGURE 10.28

Arrowhead Shape dialog box.

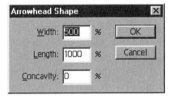

FIGURE 10.29

Varying the concavity of the arrowheads.

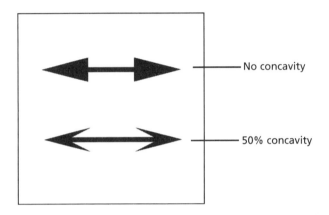

Using the Eraser Tool

Last but not least, you have the Eraser tool. This enables you to erase areas of your image. You can make the Eraser act like the various drawing tools—Paintbrush, Airbrush, Pencil, and Block. You can also choose from the various brushes and set Wet Edges and the opacity.

Another available option is called Erase to History. This option was demonstrated on Day 3, "Checking Out the New 5.0 Features."

Creating Your Own Brushes

Photoshop is quite extensible in several ways, and creating and saving your own brushes is one of the ways you can extend its capabilities.

To create a brush, simply open a new or existing image and select a portion of that image. Unlike the pattern definition, the selection doesn't have to be rectangular in nature. The brush, by definition, though, must be monochrome. You can draw it in any color, but once defined the brush will, like any other brush, draw in the current foreground color.

Optionally, you can have Photoshop help you define a new brush. To access this feature, double-click an unoccupied space on the Brushes palette. This brings up the New Brush dialog box (see Figure 10.30). Using the options available in this dialog box, you can set the Diameter, Hardness, Spacing, Angle, and Roundness of your new brush.

FIGURE 10.30

The New Brush dialog box.

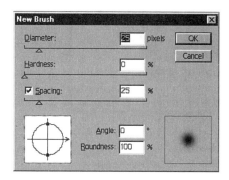

10

> You can save your new brushes by clicking the small black arrow to the right of the Brushes tab in the Brushes palette. This activates a menu from which you can choose Save Brushes.

I created the brush you see in Figure 10.31 by drawing a small gray area with the Paintbrush. I then applied a number of Photoshop's built-in textures and filters to get the rough-looking shape.

All that is needed to create the brush is to select the image using Select, All and then clicking the small black arrow next to the Brushes tab in the Brushes palette and choosing Define Brush. With the brush defined, it's a simple matter to select and use it.

I'll admit that the brush in Figure 10.31 isn't too glamorous, but you'd be surprised at what you can do with a couple of brushes like this. As an example, I used a couple of custom brushes to give a custom edge to the portrait you see in Figure 10.32.

FIGURE 10.31

A custom brush.

FIGURE 10.32

Custom brushes were used to create the custom edge.

Summary

As you can see, the painting and drawing tools you have at your disposal with Photoshop are quite powerful. I hope that you'll take a little time and explore the various settings and options to see how they work. You can do much more with them than I had the time and space to demonstrate.

Q&A

Q Can the painting and drawing tools be used to make corrections to photographs?

A Absolutely. The painting and drawing tools are very versatile. You can use them to touch up photographs, create and modify masks, and even just draw and paint.

Q How can the drawing/painting tools be used to create and modify masks?

A You can use the Pencil, the Paintbrush, and the Airbrush tools to create quick masks, for example. I'll demonstrate this in greater detail on Day 11, "Masking with Layer Masks and Quick Masks."

Workshop

`10`

The following section is a quick quiz about the chapter you have just read. If you have any problems answering any of the questions in the quiz, see the section directly following it for all the answers.

Quiz

1. What effect does a high Tolerance value have a on a fill?
2. How do you define a pattern fill?
3. How do you define a gradient fill?
4. What are the advantages of anti-aliasing?
5. How do you create a custom brush?

Quiz Answers

1. It enables the fill to cover more area. It allows the fill to spread over a greater range of underlying colors.

2. You can define a pattern fill by selecting a rectangular area and choosing Edit, Define Pattern.

3. You must click the Edit button on the Gradient Options palette and use the options in the Gradient Editor dialog box to modify an existing, or create a new, gradient fill.

4. Anti-aliasing softens the transition between contrasting edges in an image.

5. You can select an area of an image and create a brush from this selection, or you can double-click an empty space in the Brushes palette and use the options in the New Brush dialog box to help you create a new brush.

DAY 11

Masking with Layer Masks and Quick Masks

A digital mask is analogous to placing masking tape over a portion of a wall while you're painting. The masking tape protects the area it covers while allowing you to paint over the other surfaces of the wall. Digital masks, though, are much more powerful, as you'll see in this chapter. You can vary the opacity of layers, for example, allowing more or less of the underlying layers to show through. You can also use Layer modes to blend layers in different ways, as I'll demonstrate on Day 13, "Layering Your Images."

- Working with layer masks
- Understanding quick masks
- Working with Adjustment layers

Layer Masks

It may seem a little strange to be discussing layer masks before I've covered layers. On the other hand, it's not imperative that you fully understand layers and the Blending modes that accompany them to get a feel for layer masks.

Layer masks go hand in hand with the layer they are on. Each layer can have one layer mask, though it doesn't necessarily have to have one. A layer mask allows portions of the layer below to show through—how much depends on the mask.

The digital masks differ from the masking tape in that the digital mask can cover or reveal the surface (or layer, in the case of the digital mask) below in varying degrees. When the mask is black, the layer below is visible, and when the mask is white, the layer below does not show through the masked layer. As well as black and white, a mask can also have shades of gray. The darker the gray, the more the underlying layer shows through, while the lighter the gray, the less the underlying layer is visible. To get an idea of what I'm talking about, take a look at Figure 11.1.

FIGURE 11.1

Text masked with a linear gradient from black to white.

You'll notice that the text is extremely faded at the left. This is where the mask was black. The text becomes more visible as the mask becomes lighter (towards the right). The mask itself is a simple black to white gradient. If you were to look at the mask itself, it would resemble Figure 11.2.

So what exactly is going on here? For the answer to that question, take a look at the Layers palette (see Figure 11.3).

Just below the words Preserve Transparency, you can see that there are currently two layers associated with the image. The bottom layer, the background, is simply the white background that was created when I opened the new file. The top layer is the one you really want to look at.

FIGURE 11.2

The mask—a linear gradient from black to white.

FIGURE 11.3

The Layers palette showing a layer with a layer mask.

Click to turn layer on and off

Delete current layer

Create a new layer

Add layer mask

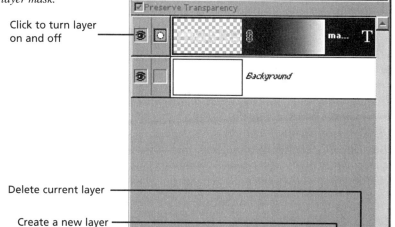

In the area that describes the layer, you can see a few icons. I'll discuss these in more depth on Day 13. The ones you need to look at for now are the third and fifth. The third icon shows a thumbnail view of the contents of the layer. It's difficult to see here, but the top layer has the word "masks" in blue over a transparent background. The fifth icon represents the contents of the mask itself. You can see how it's a linear gradient. Because of the gradient mask, the word fades into the white background layer below it.

Creating Layer Masks

Layer masks are easy to create and just as easy to delete. They needn't be linear gradients either. You can create a layer mask and punch a hole in it to reveal just the portion of the layer below that's visible through the hole.

 Note

Although using a mask changes what you see of an image or a layer, the mask does not actually change the information present under it. Rather, it just changes what you see. You should note, too, that painting on a layer that is masked affects the mask itself and not the actual layer. Just make sure the layer thumbnail indicates that you're working on the layer mask, and not the layer itself.

Layer masks can actually be used to help you construct montages and collages. I'll demonstrate these techniques on Day 19, "Compositing Two or More Images into One."

Let's look at one more example, this time one you can work through, so that you get a good idea of how a layer mask works.

1. Open a file of a portrait. If you don't have one handy, copy one of the included files off the CD-ROM that accompanies this book. I'll use the portrait you see in Figure 11.4.

2. Create a new layer by clicking the New Layer icon at the bottom of the Layers palette. You can also create a new layer by choosing Layer, New, Layer. This brings up the New Layer dialog box, which enables you to name the layer, set its opacity, its Mode, and its Group With Previous Layer check box (see Figure 11.5). For now, leave Opacity at 100%, Mode at Normal, and Group With Previous Layer unchecked.

3. Set the default foreground/background colors by clicking the small black and white squares icon below the foreground/background color swatches.

4. Press Ctrl-Backspace (Cmd-Backspace) to fill the new layer with white. This, of course, covers the portrait.

With the new layer in place and filled with white, it's time to add the Layer mask.

5. Choose Layer, Add Layer Mask. You can choose to Reveal All or Hide All. Choose Reveal All so that you still see the white layer.

FIGURE 11.4

Black and white portrait of Marianne.

11

FIGURE 11.5

New Layer dialog box.

> **Note**
>
> Choosing Reveal All creates a white mask. You won't notice any obvious change with this mask. Choosing Hide All creates a completely black mask, which reveals the portrait below the white layer. This is because, even though the white layer is still there, it's now completely transparent due to the black mask. What's happening is that you're really working with the mask, not the white layer itself.

 6. Select the Elliptical Marquee tool and draw a large oval shape that fills most of the white layer (remember, it's actually the mask that you're working on, not the layer).

7. Choose Select, Feather and enter a value of 10 in the Feather Selection dialog box.

8. Now press Alt-Backspace (Option-Backspace) to fill the selection with black.

Whoa! What's this! The portrait below is now showing through. Why? Because the black oval portion of the mask allows the layer below to show through (see Figure 11.6). This mask has produced the effect known as "vignette." If you've ever seen old photographs, you may have noticed this effect used on them.

FIGURE 11.6

Marianne through an oval, feathered mask.

At this point, you might want to save or save as to keep the changes you've made. You can do so by choosing File, Save (to save over the original image) or File, Save As (to save a new copy of the image).

There are other ways to accomplish this effect with Photoshop (as you may remember, I demonstrated another "vignette" technique using the Elliptical Marquee tool on Day 10, "Painting with Fills, Patterns, and Gradients"), but this shows you how it can be done with a simple mask.

Quick Masks

Another type of mask is the quick mask. Quick masks are actually representations of selections. With the Quick Mask mode, you can paint and erase a mask while seeing the image below. You can toggle between Standard mode and Quick Mask mode using the two icons in the second to last row of the toolbox. The icon on the left turns on Standard mode and the one on the left sets Quick Mask mode (see Figure 11.7).

FIGURE 11.7
Standard and Quick Mask modes.

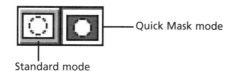

Quick Mask mode

Standard mode

The mask shows up as a semi-transparent red layer over the image. You can change the color and its opacity to suit your needs. To do so, double-click the Quick Mask icon. This brings up the Quick Mask Options dialog box (see Figure 11.8).

FIGURE 11.8
Quick Mask Options dialog box.

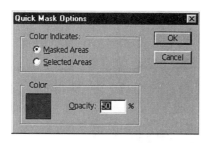

11

You can choose whether the color indicates masked areas or selected areas. You can also choose the color and set the opacity. To set the color, simply click the Color swatch. This brings up the Color dialog box, enabling you to change the color. Under most conditions, the default red at 50% will suffice. If, however, you find yourself working on an image that's predominantly red, you'll find it difficult to work in Quick Mask mode and probably will need to change the color. For now, though, just leave the defaults.

I'm going to show you a quick way to use the Quick Mask mode to select an area of a photo so that the area can be manipulated. I'll be working with the file Marianne01.psd. You'll find this file in the Day11 folder on the accompanying CD-ROM.

1. Open a portrait image of your own or use Marianne01.psd.

2. Choose Image, Mode, RGB to switch the black and white photo to RGB Color mode.

3. Click the Edit in Quick Mask icon. You won't see any changes yet, but bear with me for a moment longer.

 4. Select the Zoom tool and zoom in on the lips.

 5. Select the Paintbrush tool and make sure that the default black foreground/white background colors are selected.

6. Select a fairly small soft brush from the Brushes palette.

7. Start painting over the lips in the photograph. Instead of black, you should see red (see Figure 11.9).

FIGURE 11.9

Quick mask being applied to an image.

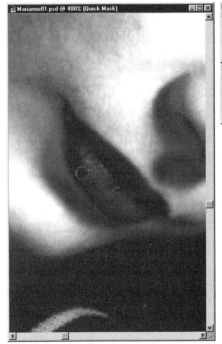

Of course, you can't see the red here in the book because the figures are in black and white, but if you're following along you'll see red...trust me. This is because you're not actually painting on the image, but you're creating a mask instead. This mask will be turned into a selection once you're done.

8. Paint as close as you can to the line between the lips and the rest of the face. If you go over or draw outside the lines, fear not; all you need do is paint over the red area with white. This erases the red. Actually what happens is that you'll be erasing the mask. Paint over the entire lip area until you're satisfied that it is completely covered.

9. Double-click the Zoom tool on the toolbox (do not double-click the image with the Zoom tool) to return the image to its normal size.

 10. Click the Edit in Standard Mode icon. The red disappears and is replaced with the familiar marching ants showing you the area you selected in Quick Mask mode.

Actually, the selection is the inverse of what you want. Everything except the lips is selected.

11. You can quickly rectify this by choosing Select, Inverse. You should now see that the lips have been selected (see Figure 11.10).

Figure 11.10

A Quick Mask turned into a selection.

Now that you've selected the lips, you can add some color to them with out affecting the rest of the image.

12. Choose Image, Adjust, Hue/Saturation.

13. In the Hue/Saturation dialog box, set the Hue to 0, the Saturation to 25, the Lightness to 0, and click the Colorize box (see Figure 11.11). Click OK and see what effect this has on the image. The portrait, though still in black and white, now has red lips.

Note

If you're following this exercise with an image of your own that's been scanned in as grayscale, you will have to adjust the mode (choose Image, Mode, RGB). Otherwise, you won't be able to add color.

FIGURE **11.11**

Hue/Saturation dialog box.

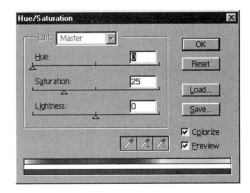

14. Choose Select, Deselect to see the effect more clearly. Not bad; just like a magazine advertisement.

Tip

> Step 14 offers one way of seeing changes against the rest of the image. In Photoshop 5, many tools and effect dialog boxes automatically turn off the marching ants of an active selection. Instead of losing an undo step by using the Deselect command, you can hide the selection temporarily using the Hide Edges command (Ctrl/Command-H). This function is particularly useful when it is necessary to see the edge of a selection when a dialog box is open.
>
> There are other keyboard shortcuts that save a lot of trouble. Since the toolbar items are not available when dialog boxes are open, you may have trouble moving to other areas of the image or zooming into the picture. Getting familiar with Ctrl+"+" (Command+"+" on the Mac) and Ctrl+"-" (Command+"-" on the Mac) to magnify or shrink the image view pays off immediately. Also, holding down the Spacebar changes the mouse pointer to the Hand tool, which allows you move to different areas of the image. To access different brush sizes, use the left and right bracket keys ("[" and "]") to toggle the current setting.

You can use the Quick Mask mode to do all kinds of magic. You can erase backgrounds from photos and subsequently replace the background with another image. Have you ever imagined yourself in front of the Leaning Tower of Pisa? No problem. Get a photo of you and another of the tower and have some fun.

It's easier to "paint" in Quick Mask mode than it is to create selections when the areas you want to select are highly varied, and other highly varied areas surround them. It's also easier to correct in Quick Mask mode than it is to correct a selection. In fact, if you find yourself struggling with a selection, simply click the Edit in Quick Mode icon. The selection turns into a quick mask, and you can apply the same techniques you used here to remedy the selection problem.

There's one more type of mask that I'd like to introduce you to before we move on. This last type of mask is known as an Adjustment layer.

Adjustment Layers

Adjustment layers are a kind of mask that enables you to see how corrections, such as brightness/contrast, color changes, and curve changes, affect your photographs. The nice thing about Adjustment layers is that they aren't permanent. You can just as easily remove an Adjustment layer as create one.

To see how these Adjustment layers work, open a photograph that needs some corrections. I'll use a color photo of Marianne that scanned a little dark and was not printed properly by the photofinisher (see Figure 11.12 and Color Plate 11.1).

FIGURE 11.12

*Scan of Marianne that
needs correcting.*

11

With the image loaded, it's time to make some adjustments. The first thing I noticed when I got this print back from the photo-finisher was that it was a little too green. This can be corrected easily in Photoshop.

1. Choose Layer, New, Adjustment Layer.

2. In the New Adjustment Layer dialog box, pull down the Type menu and choose Color Balance (see Figure 11.13). Click OK.

FIGURE **11.13**

New Adjustment Layer—Color Balance.

3. In the Color Balance dialog box, drag the sliders to add a little red, subtract some green, and subtract some blue (see Figure 11.14). This is a little better (see Figure 11.15 and Color Plate 11.2), but it's still too dark.

FIGURE **11.14**

Color Balance dialog box.

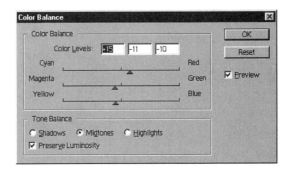

4. Add another Adjustment layer by choosing Layer, New, Adjustment Layer.

5. This time select Brightness/Contrast for the Type. In the Brightness/Contrast dialog box, bump the brightness up by about 20 or so (see Figure 11.16). This is definitely an improvement, but it still needs some work (see Figure 11.17 and Color Plate 11.3).

Now it seems a little too red. I wanted to add some red to combat the overall green tinge, but this is not quite what I had in mind. One more Adjustment layer should do it.

FIGURE 11.15

Color adjusted via Adjustment layer.

FIGURE 11.16

The Brightness/Contrast dialog box.

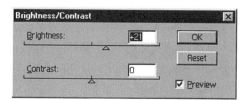

FIGURE 11.17

Brightness/Contrast adjusted.

6. Choose Layer, New, Adjustment Layer and select Curves for the Type (see Figure 11.18).

FIGURE 11.18

New Adjustment Layer—Curves.

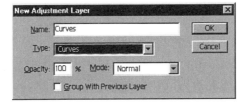

I'm just going to show you the change I made without going into details. I'll demonstrate exactly what I did on Day 16, "Correcting the Color," when I discuss color correction. You can see how I adjusted the curve in Figure 11.19.

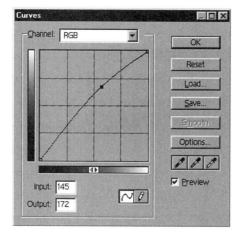

The Curves feature enables you to adjust a color cast without having too much effect on the rest of the colors that make up the image. You can see the result of all the changes in the final image (see Figure 11.20 and Color Plate 11.4).

11

You can also see all of the Adjustment layers in Figure 11.21.

FIGURE 11.21

All the Adjustment layers for the final corrected image.

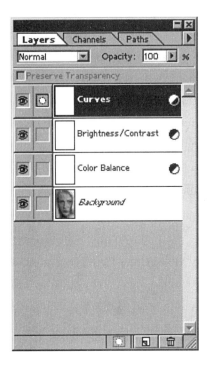

The nice thing about adjusting the image this way is that you can easily go back and make changes. Simply double-click an Adjustment layer to bring up its associated dialog box and make the changes. If you save an image with its Adjustment layers, you can pick up right where you left off. All the settings remain intact.

Workshop: Combining Masks and Adjustment Layers

As you can start to see, Photoshop allows you to accomplish your imaging tasks in a variety of ways. In the previous exercise, we used three different Adjustment layers to correct the image. Oftentimes, these effects can be done with just one Adjustment layer. The more you get to know Photoshop and its tools, the better you will be at getting results in a short amount of time.

This next exercise incorporates much of what we have covered in past chapters but in the context of what we have learned today. Our goal with this next exercise is to take a scan and get it ready for output, and we'll use the Rubber Stamp tool, quick masks, alternative selection methods, and Adjustment layers to accomplish this.

Although Adjustment layers have practically given us limitless levels of undo for tonal corrections, they can introduce some new problems. For example, if you are cloning information to a new empty layer on an image that already has a Levels Adjustment layer, how do you stack the layers? Remember, the benefit of using any adjustment tool is that we can always go back and change the settings without any tonal loss. To see what I mean, take a look at Figures 11.22 through 11.28.

FIGURE 11.22

A scan with a scratch in the upper-left corner.

The unwanted scratch

11

FIGURE 11.23

Magnified area of the scratch.

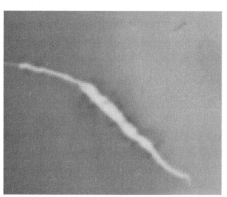

FIGURE 11.24

The flower image with a Levels Adjustment layer added.

FIGURE 11.25

An empty layer added to the flower image for cloning purposes, appropriately named Clone Layer.

FIGURE 11.26

The scratch is covered up using the Rubber Stamp tool and the Blur tool. Both tools had the Use All Layers option checked during the retouch.

FIGURE 11.27

The complete retouched and levels-adjusted image.

11

Why does this happen? Since the Levels Adjustment layer was below the clone layer during the rubber stamping process, the clone layer image data reflects the previous state of the image. We could add another Levels Adjustment layer on top of the clone layer (for a total of two Levels layers), but this could cause problems as well. If the lower Levels layer is blocking information in the shadows, that information will still not be available to the new Levels layer. In short, the second Levels Adjustment layer will not have as wide a range of tones to adjust.

So what are our options? We could manually adjust the levels of the clone layer without an Adjustment layer. If the clone information was isolated to a small area of the image like in this example, then this might be an efficient method of action. However, it would be best to simply perform the entire operation correctly from the start, which is what this workshop will show you.

Here's a brief outline of the steps we'll go through:

1. Select an image that needs retouching and that has specific color areas that you want to change.

2. Add an initial "preview" Adjustment layer.

3. Fix dust and scratch marks with a combination of filters and paint tools.

4. Using the Quick Mask mode and selection tools, select specific areas of the image that you want to change.

5. Add additional Adjustment layers with masks.

6. Duplicate the image and perform any necessary sharpening for output on a flattened version of the image.

Granted, there's much more to the exercise than what is stated here. In fact, you may want to read through the following detailed exercise before actually performing it with one of your images; you may change the image you want to work with after you have a better idea of what we're going to do.

1. Open an image in Photoshop (see Figure 11.29). Make sure the Layers and Options palettes are showing (Window, Show Layers and Window, Show Options).

FIGURE 11.29

The focus fall-off is not a Photoshop effect, although it very well could be. The image was taken with a 4×5 view camera that allows very specific control over the focus plane.

11

2. Add a Levels Adjustment layer using the Layer, New, Adjustment Layer command, or by accessing New Adjustment Layer from the Layer palette menu (see Figure 11.30).

FIGURE 11.30

The New Adjustment Layer command from the Layers palette.

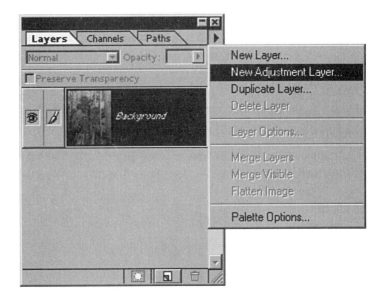

3. In the Levels dialog box, drag the shadow, midpoint, and highlight arrows to produce an overall tonally adjusted image (see Figure 11.31).

FIGURE 11.31

The Levels dialog box. Notice that the shadow point has been dragged to the first occurrence of shadow information (on the left side of the graph) and that the white point has been moved to the first spike of highlight information (on the right side of the graph).

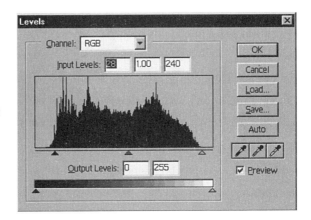

Why are we adding a Levels adjustment when this is exactly what was done in the error-prone example mentioned earlier? Adjusting the tonal information of the image first may eliminate faint scratches or dust specks in the shadow and highlight areas. Thus, we have saved ourselves from needless additional cloning.

4. With the Background layer active, click the Create New Layer icon on the Layers palette, or use the Layer, New, Layer command (Shift-Ctrl/Cmd-N). Name this layer Clone Layer in the Layer Options dialog box. You can access the Layer Options at any time by double-clicking on the layer.

Tip

Why is it important to name layers? For one thing, it keeps track of the layers better than the default Layer 1, Layer 2, and so on. But, more importantly, it allows for quicker access to overlapping layers when using the Move tool. By right-clicking with the Move tool (in Windows) or Control-clicking with the Move tool (on a Mac), you can choose which layer you are currently moving. This saves you from having to go to the Layers palette and back each time you want to switch to a different layer.

5. Make sure that clone layer appears between the Levels layer and the Background layer in the Layers palette (see figure 11.32). If it isn't, simply click and drag the clone layer between the other two.

FIGURE 11.32

The Layers palette showing the Clone Layer between the Levels and Background layers.

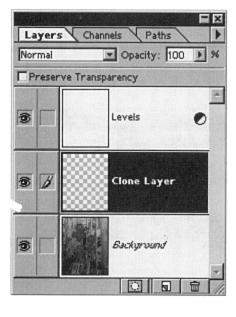

6. Now here's the tricky part. Before you start to use the Rubber Stamp tool on the clone layer, hide the Levels Adjustment layer by clicking the eyeball for that layer in the Layers palette. Failure to do so will repeat the error we're trying to avoid. See Figure 11.33 for details.

FIGURE **11.33**

The Layers palette showing the Levels layer hidden.

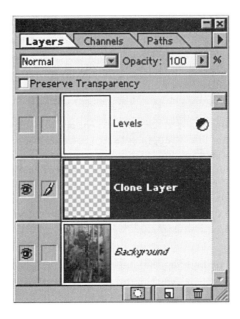

7. Click the Rubber Stamp tool on the toolbar (S on the keyboard). In the Options palette, check the box for Use All Layers (see Figure 11.34). This allows the Rubber Stamp tool to see information from any layer that is visible. Also, verify that the Aligned box is checked. For Opacity, start with a lower percentage between 25–50%. This will allow you to build up the retouching area slowly and carefully.

FIGURE **11.34**

The Options palette for the Rubber Stamp tool, with appropriate settings for this exercise.

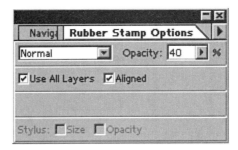

8. Find an area of the image that needs to be retouched and zoom up on it. Sample a spot next to this area by Alt+clicking on it (Option+clicking on a Mac) while using the Rubber Stamp tool. Depending on the size of the area you're retouching, you may need a smaller or bigger brush than the default. Open the Brushes palette (Window, Show Brushes) to select a different brush. See Figure 11.35 for more information.

FIGURE 11.35

For easier cloning, go into your Display & Cursors preferences (File, Preferences, Display & Cursors) and use Brush Size for Painting Cursors and Precise for Other Cursors. When you start to clone, the Rubber Stamp tool will appear as a circle, like this figure shows.

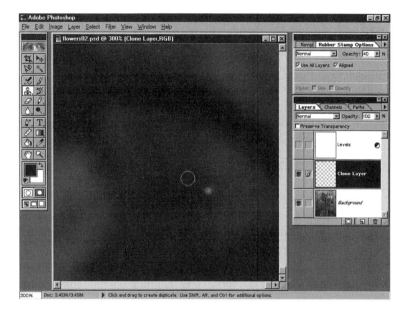

9. Hide and show the clone layer to see what effect your retouching is having on the image. Does it look better or worse? Also, zoom out using the Ctrl+0 (Cmd+0) shortcut, and look at the image from a distance. Is the error still detectable? Remember, since the clone information is on its own layer, you can always trash it and start over. If you're having difficulty getting the area to look right, try Alt+clicking (Option+clicking) in a spot directly opposite from where you first sampled. Using a low opacity again, work with the Rubber Stamp tool until the area blends more seamlessly.

10. Feel free to use any other paint tools on the clone layer to help with blending, if necessary. The Smudge, Blur, Airbrush, and Paintbrush can be very helpful. For the blending tools like Smudge or Blur, verify that the Use All Layers option is checked in the Options palette before retouching.

Note

Don't be surprised by brush size changes when you switch to a new tool. Photoshop remembers what brush size was used last with each tool. This is another good reason to use the Brush Size cursor as mentioned in the caption for Figure 11.35.

11

11. Show and hide the Levels layer. Does your level setting exacerbate the problem area? Often, if you have increased the overall contrast of an image, dust marks and scratches will be more noticeable. Hide the Levels layers when you are finished evaluating its effect.

    You may be wondering why we are hiding the Levels layer while cloning. Try this test to find out. With the Levels layer showing, click on the clone layer and try using the Rubber Stamp somewhere in the image. Can you see what's happening? The Rubber Stamp tool is re-applying the Levels settings to the information it is copying. Therefore, the clone will appear darker or smaller than the area you are actually sampling. Use the Edit, Undo (Ctrl/Cmd-Z) command to erase the mark.

12. Repeat steps 8–10 for any other areas of the image that need retouching. However, do not trash your clone layer if you make a big mistake in another area. Simply use the Eraser tool to clear that particular mistake. You wouldn't want to unnecessarily redo every retouch. Also, don't get too picky with your retouching. You may want to make a sample output to see if the errors that you see up close will indeed be noticeable in the final, especially if the output size is small.

FIGURE 11.36

The retouched and levels-corrected tulips image with the Layers and Options palettes showing.

Whew! We've come a long way since Day 1. You may want to take a short break to rest your eyes for a moment. I know I am. (But before you do that, you may want to save your image as a Photoshop (PSD) file, if you haven't done so already.) When you return, look at your Layers palette to review what we've done. Show the Levels layer, and double-click on the Levels layer icon or name (not the thumbnail) and readjust the highlight slider. Notice that both the Background and clone layers are being affected by the new setting.

Working with Precision Adjustment Layers

Excellent! Let's move on with the rest of the workshop, where we'll start to get more precise with our Adjustment layers using masks. At this point, you can leave the Levels layer showing unless you need to go back and retouch something else.

The first thing you'll need to do is find a specific part or parts of the image that you want to manipulate exclusively. For example, I want to change the hue and saturation of the tulips.

Now comes the selection part, and you can use any of the following methods:

Magic Wand tool: By far, this is one of the simplest tools to select information in Photoshop. Again, make sure the Use All Layers option is checked in the Options palette for this tool. Use a Tolerance value that is appropriate for the range of colors you want to select. When using this tool, Shift-click to add additional areas to the selection.

Lasso or Magnetic Lasso tool: If you're using a graphics tablet or have a steady hand, go ahead and try grabbing the area(s) this way. The new Magnetic feature-set of Photoshop 5 makes the task much easier.

Color Range command (See Figures 11.14-11.18): In an image like the tulips example, it may be easiest to use the Select, Color Range command. Here's a quick breakdown of the settings:

Working with the Color Range Command

Because we've already covered the use of the Magic Wand, Lasso, and Magnetic Lasso tools, let's take a moment here to introduce the options available with the Color Range command (see Figure 11.37).

- **The Select drop-down menu.** For now, let's stick to using Sampled Colors. Notice, though, its other presets: Reds, Yellows, Greens, Cyans, Blues, Magentas, Highlights, Midtones, Shadows, and Out of Gamut. Out of Gamut is particularly useful in seeing what colors will not print with standard printing inks.

11

- **Fuzziness slider.** This is similar to the Tolerance setting of other tools in Photoshop. However, the scale ranges from 0–200, not 0–255. As this number increases, the selection will include more surrounding colors from the sampled colors. Keep this value at 0 initially.

- **Selection/Image and Selection Preview options.** These settings specify what you see in the Preview pane and the image area, respectively. Choosing Selection will show you the selection in grayscale, which is preferred. Choosing Image will show the actual image in the Preview pane. If you choose this setting, make sure you change the Selection Preview setting to something other than None so that you can see exactly what you are selecting.

- **The Eyedroppers.** The one on the left allows you to select the initial color areas in the Preview pane or the image itself. The Eyedropper + allows you to add more specific colors to the selection. This is different from the Fuzziness slider in that you have greater control with the Eyedropper + tool. Fuzziness controls a range from a given set of sampled colors. You cannot control what colors will be selected in that range. However, the Eyedropper + tool does allow you to specify exact colors in the sampling set. The Eyedropper – tool subtracts a color from the sampling set.

- **Invert.** This does the same thing as the Select, Inverse command.

FIGURE 11.37

The Color Range dialog box.

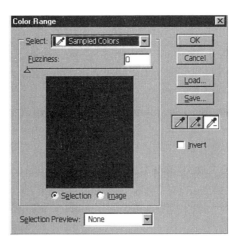

The following figures walk you through the color selection process, showing you the various option settings available with the Color Range command.

FIGURE 11.38

Using Sampled Colors as the Select preset, the normal Eyedropper tool is used to select one color in the image. This color selection is shown as white in the Preview pane. Notice that the Fuzziness slider is set to 0.

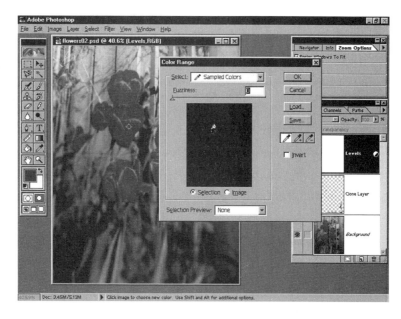

FIGURE 11.39

Using the Eyedropper + tool, more colors in the tulips were selected in the image area.

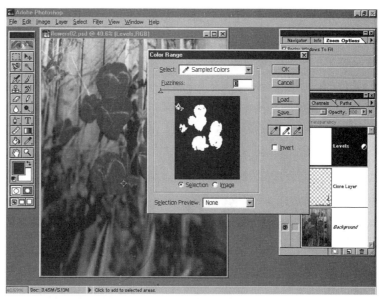

11

FIGURE 11.40

Now, in order to grab some extra edge pixels, the Fuzziness slider is set to 10. The Eyedropper + tool was used to add more colors within the Preview pane.

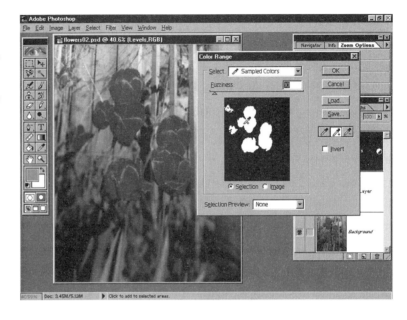

FIGURE 11.41

The selection after the Color Range command is applied.

Making the Final Adjustments

 After using the Color Range command (or any other selection tool) to make your selection, convert the selection mode to Edit in Quick Mask mode by clicking the Quick Mask Mode icon.

If necessary, use the painting tools to add or subtract any areas to or from the current selection. The tulips selection in Quick Mask mode is shown in Figure 11.42.

FIGURE 11.42

Here, since the tulips are red, the color of the quick mask overlay was changed to green to more easily see the areas that were not selected by the Color Range command.

 Now, return to Standard mode by clicking the Edit in Standard Mode icon on the toolbar. Then, click on the Levels layer (or the topmost layer). With the selection active, add another Adjustment layer (Layer, New, Adjustment Layer) for the effect you need. In the tulips image, a Hue/Saturation Adjustment layer was added.

Did you notice what happened to the Hue/Saturation layer in the Layers palette? Since a selection was active when we initiated a Hue/Saturation Adjustment layer, it was used as a mask for that adjustment. Refer to Figure 11.43 for an example.

To load a "selection" contained in any mask or layer, simply Ctrl+click (Cmd-click) its layer or channel thumbnail. You will notice that the mouse pointer changes into the Load Selection Pointer, shown below.

Another way of accessing the selection of a mask is to highlight a given layer and go to the Channels palette. There you will find a temporary alpha channel (indicated by the italicized name of the channel) for the mask, as shown in Figure 11.44. Since Photoshop knows the selection of each mask, layer and channel, it cuts down on the number of saved selections that you need to store in the Channels palette.

FIGURE **11.43**

The Layers palette with a mask for the Hue/Saturation layer.

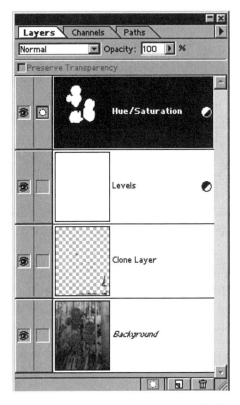

By now, you've realized that Adjustment layers have editable masks associated with them. Even the Levels layer has a mask. Currently, the mask is filled with white, which means that the settings we entered in the Levels layer is affecting everything that is showing and beneath it. So, if you want to protect any area from being affected by an Adjustment layer, simply fill that area with black (or a variation of gray). This is extremely useful, not to mention time saving and offering limitless levels of undo.

FIGURE 11.44

The Channels palette with a temporary alpha channel for the Hue/Saturation layer.

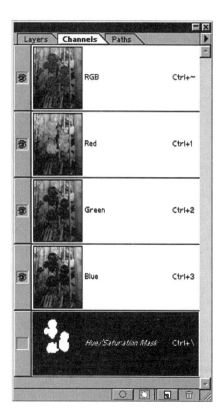

Now you're ready to make any additional modifications to the image. In the tulips example, another Hue/Saturation Adjustment layer was added to desaturate the two tulips in the left background (see Figure 11.45). When you're happy with the results, save the final image as a Photoshop (PSD) file. If you want to place this image in another document or have it printed, you may decide to save a flattened TIFF copy as well (File, Save a Copy).

Excellent work! We've gone through a few complex methods to master control of the image. If you followed the directions at the beginning of the exercise, you're just finishing the read-through now. So, find an image that's worth this time and effort and be amazed by what you can do.

FIGURE 11.45

The final tulips image, with the background tulips desaturated.

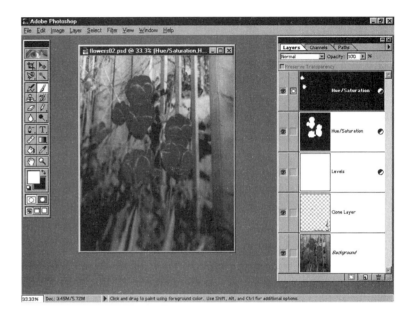

Summary

You've covered a lot of ground today. Masks are fairly complex and can be used to create magic. I hope you'll spend some time going over the material I demonstrated today and that you'll try to put some of it into action. The rewards will be worth the effort.

Q&A

Q **Can Adjustment layers be used for purposes other than adjusting and correcting an image?**

A No. The whole idea behind Adjustment layers is to enable you to see how certain changes affect an image. Because the adjustments are made using the Adjustment layers, though, you can keep changing, correcting, and adding different changes without worrying that you're affecting the original image. You can even save the file and come back to it later. At that time, you can continue applying corrections or even reverse all the corrections you made by deleting the Adjustment layers.

Q **Why are there so many ways to do the same thing in Photoshop, particularly with layer masks and Adjustment layers?**

A One of the reasons Photoshop is so great is that it allows people to adapt to their preferred working methods and skill levels. Often, you can do the same thing with color balance that you can with curves. There's absolutely nothing wrong with using three Adjustment layers, even though someone else might be able to do it in one. Photoshop was built for novices and experts alike. The usefulness of layer masks and Adjustment layers is that these changes are never permanent. You can always change your mind without losing precious image information. The last thing we want to do is go back to the original scan and start over.

Q If I use a selection to make a mask and that selection is no longer active, how do I get it back?

A You can load the selection for any mask or channel by Ctrl-/Cmd-clicking the thumbnail of the layer, layer mask, or channel.

Workshop

The following section is a quick quiz about this chapter. If you have any problems answering any of the questions in the quiz, see the section directly following it for all the answers.

Quiz

1. What are the three types of masks?
2. How do you create a layer mask?
3. What is a quick mask?
4. What is an Adjustment layer?
5. How do you create a new Adjustment layer?
6. How can you easily select a set of colors?
7. How do you use a mask for an Adjustment layer?

Quiz Answers

1. Adjustment layers, layer masks, and the Quick Mask mode.
2. You choose Layer, Add Layer Mask, and either Reveal All or Hide All.
3. Quick Mask is an editing mode that enables you to literally "paint" a mask onto an image. This mask will be converted to a selection when you go back to the Standard editing mode.
4. An Adjustment layer enables you to make adjustments to an image, such as brightness/contrast and color adjustments, without changing the actual image. The mask shows you how these changes affect an image but don't actually change the image in any way.

11

5. Choose Layer, New, Adjustment Layer. You'll then be given the choice of which type of Adjustment layer you'd like to create. The choices are: Levels, Curves, Brightness/Contrast, Color Balance, Hue/Saturation, Selective Color, Channel Mixer, Invert, Threshold, and Posterize.

6. There are many ways to select a set of colors in Photoshop. By far, one of the most powerful selection tools is the Color Range command (Select, Color Range). You can also use the Magic Wand or Lasso tools. In the next chapter, we'll look at using channels to select colors as well.

7. By default, all Adjustment layers have masks that are filled with white. However, if you have a selection active before you add an Adjustment layer, the selection will turn into a mask. Also, you can paint on an Adjustment layer. Treat it like any other mask.

Photoshop in Color

This color section is broken into two parts. The first portion will help you follow along with those exercises that contain color-critical information. In other words, if color plays a big part in understanding a particular exercise, I've added the color images to this section.

The second part of this section will showcase some of the final projects and show you where to turn to create the effects that have been highlighted. From color correction to special color effects, you'll find examples of it here.

The Color Picker dialog box, which you can bring up by clicking on either the foreground or background swatch in the toolbox, enables you to choose a new foreground or background color. To choose a new color, drag the white arrows along the color slider (the spectrum) and click OK. Or, click somewhere within the color slider to get close to the color you want, then click-and-drag in the color field (the main color swatch) to fine-tune the color, and then click OK.

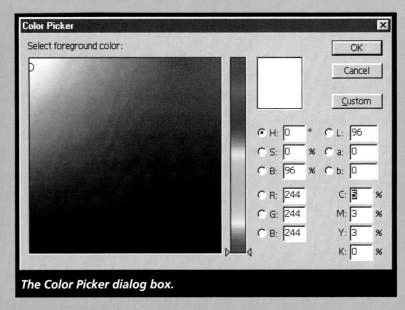

The Color Picker dialog box.

As an alternative you can specify the color explicitly by entering numbers directly into the fields alongside the different color models. You can enter numbers for HSL (Hue, Saturation & Brightness), Lab (a Photoshop specific color model), RGB (Red, Green & Blue – intended for onscreen images), or CMYK (Cyan, Magenta, Yellow & percentage of Black – intended for print). Entering exact numbers will help when following along with some of the examples in the book.

The Color Table dialog box.

Palettes are a subset of the available colors. The web palette, for example, is a collection of 216 specific colors that will appear the same on PCs or Macs with either Netscape or Internet Explorer. Photoshop refers to restricted palettes, such as the Web palette, as color tables. You can access a color table for any indexed color image by choosing Image, Mode, Color Table. You can also change any of the colors in the table by clicking on the color entry. Doing so will bring up the Color Picker dialog box enabling you to choose a new color to replace the one you clicked on. Beware, though, that changing a color in the table will change every instance of the color in your image.

Note Although both the PC and the Macintosh have their own versions of the Color Picker, I recommend that you stick with the Photoshop Color Picker. To choose the Photoshop Color Picker as your default Color Picker, choose File, Preferences, General and then select Photoshop.

The figures on this page, created by digital artist Laren Leonard, give you an idea of just what kind of unique art you can create with various Photoshop filters. Laren started with a scan of some fall leaves that she photographed, added an Impressionist filter to the entire image, and then applied various filters—including Alien Skin's Fire—to selected portions of the image to until she was happy with the result, which is titled "Fireman."

Original image.

Image with filters.

Final image.

RGB image (printed in CMYK).

Grayscale image.

For more information about working with Photoshop's built-in and third-party-compatible filters, see Days 15, "Applying Filter Effects," and 20, "Adding All Kinds of Special Effects."

Bitmap image.

The images on these pages represent how the different image modes affect an image area. The first image above is the original RGB mode (naturally it was converted to CMYK for printing). It would be exactly (more or less) the same in CMYK mode. The second rendition is what the image would look like when converted to grayscale. The major difference between this version and the first is that this image is what you would call black and white in photography while the original is in color. The bottom image is a bitmap version. This image is not grayscale but is instead truly black and white.

Duotone, with sepia tone added.

Indexed (Adaptive palette).

Indexed (Web palette).

Indexed (Web palette, dithered).

The first image above is a duotone. I used a sepia tone as the second color to give the image its rich brown appearance. The remaining images are all in Indexed Color mode. The first of these images is in Indexed color (256 color) mode. I used the Adaptive palette—which doesn't look too bad—followed by the image Indexed mode with the Web palette. Notice the degradation of the image. This is what will happen to your images if you save them all as web-ready GIFs. The last image also uses the Web palette, but with a small twist. I allowed the program to dither the image. This results in an apparent increase in the number of colors. It also results in an increase in the final size of the GIF image.

Image with pure colors.

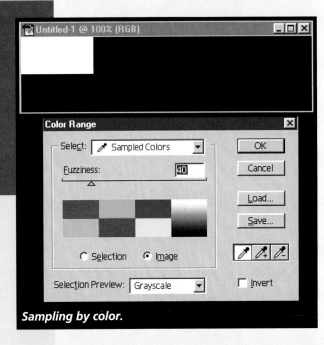

Sampling by color.

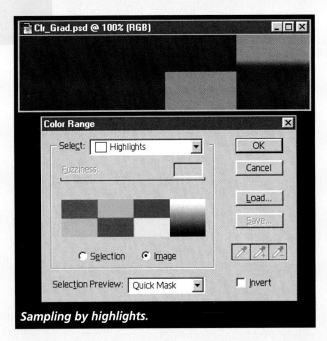

Sampling by highlights.

Sometimes you'll find it necessary to make a selection by choosing a range of color, and this is where the Color Sampler tool comes in. In the first image, all of the colors are pure. That is to say, the red is 255, 0, 0 in the RGB palette. The Green is 0, 255, 0, and so on. The same is true for the cyan, magenta, and yellow except that their values are in the CMYK space.

With the original open, you can choose Select, Color Range to bring up the Color Range dialog box. What you see is the result of selecting the red area of the image. The selected area shows up as white whereas the unselected area shows up as black. In addition to sampling colors, you can select highlights, midtones, and shadows. When you click OK, the areas you selected will translate to selections.

For more information about color, see Days 7, "Calibrating Your System and Setting the Color Modes," and 16, "Correcting the Color;" for more information about selections, see Day 9, "Creating Selections and Defining Paths."

Original image.

Final image, with brightness increased and curves adjustment.

On this page, we use a photograph that needs color correction in order to show how Adjustment layers work. The image we started with is a bit too dark and a bit too green. By adjusting the curves, we're able to adjust the color cast without drastically altering the remainder of the colors in the image.

Working with Adjustment layers is just one of the processes you may need to work through in order to achieve that perfect image. In Day 11, you'll practice using adjustment layers, but you'll also learn to work with the Rubber Stamp tool, quick masks, and alternative selection methods.

For more information about adjustment layers, see Day 11, "Masking with Layer Masks, Quick Masks, and Adjustment Masks;" for more information about color correction, see Day 16, "Correcting the Color."

Original image.

Red channel.

Green channel.

Channels are an important, and extremely powerful, feature of Photoshop, and they are of great help in creating exacting masks, photo restoration, and for creating special effects in Photoshop. This RGB image contains four channels: one for red, one for green, one for blue, and one for the composite image. As you'll learn in Day 12, "Working with Channels," there are many advantages to working with channels, including cleaning up scans and creating selections.

Blue channel.

Also in Day 12, you'll learn how to isolate a section of an image that is contained primarily in one color channel. Once it's isolated, you will then apply tonal corrections to that isolated area. As a bonus, you'll also learn to replace that area with a different image or Photoshop creation. Here we've chosen to demonstrate with the sand dunes, but you can apply these same techniques to your images just as easily.

Original image.

Photoshop includes many great tools and features to help you adjust the color of your photographs, and Day 16, "Correcting the Color," shows you many of these tips and techniques. As you'll see in the original scan, there are some obvious problems: the entire scan is a little too dark and has an overall green cast. Luckily, the green cast—and the brightness and contrast—are pretty even throughout the image.

By using the Variations dialog box, you can preview the effect of the changes you're making. You can choose to edit the shadows, midtones, highlights, and saturation; you can change the colors; you can change the overall brightness. The third image here shows a more yellow, more blue, more light version of the image. Notice how the image is obviously brighter and that you can see more detail in the shadows.

Editing the image.

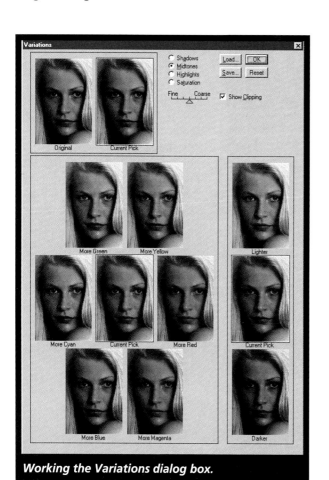

Working the Variations dialog box.

Changing the color balance.

Final image.

Although the image is noticeably better, the skin is a little too red and the hair still seems a little too green. By using Photoshop's Color Balance feature, you can easily fine-tune some of these color changes. The top image above shows the figure with more cyan overall and more magenta added to the midtones.

Even with all of these changes, you may notice that the face appears a bit too red. By editing the curves, we're easily able to correct this and achieve a markedly improved final photograph.

When you finally decide to output your image to a device other than your monitor, you'll find that digital imaging and Photoshop present many challenges. Depending on the range of the gamut of your output device, your output may look much different from what you saw on your monitor. In order to make what you see onscreen appear closer to what you get in the final printed piece, Day 16 walks you through the process of color output testing, including how to create an image output template.

Original image.

Using a Casio QV-100 digital camera, I photographed these carnations. Then, using the Artistic, Underpainting filter, I created the resulting "watercolor." For more information about digital cameras, see Day 5, "Importing Existing Images and Creating New Ones." For more information about working with filters, see Day 20, "Adding All Kinds of Special Effects."

Final "watercolor" image.

Image with the leash.

After you get your pictures developed, you may find that you have unwanted telephone poles, people, or dog leashes creeping into your masterpiece. Day 8, "Understanding the Editing Tools," shows you just how easy it is to clean up those unwanted items that tend to detract from an otherwise beautiful piece of art.

Image without the leash.

When a rectangular border just becomes too square, try an oval. In Day 9, "Creating Selections and Defining Paths," you learn how to add oval borders to your figures, and in Day 10, "Painting with Fills, Patterns, and Gradients," you learn to customize your paint brushes so that you can use patterned and feathered borders.

Using oval borders for variety.

Using custom brushes to create unique borders.

With Photoshop 5.0, the text capabilities are greatly enhanced. You can place text horizontally and vertically. You can even edit and rotate text. The possibilities for great text effects are endless, and Day 14, "Typing In Great Type Effects," shows you just a smattering of the myriad options.

Beveled and embossed text with drop shadow.

Text with a photograph fill.

Adding vertical text.

In the first shot shown here, you'll notice that the lighting is terribly uneven—the result of a flash working overtime no doubt—and the overall contrast is poor. Pictures like these probably turn up more than not, but fortunately, there's the Photoshop to the rescue. All you need to do is even out the brightness, adjust the shadows, gray levels, and highlights, and clean off the scratches and dust marks. Voila. You have a new photo in no time.

Original image.

Editing the overall contrast.

Cleaning off dust and scratches.

Final image.

Image compositing, whether it be a collage or montage, is pretty simple if you start with the right types of images. Day 19, "Compositing Two or More Images into One," walks you through the process of creating image composites and provides you with lots of tips on how to go about blending two or more images seamlessly.

Original, background image.

Composited image, including text.

Most of the time, you won't have to worry about linking your layers to each other. For certain tasks, though, such as positioning multiple layers on top of a background or transform effects, layer links can be extremely useful. In Day 13, you'll learn multiple methods for linking your layers as well as how to create a new background from two existing images.

With the help of filters, both built-in and third-party, it's easy to achieve many different looks for the same image. Day 15, "Applying Filter Effects," takes you through the installation process and shows you how to use filters to create various artistic effects, some of which can be created only by combining multiple filters.

DAY 12

Working with Channels

Channels are an important and extremely powerful feature of Photoshop. Channels are also one of the most overlooked and underused features. This is true not only of beginners and intermediate users but also of some advanced users as well. Channels can be of great help in creating exacting masks, photo restoration, and for creating special effects in Photoshop. In fact, many of the effects that can be accomplished with third-party plug-ins can be done with channels. Using channels to replicate these effects can be more time-consuming but can provide better results. In this chapter, I'll introduce you to channels, demonstrate how you can use them to create and save selections, and demonstrate how you can use them to create some awesome effects. This chapter covers the following topics:

- Understanding what a channel is
- Creating selections with the help of channels
- Editing with channels
- Using channels for lighting effects

What Is a Channel?

Every image has at least one channel. Channels contain the information that makes up an image. A grayscale image, such as a black-and-white photo, contains one channel. An RGB image contains four channels: one for the red information in your image, one for the green, one for the blue, and a composite channel that contains all the information contained in the other three channels.

Each channel is grayscale and, therefore, contains 256 levels of gray from white to black, inclusive. Every image can contain up to 24 channels. These 24 channels are the default channels that make up the image and any that you create to hold selections or other information you may need in the creation or manipulation of your images. If your image has multiple layers, each layer has its own channels.

Channels that you create are sometimes referred to as alpha channels. Although you can arrange the order of any alpha channel you create by clicking and dragging them within the Channels palette, you cannot rearrange the default Color channels.

The Channels Palette

The Channels palette is normally grouped with the Layers and Paths palettes. As you read earlier on Day 1, "Introducing the Photoshop Interface," you can separate the Channels palette from its partners and move it around your work area. This can be helpful if you need to see, for example, the Layers palette and the Channels palette at the same time. For the most part, though, the default setting works well.

To view the Channels palette, you can click its tab or choose Window, Show Channels from the menu. The Channels palette contains all the current channels associated with the current image (see Figure 12.1).

You can turn channels on and off by clicking the small eye icon to the left of the thumbnail in each channel. You can add and delete channels (except for the default channels that make up an image). As well, you can manipulate the channels separately as you would an entire image. You can draw and paint on a channel, make selections of portions of a channel, and so on. I'll demonstrate the usefulness of some of these processes as you read through this chapter.

So what are these channels and what type of information do they contain? That depends, to some degree, on the image's mode. An RGB image contains four default channels when it is first created. One channel contains all the red, green, and blue information present in the image. In other words, it contains the complete image. The other three channels contain the separate information of the three colors that make up the image. One contains the red information, one the green information, and the last holds the blue information. I'll demonstrate this in a moment.

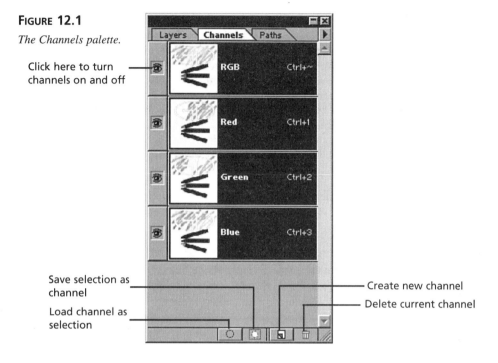

FIGURE **12.1**

The Channels palette.

Click here to turn
channels on and off

Save selection as
channel

Load channel as
selection

Create new channel

Delete current channel

Other image modes contain different numbers and types of channels. For example, a CMYK image has five channels. The first contains all the image's color information and the other four contain the cyan, magenta, yellow, and black information.

Note

Strictly speaking, non-Photoshop file formats that support multiple channels (like TIFF) only store one data channel for each color and do not store a channel for a composite. Technically, Photoshop doesn't store an additional composite channel either. It lists the combined colors as a channel to quickly turn on all color channels at once.

A black-and-white photograph scanned into Photoshop contains only a black channel when it is first created.

As a quick exercise, open an RGB or CMYK file and open the Channels palette. Choose File, Preferences, Display & Cursors, and then toggle the Color Channels in Color option. Click OK and see how the Channels thumbnails change. When finished, you can set this back to the default or, if you prefer, leave the new setting.

12

Because a channel represents the information of one certain color in an image, the channel can be represented in grayscale. In fact, unless you specify Color Channels in Color under Preferences, Display, & Cursors, the thumbnails you see in the Channels palette are in black-and-white (grayscale, actually). If you turn the option on, you see the different channels represented by their colors. In other words, the Red channel's thumbnail is red, the Green one is green, and so on. This doesn't make a difference with how the channels work or what information they display. It's just a different way of seeing the information.

A Closer Look

To see what kind of information is kept in a channel and how it's represented, open the file Gdcrayons.psd from the Day12 folder on the CD-ROM (see Figure 12.2). Notice how there are three crayons: one red, one green, and one blue.

FIGURE 12.2

Red, green, and blue crayons.

Open the Channels palette and you'll see four channels: the RGB, the Red, the Green, and the Blue channels. In the thumbnail views, they all look pretty similar, right? To get a better view of each channel, you can split the image into its separate channels.

Click the small black arrow to the right of the palette tabs. In the pull-down menu, choose Split Channels. The full-color image disappears and is replaced by three grayscale images. Each of these is one of the separate Color channels of the original image (see Figure 12.3).

FIGURE 12.3

The RGB channels.

Red channel

Blue channel

12

Green channel

If you look at each separate channel now, you'll notice something interesting. Look at the Red channel and note how the red portions of the original image seem lighter than the green or blue portions. The red crayon, for example, is much lighter than the green and blue crayons. You may notice, too, that the red portion of the drawing behind the logo has turned completely white. This is because white is represented by the value 255, or the full capacity of the channel (remember how I said that a channel is grayscale where white is 255 and black is 0).

This is true for the corresponding green and blue scribble marks on the Green and Blue channels. The blue scribble is not completely white, though, which means that the blue I used is not pure blue. It may have had a little green in it as well.

So what does all this mean in the grand scheme of what you can do with Photoshop? Well, it means that you can look at an image's information in different ways, and that you can use this information in different ways, too.

For example, there are methods of cleaning up scans or digital photographs that take advantage of how some channels are not as good at representing the information that makes up an image as some of the others. In a digital photograph, where the information that makes up the image is captured by a CCD (Charge-Coupled Device), the Blue channel is normally not as good as the Red and Green channels.

Using a Channel to Create a Selection: Example I

Whole chapters in advanced Photoshop books have been written on this subject, and I'm not going to pretend that you'll be an expert after this one exercise, but it will certainly give you a headstart on how to effectively use channels to make difficult selections an easier process.

Have you ever wondered how to change the color of one portion of an image while leaving the rest unchanged? Here's how to accomplish that effect.

Open an image that you'd like to change. You can use any of the photographs on the CD-ROM, but I'll be demonstrating using a color portrait of Marianne.

   1. Open the Channels palette.

   2. Zoom in on the eye on the right using the Zoom tool.

Now look at the separate channels. Which one shows the most contrast between the colored portion of the eye and the surrounding areas? Because the eye, in the photo I've chosen, is green, the Red channel shows the greatest contrast (see Figure 12.4).

FIGURE 12.4

*Zoom in on the area
you want to select.*

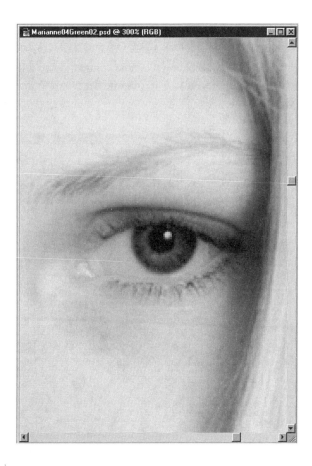

12

The Red channel has the greatest contrast because human skin contains a lot of red, so the red portion is quite pale in the Red channel. Also, because the green in the model's eye doesn't contain much if any red, the green of the iris is quite dark in the Red channel.

 3. Now that you've selected the channel with the greatest contrast for the area you want to select, select the Magnetic Lasso tool and simply click and drag it around the colored portion of the eye.

If the selection doesn't work out too well, a couple of tricks can help. You could bump up the contrast of the channel, but that affects the entire image. What you can do instead is work on a copy of the channel.

   4. Click and drag the Red channel onto the Create New Channel icon at the bottom of the Channels palette. The icon you're looking for is the small rectangle with a bent bottom-left corner. Doing so creates and makes current a new channel called, appropriately enough, Red Copy.

5. With this channel active, choose Image, Adjust, Brightness/Contrast and bump the contrast up by about 10% or so. Click OK and try the Magnetic Lasso tool again.

    Another trick is to try adjusting the edge contrast down a little in the Magnetic Lasso options. I adjusted it to 5% from the default 10% and made the selection you see in Figure 12.5.

FIGURE 12.5

Selecting the iris only.

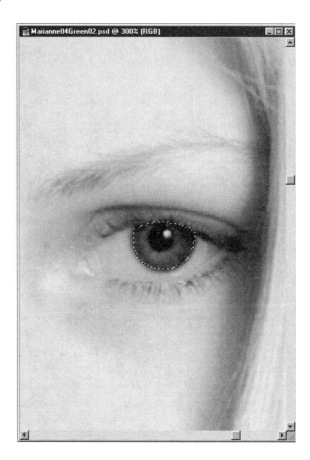

Now that the new channel has done its job, you can delete it by dragging it onto the small garbage can icon.

6. You can save the selection you've made in order to access it again later without going through all the previous steps. To do so, simply choose Select, Save Selection, which brings up the Save Selection dialog box (see Figure 12.6).

FIGURE 12.6

The Save Selection dialog box.

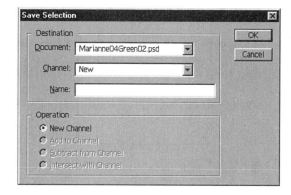

7. Enter the document name and the channel name. For now, just leave the defaults, which creates a new channel called Alpha 1 (see Figure 12.7). This new channel contains your selection, and it is saved along with the image so that you can access it in later sessions.

With your selection made and safely stored in a new channel, it's time to make some magic.

8. Click the Layers tab to go back to the image. You may notice that you're still viewing the grayscale version of the image. No problem. Click the layer in the Layers palette and the image returns to the screen. You should now see the full-color image with the eye selected.

9. Choose Image, Adjust, Variations to bring up the Variations dialog box (see Figure 12.8).

10. Click More Magenta twice and then click OK. You've just changed the model's eye color from green to a stunning mauve (see Figure 12.9).

Of course, you won't see the difference here in black and white, but take another look at the Red channel (see Figure 12.10).

Notice how the eye on the left (the one that's still green) is quite dark compared to the one you changed. This is because by adding magenta, you've also added some red (magenta is a combination of red and blue). Because you're looking at the Red channel, the magenta- (or mauve) colored eye appears lighter than the original green one.

You've just had a glimpse at how you can use the channels to make more accurate selections with a little more ease than before.

12

FIGURE 12.7

*The new alpha chan-
nel containing the
selection.*

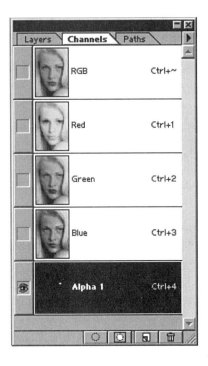

FIGURE 12.8

*The Variations dialog
box.*

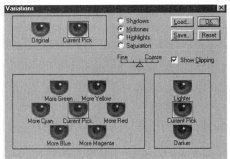

What else can you do with channels? Much more! You can use channels to help repair images, for example. You could use the same techniques described in the last exercise to help you remove the dreaded red-eye from portraits taken with on-camera flashes. The red stands out more in one of the channels than it does in the others, and this enables you to accurately select the offending portion so that you can correct it. As you'll see in the next section, we'll use a color channel to make tonal changes to an entire sky.

FIGURE 12.9

*The model's eye color
changed.*

FIGURE 12.10

*Close-up of the Red
channel with the
model's eye color
changed.*

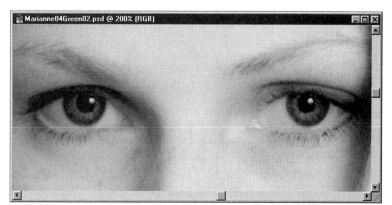

12

Using a Channel to Create a Selection: Example II

In the previous section, you learned how to change a selection (derived from a color channel) with the Variations command. Although the Variations dialog box is an excellent visual interface to see color changes, we don't have it available as an Adjustment layer. This may seem like a minor point, but you could throw away potentially useful information anytime you use a tonal effect in Photoshop.

Why is this so? Every time you compress a range of tones with curves, levels, brightness, contrast, and so forth, you are telling Photoshop to throw away image information. This is not the case with Adjustment layers. Again, you might question the importance of keeping information that appears to be garbage. Quite frankly, you can never trust what you see on your monitor 100%. What a disappointment it would be if you spent a great length of time tweaking an image, only to see it print horribly! This is where Adjustment layers come to the rescue: We can use the monitor as a starting point and come back to the Adjustment layer settings if we need to. Having said that, let's start the exercise for this section.

Similar to the last section, you isolate a section of the image that is contained primarily in one color channel. Once it is isolated, you apply tonal corrections to that isolated area. As a bonus, you also replace that area with some other image or Photoshop creation. You may want to read through the entire exercise before you actually perform it with one of your images.

1. Find an image that has a solid color field that needs correcting and can be replaced with some other image. In this exercise, an image of a deep blue sky and a sand dune from Baja California, Mexico, will be used.

2. Open the image in Photoshop and perform any major retouching with the Paint tools in Photoshop; don't concern yourself with very small dust marks or scratches yet. (Refer back to Days 8 and 11 for details on retouching images.) Remember to contain your retouching to its own layer, just in case you make a mistake. As you can see in Figure 12.11, the example image already has a clone layer.

3. Add a Levels or Curves Adjustment layer (Layer, New, Adjustment Layer) to the image. Make sure the topmost layer is active before doing so. Set the black and white points somewhere close to the first signs of image information on the left and right sides of the graph, respectively. Figure 12.12 shows a basic tonal correction for the sand dune image and Figure 12.13 shows the sand dune image after the changes have been applied.

FIGURE 12.11

*The sand dune image
with Layers palette.*

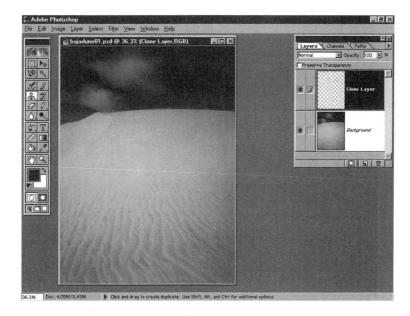

FIGURE 12.12

*The Levels dialog box
for the sand dune
image.*

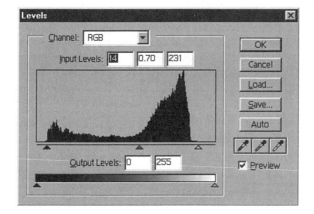

12

It may be a bit harder to see in black and white, but the effect of the Levels layer looks
fine for the sand dune. It's the sky and white clouds that are too dark. There's no reason
to waste precious time trying to find one effect or command that will satisfy the entire
image. You may run into many images that require specific tonal correction in more than
one area. The next part of the exercise will be spent isolating the sky and clouds. Using
color channels as a guide for the selection, this should be relatively easy.

FIGURE 12.13

The sand dune image after the Levels Adjustment layer has been added.

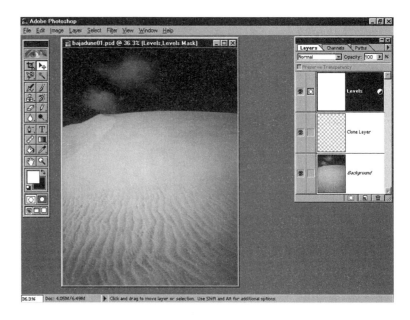

Note

Depending on the content of the image you choose, it may be just as easy with your particular image to use the Magic Wand tool or the Color Range command to isolate areas you want to change. But for this exercise, we want to maximize our use of channels.

4. Click any layer besides an Adjustment layer (either the clone or Background layer). Make sure all the layers are showing and none are hiding. Now click the Channels tab of the Layers palette (see Figure 12.14). If you've separated your palettes from the default Photoshop settings, you can use the Window, Show Channels command to bring up the Channels palette.

5. Find a color channel that shows the most contrast in the area of the image you wish to isolate. If you set the Display & Cursors preferences to show color channels in color, you may want to revert to the default grayscale settings. This enables you to see the contrast in each channel more easily. For the sand dune image, the red channel isolates the blue sky most completely. Technically, if the sky is a pure blue, either the red or green channel would isolate the sky well. Why? Because pure blue contains no red or green, the red and green channels represent blue information with the color black. See the sidebar for more details.

FIGURE 12.14

Both the Layers and Channels palettes with appropriate View settings.

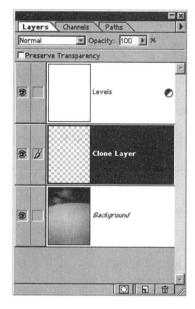
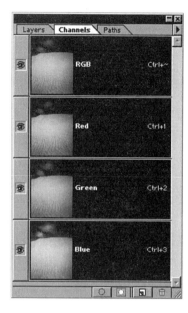

Note

How is color represented in channels? Well, remember how masks represent transparency? Black represents "0" or no opacity, while white represents "255" or 100% opacity. The same concept is true for color channels. Black in any color channel represents the absence of that color. For example, if you see black in the green channel, that area is either pure red, pure blue, or black. Likewise, white in any color channel represents the full value of that color. If you see white in the red channel, then that area of the image is either pure red or white. When you want to isolate a color area using channels, you may want to choose the color complement instead of the actual color. In the sand dune image, the red channel is used instead of the blue channel because the lightness value of the sand is close to the intensity of blue in the sky. Therefore, little contrast is available in the blue channel. The red channel, however, has a suitable amount of contrast to isolate the sky.

12

6. Once you've found a color channel that effectively isolates the area you wish to change, click the channel name in the Channels palette. Now click and drag the channel to the Create New Channel icon at the bottom of the Channels palette. This duplicates the channel.

7. Double-click the new channel (called "Alpha 1") and give it a more descriptive name. The duplicated red channel of the sand dune image is named "Sky" (see Figure 12.15).

FIGURE 12.15

*The red channel is
duplicated and named
"Sky."*

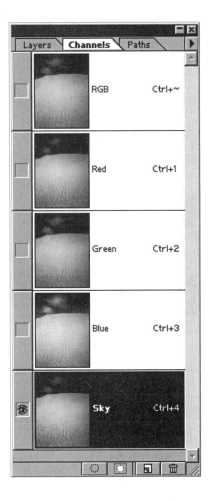

8. Now that we have a copy of the red channel to use as a template, we need to make the area of the channel that the sky occupies stand out more clearly. To do this, you need to apply a Levels command (Image, Adjust, Levels) to the Sky channel. See Figures 12.16, 12.17, and 12.18 for a "before and after" look at the Sky channel, as well as the Level settings used to accomplish the "after" version.

FIGURE 12.16

The Sky channel before the Levels command is applied.

FIGURE 12.17

The Levels dialog box with settings used for the "after" version. Try to get the black and white points as close together as possible, while maintaining smooth edges along major objects in the image.

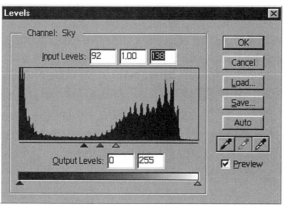

12

FIGURE **12.18**

The Sky channel after the Levels command is applied.

9. Except for the lower areas of the dune and the clouds, the sky is completely black. Now let's edit the Sky channel with the Paintbrush tool (or your preferred Painting tool). Because the Sky channel is already an alpha (or mask) channel, paint directly on the Sky channel with either black or white. If you paint into the sky area with white accidentally, immediately undo (Edit, Undo or Ctrl/Cmd-Z) your last paint stroke. See Figure 12.19 to see the dune area being painted with white and Figure 12.20 for the finished channel touch-up.

FIGURE 12.19

Some areas of the Sky channel need to be cleaned up with the Paintbrush tool.

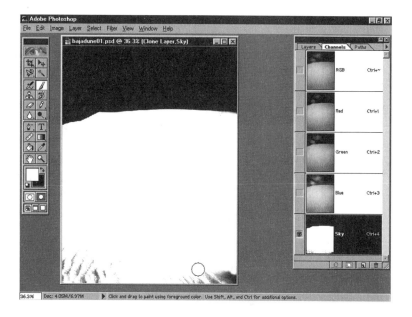

FIGURE 12.20

The Sky channel with the sand dune filled with white and the sky isolated in black.

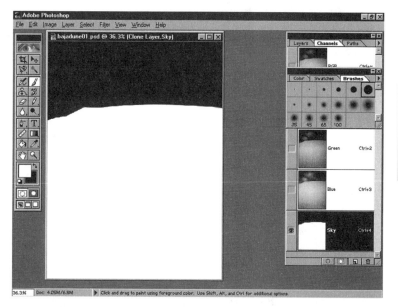

12

Excellent! Save your image as a Photoshop (PSD) file and take a quick break to rest your eyes. We're halfway done with the exercise. When you get back, review your work in the Layers and Channels palettes.

1. Picking up where you left off after step 9, click and drag the Sky channel to the Load channel as a selection icon. The channel information will now be used to create a selection. Whatever is white in the channel (the sand dune) is selected (see Figure 12.21).

FIGURE 12.21

The selection loaded from the Sky channel outlines the sand dune foreground.

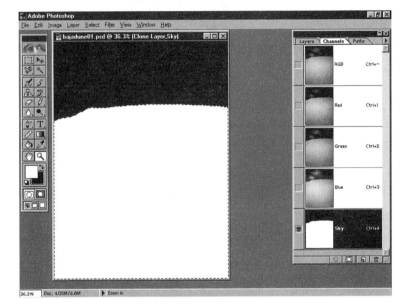

2. In order to get a better blended edge for the sand dune, the selection is expanded by one pixel using the Select, Modify, Expand command and feathered by two pixels using the Select, Feather command. For a "before and after" look of the selection, see Figures 12.22 and 12.23.

3. Click the RGB channel name or thumbnail to hide the Sky channel. Don't worry about the selection—it won't go away. We have to reactivate all the color channels before we go back to the Layers palette. The RGB, Red, Green and Blue channels should all be showing now. If the Sky channel is still on, click the eyeball next to its channel thumbnail.

4. Go back to the Layers palette and click the Levels layer, which should be the topmost layer. Invert the sand dune selection by choosing Select, Inverse and then use the Ctrl-Backspace (Cmd-Backspace) keyboard shortcut to fill the inverted selection with black. Because this is a mask on the Levels layer, this action excludes the sky from the effect of this layer's settings. Why is this important? It's because we want to have the widest range of tonal values to use on our next Adjustment layer for the sky and clouds.

FIGURE 12.22

A close-up of the selection from Figure 12.21.

FIGURE 12.23

The selection after it's expanded and feathered.

12

5. With the selection still active and the Levels layer highlighted, add a new Levels
    Adjustment layer. In the name field for the first dialog box, give a better descrip-
    tion than "Levels." For this example, it was named "Sky and Cloud Levels." Use
    whatever settings for the black, white, and midpoints that you prefer. Refer to
    Figure 12.24 to see the effect on the image and the layer stacking.

FIGURE 12.24

*The sand dune image
with a new Levels
Adjustment layer
added selectively to the
sky. Notice the oppo-
site masks in each
Levels Adjustment
layer.*

Note

To see why additional Adjustment layers can be necessary, try Shift-clicking
the Adjustment layer's thumbnail. Doing so deactivates the selective mask
(putting a red "X" through the thumbnail) and applies the Adjustment layer
settings to the entire image. Be sure to hide other Adjustment layers,
though, to see the effect of an individual Adjustment layer. To bring back
the selective mask, Shift-click the thumbnail again. This function can be
accomplished on any mask or layer with transparency.

6. Re-evaluate the retouching you did earlier. In the sand dune example, the second
   Levels layer has brought out more dust marks and scratches. Perform any additional retouching that you consider necessary; just remember to turn off all Adjustment
   layers before you do so. You might be wondering why such an image with so many
   dust marks was picked for this exercise. You'll see in the last part of this exercise.

Even though the Paint tools in Photoshop can do wonders, they can't always save the
day. After spending some time retouching the sand dune image, there are still some fine
hairs causing problems. To remedy this, we're going to try another approach besides
retouching. Next, you'll replace the sky with one made in Photoshop using gradients.

7. Reload the selection of the sky from the Sky and Cloud Levels layer by Ctrl-
   clicking (Cmd-clicking) the Levels thumbnail (see Figure 12.25).

FIGURE 12.25

The sky selection loaded from the "Sky and Cloud Levels" layer.

8. Double-click the Background layer to bring up the Layer Options dialog box. Give the Background layer a new name. For the sand dune image, the Background layer is renamed "Sand Dune." Why is this important or necessary? If you do not rename the Background layer, Photoshop does not let any layers be stacked under it. Additionally, you will not be able to add a layer mask to the Background layer unless it is renamed.

9. With the renamed Background layer highlighted and the selection of the sky active, Alt-click (Option-click on a Mac) the Add Layer Mask icon. Holding Alt (Option) while clicking tells Photoshop to hide the selected area for this layer. As you can see in Figure 12.26, the sky now shows the default transparency grid.

10. Click the Create New Layer icon to add an empty layer. Double-click the "Layer 1" name and give the layer a new descriptive name. For the sand dune example, the new layer is given the name "New Sky."

11. Drag the new layer titled New Sky below the renamed Background layer (Sand Dune). See Figure 12.27 for the correct layer stacking. Also, hide both Adjustment layers.

12

FIGURE **12.26**

The sand dune image with a transparent sky area. Notice the layer mask attached to the Sand Dune layer. Because the Clone layer has information in both the sky and the sand dune, a layer mask is added to it as well.

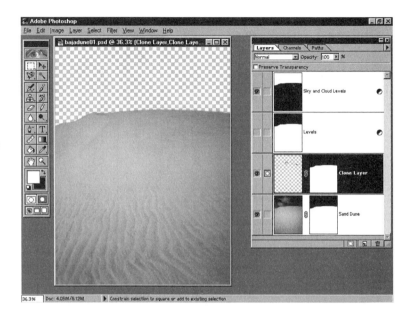

FIGURE **12.27**

The Layers palette for the sand dune image.

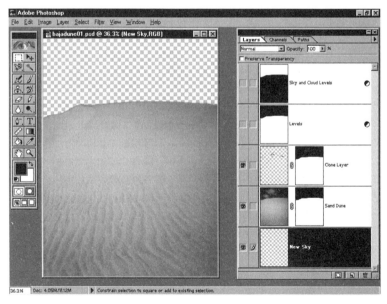

12. Click the Sand Dune layer to make it active. Shift-click the layer mask for the Sand Dune layer to temporarily hide it. You should see a red "X" appear through the mask thumbnail. Click the layer thumbnail for the Sand Dune layer to exit the Mask mode (see Figure 12.28).

FIGURE **12.28**

The layer mask of the Sand Dune layer is hidden. The Paintbrush icon for the Sand Dune layer indicates that we are working on the layer and not the mask.

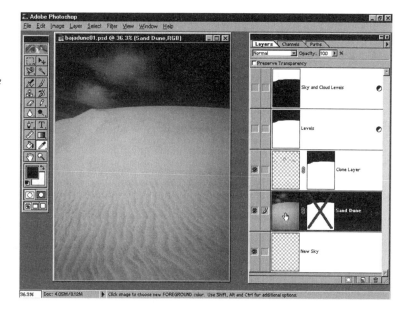

13. With the Eyedropper tool on the toolbar, click the darkest area of the sky. Press the X key on the keyboard to flip the foreground and background colors. Now sample the lightest color of the sky with the Eyedropper tool. Press the X key again to flip the colors on the toolbar. Reactivate the layer mask for the Sand Dune layer by Shift-clicking the thumbnail with the red X.

14. Click the Gradient tool icon on the toolbar. Make sure your options look like those in Figure 12.29. With the New Sky layer active, draw a vertical line starting at the top of the sky and ending just below the sand dunes. You should have something similar to Figure 12.30.

12

FIGURE **12.29**

The Gradient tool options.

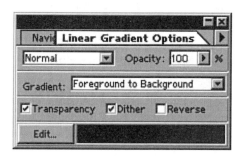

FIGURE 12.30

*The New Sky layer
with a gradient fill.*

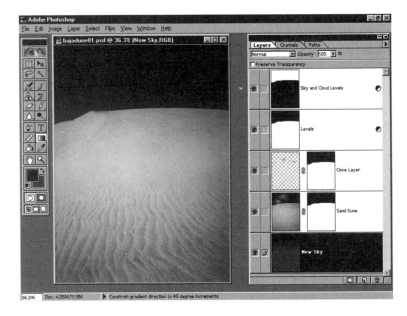

This image is acceptable, but we have lost our cool-looking clouds. Using the color channels as a template, you could isolate the clouds and use the channel as a selection to fill with white. We won't re-create the clouds for this exercise though. If you want to try a cheap and easy way to fill a scene with clouds, try steps 24 and 25, or see "Applying Filter Effects" in Day 20.

15. Create a new layer, name it Clouds, and position it above the New Sky layer. Set the foreground and background colors to the black and white default by pressing the D key. Use the Filter, Render, Clouds command to add clouds to the new layer. You may not like the position of the clouds, so feel free to use the Move tool to find an area of rendered clouds that blends in well with the landscape.

16. Change the Layer mode (discussed in the next chapter) to "Soft Light" and reduce the Opacity to 50–70%. Add a layer mask to the Clouds layer and paint out undesired clouds with black. See Figure 12.31 to see the effect with the sand dune image.

Whoa! That was pretty cool. Admittedly, the fake clouds aren't as nice as the original clouds, but they'll suffice. We've covered a few methods in this exercise that you may not understand fully until you get further in the book, but the more you practice, the better you'll become.

FIGURE 12.31

The sand dune image with a new sky and clouds backdrop.

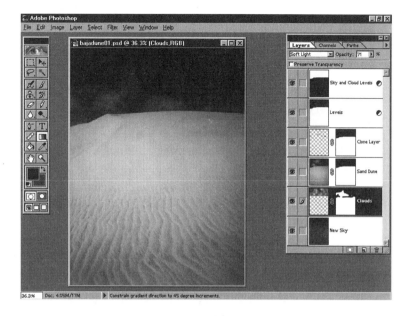

Using Channels for Special Effects

You can also use channels to create special effects. Although Photoshop is not a 3D program, there are still some techniques you can use to give the illusion of 3D to your images.

One of the coolest built-in filters that Photoshop has is the Render Lighting filter. This filter casts light on your image and can be used to add drama, coloring, texture, and many more effects to your images. I'll demonstrate some of these on Day 15, "Applying Filter Effects," but for now I'll show you how to use this filter in conjunction with an alpha channel to create the illusion of 3D.

1. Choose File, New and enter 100 for the width, 50 for the height, 72 dpi for the resolution, and RGB as the mode.

2. Choose a color for the button by clicking the foreground color swatch and choosing a color from the Color Picker dialog box. I chose a light blue.

3. Press Alt-Backspace (Option-Backspace) to fill the image with your chosen color.

4. Open the Channels palette by clicking the Channels tab.

5. Click the Create New Channel icon to create a new alpha channel. Your image turns black and the foreground/background color swatches show dark gray and black.

12

6. Click the default foreground/background color icon. You may notice that this sets the foreground/background to white and black, which is, if you remember, the opposite of the default when you're viewing the image rather than its alpha channel.

7. With the default foreground set to white, press Alt-Backspace (Option-Backspace) to fill the alpha channel with white.

8. Choose Select, All to select the entire image.

9. Click the foreground color swatch to bring up the Color Picker dialog box and choose a light gray (see Figure 12.32).

FIGURE 12.32

The Color Picker dialog box with a light gray color selected.

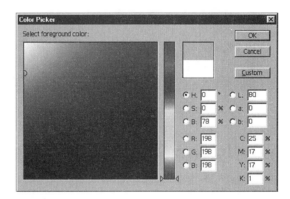

10. Choose Edit, Stroke. Set the Width to 8, the Location to Inside, the Opacity to 100%, and the Mode to Normal. Click OK. You should now have a white rectangle with a gray edge as seen in Figure 12.33.

FIGURE 12.33

Building an alpha channel for a 3D effect.

11. Set the foreground color to a darker gray, choose Edit, Stroke, and change the Width to 6.

12. Repeat with a darker gray, a Width of 4, once more with a really dark gray (almost black), and a Width of 2. You should now have something that resembles Figure 12.34.

FIGURE 12.34

Creating the Bump
map for the Lighting

The image you now have (or the channel at any rate) is sometimes referred to as a Bump map, which is often used to give depth to the image. You might, however, want to soften the transition between the gray shades. This is easily accomplished.

13. Choose Filter, Blur, Gaussian Blur and set the value to about 1.0. This blurs the grays together and makes the transition between them smoother (see Figure 12.35). You now have your final Bump map.

14. Click the Layers tab to go back to your button.

15. Click the layer itself to switch back to the full-color view of your image.

16. Choose Filter, Render, Lighting Effects to bring up the Lighting Effects dialog box. Set the values shown in Figure 12.36.

FIGURE 12.35

The final Bump map
for the Lighting filter.

FIGURE 12.36

The Lighting Effects
dialog box.

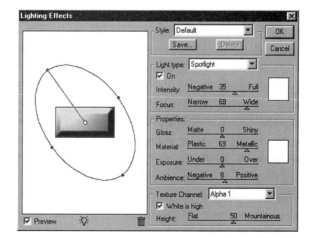

12

The most important value that you need to set here is the Texture channel. You must point this option to the Alpha 1 channel that holds your Bump map. You must also set White to on. For now, leave the default Height of 50.

 Note

> You'll find many fascinating options in the Lighting Effects dialog box. You can choose a style and a light type. You can set the Intensity, the Focus, and the color of the light. You can set the Gloss and the Material properties, as well as the Exposure and Ambiance. I'll demonstrate these options, and others, on Day 15.

17. Move the oval that describes the light direction and height into the same position as you see in Figure 12.36. You can move the oval by clicking and dragging it.

18. Click OK and you should now have a button that you can use for kiosks, multimedia presentations, multimedia CD-ROMs, and Web pages (see Figure 12.37).

FIGURE 12.37

The 3D button created with an alpha channel and the Lighting Effects filter.

You should save a copy of this image as a PSD file. You'll then be able to add text, apply textures to it, and more later on.

Summary

Channels are a feature that many users often overlook. Although they can be difficult to get a handle on, I hope that you'll explore some of the possibilities that a good knowledge of them can bring. Being able to manipulate channels well is what can separate the level of one Photoshop user from another.

Q&A

Q Is there a limit to the number of channels an image can have?

A An image can have up to 24 channels.

Q **Can grayscale images have channels as well as color (RGB and CMYK) images?**

A Yes, grayscale images can have channels. They start out with one but can have more added. Some modes, though, such as bitmap, don't support channels.

Q **Is it possible to merge two channels?**

A Yes, you can merge channels. Normally this would be done if you had split the channels to perform some operation on one or more of the channels without affecting the others. Once you completed the work, you could merge the channels back together to form the composite image.

Q **Should all selections be saved as alpha channels?**

A Not necessarily. If you have spent a lot of time adding finesse to a selection, you should save the selection as a channel. However, if you use the selection to create a layer or adjustment layer mask, then you do not need to save the selection as a channel. The selection can be reloaded from the mask by Ctrl-clicking (Cmd-clicking on a Mac) the mask thumbnail.

Workshop

The following section is a quick quiz about the chapter you have just read. If you have any problems answering any of the questions in the quiz, see the section directly following it for all the answers.

Quiz

1. How do you add a channel to an image?
2. How many channels are there in an RGB image?
3. How do you delete a channel?
4. How do you change the Channels palette thumbnails from grayscale to color?
5. What's the difference between a channel and an alpha channel?
6. How do you alter a duplicated channel to isolate a color area?

Quiz Answers

1. You can add a new channel by clicking the New Channel icon at the bottom of the Channels palette. You can also copy an existing channel by clicking and dragging the channel onto the New Channel icon.
2. Initially there are four: the RGB channel, the Red, the Green, and the Blue channels. You can add more channels to the image, though.

12

3. You can delete a channel by dragging it to the small garbage can icon at the bottom of the Channels palette.

4. You can do so via Preferences. Choose File, Preferences, Display & Cursors and place a checkmark in the Color channels in Color option.

5. A channel is how you would commonly refer to a default channel that stores part of the information that makes up your image. An alpha channel is what you'd call a channel that you create for other purposes, such as saving a selection.

6. You can use any Paint tool or tone effect on a duplicated channel. Remember, it is essentially a mask. You can paint in any grayscale color on a mask, or use commands like Levels or Curves to isolate a given area.

DAY **13**

Layering Your Images

You can think of layers as sheets of tracing paper placed one over the other, because this is what layers in a Photoshop image are like. However, they are much more than what this simple analogy alludes to because you can add, delete, or copy layers with a simple click and drag. More than this, though, you can change the opacity of a layer so that the layer, or layers, underneath it show through. You can also change the Layering mode of layers so that they interact with each other in weird and wonderful ways. In this chapter, I'll demonstrate the layer options and show you how to utilize them to improve your images. This chapter covers

- Working with the Layers palette
- Creating and applying multiple layers
- Understanding the Layering modes

The Anatomy of the Layers Palette

The Layers palette is where you'll do a lot of your work with layers. You can access the Layers options via the menu as well, but I feel that it's easier to access the layers visually through the Layers palette (see Figure 13.1).

FIGURE 13.1

The Layers palette.

Indicates active layer

Click here to turn layers on and off

Add Layer Mask icon

Create New Layer icon

Delete Current Layer icon

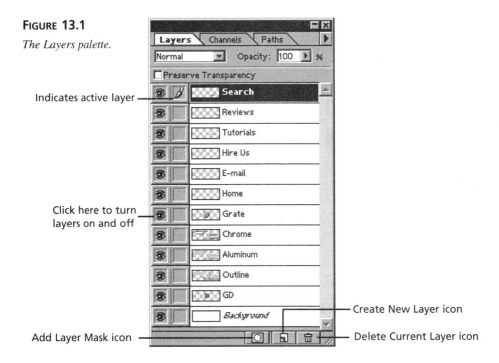

Beneath the Layers tab, you'll see the Layering mode of the current or active layer. The active layer is the one that has its title in a darker shade than the others. In Figure 13.1, the active layer is the top one (titled Search).

Next to the Layering Mode pull-down menu you can see the opacity of the current layer. Below and to the left is the Preserve Transparency option. In Figure 13.1, this option is currently off.

The image I'm working on has 12 layers. Each layer has a couple of different icons associated with it. The first icon, which resembles an eye, signifies whether the layer is visible or not. All the layers in Figure 13.1 are on. The eye icon works as a toggle, toggling the visibility of a layer on and off.

Next to the eye icon on the Search layer is a small paintbrush. This indicates that this is the layer you're working on. This icon can also contain a small link. You can link layers together and later merge these layers via an option in the Layers palette. After the two icons, there is an icon that represents the contents of the layer. You can choose from three sizes for this icon. To do so, click the small black arrow to the right of the Layers tab and choose Palette options. You then get a small dialog box that enables you to choose the size of the icon or turn it off altogether.

Lastly, the name you give a layer is visible to the right of the layer's icon. You can change the name by double-clicking a layer's title bar and setting the name in the dialog box that appears.

At the bottom of the palette are three icons. The first is the Add Layer Mask icon (you can refresh your memory about layer masks by thumbing through Day 11, "Masking with Layer Masks and Quick Masks"), the second is the Create New Layer icon, and the third is the Delete Current Layer icon.

As well as clicking the last two icons to activate them, you can use them in conjunction with the layers themselves. You can click and drag a layer onto the Create New Layer icon to duplicate a layer, and you can click and drag a layer onto the Delete Current Layer icon to delete it.

Caution

The Add Layer Mask icon produces different results depending on the conditions for which you use it. If you have an image floating in a transparent layer, dragging that layer to the Add Layer Mask icon adds an exact mask around the image. That is, you can accomplish the same effect by loading the selection of that layer (Ctrl/Cmd-clicking it) and using the Layer, Add Layer Mask, Reveal Selection command. However, if you simply make that same layer active and then click the Add Layer Mask icon, an empty mask is applied to the whole layer. Visually, you will not notice any change to the image information on that layer, but because masks can be "unlinked" from the layer, you can produce some interesting results by making an exact mask around the image.

We will look at layer and mask linking in more detail later in this chapter. You can also change the effect of the Add Layer Mask icon by using modifier keys (Alt/Option, Ctrl/Cmd, Shift and combinations of them).

13

Working with Layers

The following exercise will walk you through some of the basic options and functions of layers. Here's a quick exercise you can try to get a better idea of how layers work.

1. Open the file Layers01.psd from the Day 13 folder on the accompanying CD-ROM.

2. Figure 13.2 is the image and Figure 13.3 is the Layers palette as you should see it after opening the Layers01.psd image.

FIGURE 13.2

Layers01.psd image.

FIGURE 13.3

The Layers palette for the Layers01.psd image.

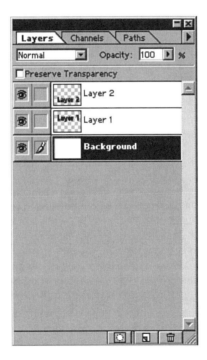

You will notice that all the layers are visible and that they are named from the top down Layer 2, Layer 1, and Background. The Background layer is active.

3. Click the eye icon of the layer named Layer 2. The eye then disappears and is replaced by a blank box. The words "Layer 2" disappear from the image as well (see Figures 13.4 and 13.5). Layer 2 is still there, of course; it's just not currently visible.

FIGURE 13.4

*Layers01.psd image
with Layer 2 off.*

FIGURE 13.5

*The Layers palette for
the Layers01.psd
image with Layer 2
off.*

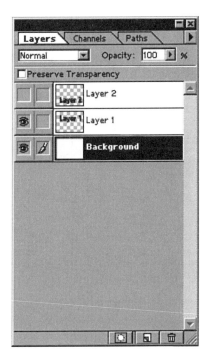

4. Now click the eye icon of Layer 1 and then click the eye icon of Layer 2. Layer 1 disappears and Layer 2 comes back. All that you're doing is toggling the layer visibility on and off.

5. Click Layer 1's eye icon again so that all the layers are visible. Make Layer 1 the current or active layer by clicking the Layer 1 title bar, not to be confused with the Layers tab or the colored bar at the top of the palette. Each layer has a title; the active layer is a dark color while the others, or inactive layers, are gray.

6. Now click the small black arrow next to the layer's Opacity setting, which causes a small slider to drop down (see Figure 13.6).

13

Note

The way palettes show up on your desktop may differ from the ones used here. In Windows 95, go to the Display Properties in the Control Panel to change the colors of the Windows interface. In the Mac OS, go to Appearance in the Control Panels menu. In the OS 8.0 version, click the Color button. Particularly for Photoshop, you may wish to change the Highlight Color setting to something other than black. Many Photoshop users prefer to use a color like yellow. See Figure 13.7 for an example of the Appearance dialog box under Mac OS 8.0.

FIGURE 13.6

The Layers palette showing the Opacity slider.

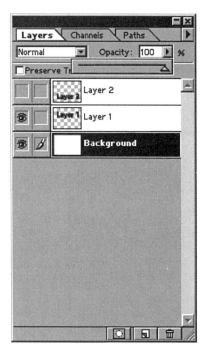

FIGURE 13.7

The Appearance dialog box in Mac OS 8.0.

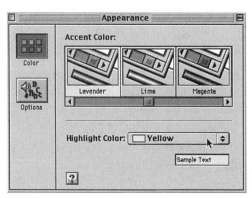

7. Drag the slider to the left until it's at about 50%. Now look at the image (see Figure 13.8). You won't see much of a difference, but Layer 1 is only 50% as opaque as the other two layers.

FIGURE 13.8

The Layers01.psd image with Layer 1 at 50% opacity.

To see the real difference, try this:

8. Click the Preserve Transparency box to preserve the transparent part of Layer 1.

9. Click the foreground color swatch and select a color. I chose a pale blue. Press Alt-Backspace (Option-Backspace on a Mac) to fill the text with the new color. Other than the change in the color of the text in Layer 1, you still won't see much change. Wait, though, it's coming.

10. Press the Ctrl (Cmd) key and drag the text in Layer 1 so that it overlaps the text on Layer 2 (see Figure 13.9).

Still not really evident, right? One last step will bring it all into perspective:

FIGURE 13.9

The Layers01.psd image with Layer 2 overlapping Layer 1.

13

11. Click and drag the title bar of Layer 1 (in the Layers palette), so that it's above Layer 2, and release the mouse. You've just rearranged the layers (see Figure 13.10).

Layer 1 is now on top of Layer 2. If you look more closely at the image you'll see how Layer 2 now shows through Layer 1 (see Figure 13.11).

The Layers01.psd
Layers palette show-
ing the rearranged
layers.

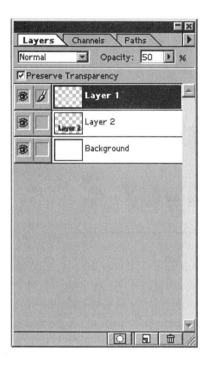

The Layers01.psd
image with Layer 2
partly visible through
Layer 1.

Wow! You've just covered quite a lot. You've turned layers on and off, changed the color
of the text on a layer without disturbing the transparent portion of that layer, changed the
opacity of a layer, and switched the order of the layers. But there are other properties of
Photoshop layers that you still haven't covered, such as the Layering modes.

Using Layer Links to Your Advantage

Most of the time, you will not have to worry about linking your layers to each other. For certain tasks, though, such as positioning multiple layers on top of a background or transform effects, layer links can be extremely useful. In this section, we'll look at three areas where links can be advantageous.

Moving Layers Together

If you have an image with two or more layers on top of a background, linking them together can facilitate easier positioning. This is crucial if you have already spent time positioning two layers relative to one another. In Figure 13.12, you can see an image of two monkeys with two layers: the monkeys and their shadow. This image, monkey01.psd, can be found in the Day13 folder of the CD-ROM.

FIGURE 13.12

Image of a mother and child monkey and their shadow.

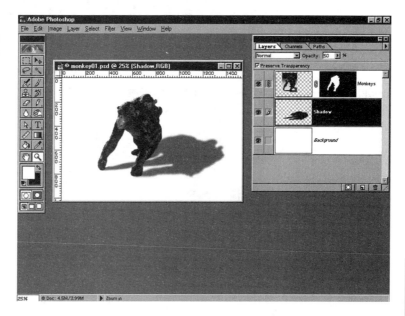

Because the image is meant to be used on a number of backdrops, it would not make sense to combine the shadow and monkey layers together. Let's add a new background to the image (see Figure 13.13). You can find the background file shell01.psd used for this exercise in the Day13 folder of the CD-ROM.

Now the monkeys and the shadow need to be moved. With the Monkeys layer highlighted, simply click the box immediately left of the Shadow layer's thumbnail. The Layer palette with the linked layers is shown in Figure 13.14.

13

FIGURE **13.13**

*The monkey and its
shadow on a new
"shells" background.*

FIGURE **13.14**

*The Monkeys and
Shadow layers are
linked.*

By switching to the Move tool (V on the keyboard), we can position the monkeys with
their shadow somewhere else on the background. See Figure 13.15 to see the monkeys
and their shadow positioned over the shell foreground.

If the layers had not been linked, each layer would have to be moved individually and re-
aligned, which would have ended up taking a lot more time than necessary. That's just
one thing that layer linking can do for you. Let's move on to some of the other advantages.

FIGURE 13.15

The monkeys and their shadow moved to the foreground.

Transform Effects

Linking layers together for transform effects can save time, too. In the next example, another set of monkeys and shadows is added to the image.

1. To begin, duplicate the original Monkeys and Shadow layers by dragging each layer to the Create new layer icon.

2. In this example, the original layers are given a prefix of "1," and the copies are given a prefix of "2." Order the layers as shown in Figure 13.16.

3. Link the second set of monkeys and their shadows to each other. Then use the Edit, Transform, Flip Horizontal command. Because the layers are linked, both the shadow and the monkeys flip together.

4. Using the Move tool, position them to the left of the original monkeys. You should have a composition similar to Figure 13.17.

13

FIGURE 13.16

Two sets of monkeys and their shadows. Because the layers are directly on top of one another, the only visual difference seen is the double opacity of the Shadow layers.

FIGURE 13.17

The second set of monkeys flipped and moved to the left.

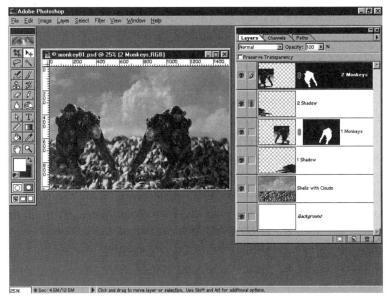

5. To add some variation to the second set of monkeys, use the Edit, Free Transform command (Ctrl/Cmd-T) to shrink and rotate them (see the following Note for more information about the Free Transform tool). Notice again that, because the layers

are linked, both the shadow and the monkeys are affected. See Figure 13.18 for an example of the Free Transform bounding box surrounding the monkeys.

FIGURE 13.18

The Free Transform bounding box around the second set of monkeys. Although the bounding box does not extend to include the shadows, the shadows are affected because they are linked to the Monkeys layer.

Note

The Free Transform tool is an excellent way to command total control over the shape, size, and position of any of your layers. Once the Free Transform command is initiated, you will see a bounding box around the layer image (see Figure 13.18). To scale the layer image, grab a corner node; to scale proportionally, hold down the Shift key while dragging a corner node. To rotate the layer image, grab the bounding box between any two nodes (or just outside of the bounding box). You'll know you are rotating if you see the cursor change to an L-shaped line with two arrowheads. To drag the layer image somewhere else in the composition, click and drag inside the bounding box but not on the center point icon. For more advanced options like Distort, Perspective, and Skew, right-click inside the bounding box for the advanced menu (on a Mac, Ctrl-click inside the bounding box).

When you've finished transforming the second set of monkeys, save your work as a PSD file. We'll come back to this image later. By now, I'm sure you realize what linking does to maximize commands on multiple layers, but what about links between layers and layer masks?

Links Between Layers and Layer Masks

By default, any layer mask added to a layer is linked (see Figure 13.19). It's generally a good thing to have a layer mask linked to its layer image. When you move the layer image, the mask moves with it. Sometimes, however, you may want to create a mask

13

that functions more like a window frame. The layer image then becomes an object that shows through that window frame. Unlinking the layer image from the layer mask allows you to position the layer image off to the side of a layer mask, so that a portion of the layer image is cropped. Open hallway01.psd in the Day 13 folder to see an example, or see Figures 13.19 through 13.21.

Notice that the top "Portrait" layer looks like it's behind the Hallway layer. Look at the layer mask for the Portrait layer: it's in the shape of the door frame. Because the layer mask is not linked to the layer image, the portrait image can be moved anywhere within the door frame without having to be remasked. Go ahead and use the Move tool on the Portrait layer image. Make sure the layer is in Paint mode and not in Mask mode.

FIGURE 13.19

The original hall-way01.psd image.

FIGURE 13.20

Close-up of the door frame.

FIGURE 13.21

The Layers palette of the hallway01.psd image (for example purposes, some of the other layers are merged with the Hallway layer—more on layer merging is in the next section).

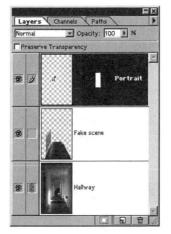

13

Layer Merging

Merging two or more layers is usually a task left for the end of the editing cycle. Why? Because usually merging one layer with another means that information in the lower layer will be discarded. With Photoshop, there are few situations where it is necessary to throw away image information.

Merging layers has a couple of advantages. First, it saves file space. One less layer can mean a lot less megabytes. Retouch or clone layers can be merged with the background when you're sure it's perfect. Once you've gotten a color-correct output from your image file, you might want to merge any selective adjustment layers with their corresponding image layers. Another advantage to merging layers is filter use. Applying one filter to one layer can take a lot less time than applying the same filter to two different layers, especially for slower machines.

Let's practice merging with the last saved version of the monkeys image. To add some realism to all the monkeys' shadows, a Gaussian blur filter will be applied to all the shadows at the same time. Before we apply the filter, though, you need to merge the shadows together. There are three ways to merge layers in Photoshop: merge linked, merge down, and merge visible. We'll try all three. You'll notice that the Shadow layer for the second monkey set was cleaned up with a layer mask. Now the shadow isn't awkwardly exposed on the sky background. For more information on layer masking, see Day 11.

1. For the merge linked option, highlight the 2 Shadow layer and unlink it from the 2 Monkeys layer. Also make sure there are no other linked layers. Now link the 2 Shadow layer to the 1 Shadow layer by clicking the square just to the left of the 1 Shadow layer thumbnail. From the Layer palette drop-down menu, select Merge Linked. Or, if you prefer, use the Layer, Merge Linked command (Ctrl/Cmd-E). Voila! The two shadows are merged into one layer. Reorder the 2 Shadow layer underneath the 1 Monkeys layer so that the shadow doesn't appear on top of the "1 Monkeys" image.

2. Now let's try the merge down method. Undo the last "merge linked" step. Whoops! We lost our undo step! No worry. Simply open your History palette (Window, Show History) and highlight the first step, Open. Your History palette should look similar to Figure 13.22.

FIGURE 13.22

The History palette for the monkey image after the linked layers are merged and re-ordered.

Perform the first part of the "merge linked" steps by unlinking the 2 Monkeys layer from the 2 Shadows layer. Also, unlink any other layers. Click and drag the 2 Shadows layer under the 1 Monkeys layer. From the Layers palette drop-down menu, select Merge Down or use the Layer, Merge Down command (Ctrl/Cmd-E). Again, our two shadow layers have formed one layer.

3. And now, let's try merge visible. As the name implies, the Merge Visible command merges any layers that are visible. Using the History palette, bring the image back to its "unmerged" state. Hide all layers—including the white *Background* layer—except the 2 Shadow layer and the 1 Shadow layer. Be certain that the 1 Shadow layer is currently active so that you won't have to reorder the final merged layer. Choose the Merge Visible command from the Layer palette drop-down menu or use the Layer, Merge Visible command (Shift-Ctrl/Cmd-E). As expected, our two Shadow layers have become one. Notice that the name inheritance is different for each merge method. When you merge down, the lower layer's name is used for the final layer. When you merge linked or visible layers, the final layer inherits its name and position from whichever layer was active when the command initiated.

Now that we've practiced all three methods of merging, let's add the Gaussian blur filter to the merged Shadow layer. If you haven't done so already, make all layers in the image visible.

4. Highlight the Shadow layer and apply the Gaussian Blur filter (Filter, Blur, Gaussian Blur). You may also want to apply a Ripple distortion filter (Filter, Distort, Ripple) to the Shadow layer to blend the shadow more unevenly with the shell background. See Figures 13.23 and 13.24 for the settings used in the example.

FIGURE 13.23

The Gaussian Blur fil-ter dialog box.

13

FIGURE **13.24**

The Ripple filter dialog box.

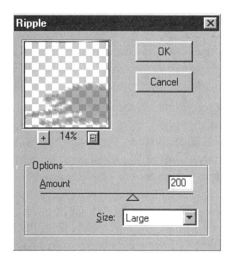

For a more realistic picture, another Gaussian Blur was applied to the 2 Monkeys layer. Figure 13.25 is the final image. To see the final Photoshop image, open the file "monkey02.psd" in the Day 13 folder of the CD-ROM.

And that's all there is to it. The final image, shown in Figure 13.25, has a Gaussian Blur applied to the second monkey set.

FIGURE **13.25**

The final monkey image.

As you experienced in this exercise, Photoshop has many built-in time saving devices, such as layer linking and merging. There's still a little more to cover on layers today, so you might want to take a quick break before you continue.

Layering Modes

Layering modes are something that even some seasoned Photoshop users have a hard time getting a handle on. A number of Layering modes are available, and I'll list them here with a short explanation of each. I'll also demonstrate each mode through the use of a two-layer image. The top layer has a photo of a tree with its leaves in full autumn splendor, and the bottom layer contains a photo of a wood texture. I've included the image in the Day 13 folder so you can follow along. The two separate images are seen in Figures 13.26 and 13.27.

FIGURE 13.26

Photo of a tree in the fall.

FIGURE 13.27

Photo of a wood texture.

13

The following sections cover the different Layering modes.

Normal

Normal applies the layer exactly. No changes or effects take place. Top layers obscure those below (see Figure 13.28).

FIGURE 13.28

Normal mode.

Dissolve

The Dissolve mode scatters pixels based on their transparency. Feathered selections and anti-aliased portions of an image dissolve more than 100% opaque portions, which do not dissolve at all (see Figure 13.29).

FIGURE 13.29

Dissolve mode.

Multiply

This mode multiplies the value of the current layer with the value of the pixels in the layer or layers below, effectively darkening them (see Figure 13.30).

FIGURE 13.30

Multiply mode.

Screen

Screen mode adds the values of the pixels of the current layer to the values of the pixels of the layer(s) below. This value cannot exceed the maximum value that a pixel can contain, which is 255 (see Figure 13.31).

FIGURE 13.31

Screen mode.

13

Overlay

With the Overlay mode, lighter areas in the upper layer are "screened" with those in the layers below, and darker areas are multiplied (see Figure 13.32).

FIGURE **13.32**

Overlay mode.

Soft Light

This mode treats black and white as burning and dodging, respectively. This mode can be used to correct exposure problems on an image (see Figure 13.33).

FIGURE **13.33**

Soft Light mode.

Hard Light

Hard Light is similar to Overlay. It multiplies dark areas and screens light areas. However, the operations performed are based on the color of the Hard Light layer rather than the layers below (see Figure 13.34).

FIGURE 13.34

Hard Light mode.

Color Dodge

Color Dodge is similar to both Screen and Lighten. The affected layers tend to lighten (see Figure 13.35).

FIGURE 13.35

Color Dodge mode.

13

Color Burn

Color Burn is the opposite of Color Dodge (see Figure 13.36).

FIGURE **13.36**

Color Burn mode.

Darken

This chooses the darkest value of the affected pixels (see Figure 13.37).

FIGURE **13.37**

Darken mode.

Lighten

Chooses the lightest value of the affected pixels (see Figure 13.38).

FIGURE **13.38**

Lighten mode.

Difference

This displays the difference between two pixels based on their hue and brightness. Two identical pixels display as black, while a black pixel and a white pixel display as white (see Figure 13.39).

FIGURE **13.39**

Difference mode.

13

Exclusion

The Exclusion mode inverts color areas in the underlying layer, based on the lighter areas in the layer above (see Figure 13.40).

FIGURE **13.40**

Exclusion mode.

Hue

The Hue mode leaves brightness and saturation unchanged while affecting only the hue, of the two layers (see Figure 13.41).

FIGURE **13.41**

Hue mode.

Saturation

The saturation of the upper layer replaces that of the underlying layer (see Figure 13.42).

FIGURE **13.42**

Saturation mode.

Color

Brightness remains unchanged while the hue and saturation of the underlying layer are affected by the colors of the upper layer (see Figure 13.43).

FIGURE **13.43**

Color mode.

13

Luminosity

This mode retains the underlying layer(s)'s hue and saturation, while affecting the brightness, based on the upper layer (see Figure 13.44).

FIGURE 13.44

Luminosity mode.

Using Layers to Create Special Effects

As always, I invite you to play around with the different settings. Using Layering modes, the possibilities are endless. You'd be surprised what you can come up with. For example, Figure 13.33 would make a great start for creating a rusted metal texture, even though the two images it was created from are some old wood and some fall leaves.

The Layering modes can be used for certain effects as well. Here's one quick idea to try before you move on to the next chapter:

1. Open a new image of 100×100 pixels at 72 dpi with the contents set to White.
2. Create two new layers by clicking twice on the New Layer icon at the bottom of the Layers palette.
3. Select the Elliptical Marquee tool and set the mode to Constrained Aspect Ratio in the Marquee Options palette.
4. Draw a circular selection in Layer 2 (the first layer is the original, or background layer, created when you opened the new image).
5. Set the default colors (black and white foreground/background).
6. Reverse the colors by clicking the small, two-headed, curved arrow to the upper right of the foreground/background color swatches.
7. Select the Radial Gradient tool and set the Gradient to Foreground to Background in the Radial Gradient Options palette.
8. Place the cursor in the upper-left of the circular selection and click and drag it towards the lower-right of the selection. You should have a radial gradient similar to Figure 13.45.

Figure **13.45**

Radial gradient.

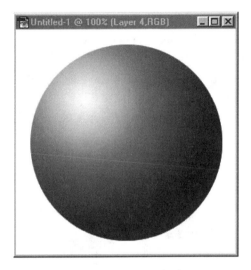

9. Choose Filter, Distort, Spherize. In the Spherize dialog box, set the Amount to 100% and the Mode to Normal. Click OK. This makes the spherical gradient more button-like (see Figure 13.46).

Figure **13.46**

Radial gradient with Spherize filter applied.

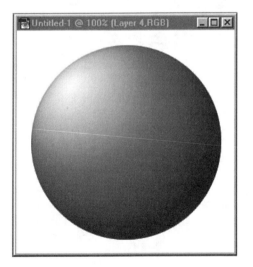

13

10. Open a texture file and select it by choosing Select, All.

11. Choose Edit, Define Pattern.

12. Make the first image current by clicking its title bar.

13. Select the Paint Bucket tool and set the Contents to Pattern in the Paint Bucket Options palette.

14. Click Layer 3's title bar to make it the active layer and then click anywhere in the circular selection.

You'll now have a round area filled with your texture. Mine is filled with a wood pattern (see Figure 13.47).

FIGURE **13.47**

Circular selection filled with a wood pattern.

Here comes the magic.

With the top layer active, set the Layering mode to Overlay. You should now have something that resembles a button you might pin to your lapel (see Figure 13.48).

You could use this trick with some clip art or an illustration to create images of buttons to use on flyers and newsletters or to create buttons for a Web page. This one little trick was all that was needed to create a sense of 3D out of a flat two-dimensional pattern.

FIGURE 13.48

A round wooden button.

Summary

Layers are a powerful feature of Photoshop. Yet unlike some of the other powerful features, layers aren't that hard a concept to work with. A little practice will have you working with layers as if you were an old pro.

Q&A

Q **Is it possible to change the order of my layers?**

A You can reorder the layers by clicking and dragging their title bars into position in the Layers palette. You can also reorder layers by choosing Layer, Arrange. This gives you the option of moving a layer to the front, the back, backward one position, or forward one position.

Q **Why would I want to link layers to one another?**

A Layer linking can facilitate quick synchronized movement of multiple image layers within the composition. Also, certain Photoshop commands like Free Transform can be applied to multiple layers by linking them together.

Workshop

The following section is a quick quiz about the chapter you have just read. If you have any problems answering any of the questions in the quiz, see the section directly following it for all the answers.

13

Quiz

1. How do you create a new layer?
2. How do you delete a layer?
3. How do you duplicate a layer?
4. What's the difference between the Color Dodge mode and the Color Burn mode?
5. What does the Exclusion mode do?
6. How do you link layers together?
7. Why would you want to merge layers together?

Quiz Answers

1. You can create a new layer by clicking the Create New Layer icon at the bottom of the Layers palette. You can also choose Layer, New, Layer or click the small black arrow to the right of the Layers palette tab and choose New Layer.

2. You can delete the current layer by clicking the Delete Current Layer icon at the bottom of the Layers palette. You can also drag and drop a layer onto the Delete Current Layer icon. You can also choose Layer, Delete Layer from the menu. Lastly, you can click the small black arrow to the right of the Layers tab and choose Delete Layer.

3. You can choose Layer, Duplicate Layer from the menu. You can also click the small black arrow to the right of the Layers tab and choose Duplicate Layer. Lastly, you can drag and drop a layer onto the Create New Layer icon at the bottom of the Layers palette.

4. Color Dodge lightens the combined layers based on the value of the pixels in the upper layer, and Color Burn darkens the layers.

5. The Exclusion mode is similar to the Difference mode in that it compares the pixels in each layer and subtracts the lighter from the brighter. The Exclusion mode provides a softer, or less harsh, effect, though.

6. You can link layers to one another by highlighting one layer then clicking the square immediately to the left of other layer's thumbnails.

7. Merging layers can save file space used by an image. Also, applying filters to just one layer often takes less time than applying them to individual layers.

DAY 14

Typing in Great Type Effects

This is the last day of Week 2. Today covers the Type tool, which Adobe has made some significant changes to. Although Photoshop is still not a layout program, the new features of the Type tool make entering, editing, and managing type much easier. Adobe has even added a couple of built-in filters that are meant just for text. Today, I'll demonstrate the following:

- Creating, selecting, and editing text
- Creating special effects with type
- Importing text from vector programs

Creating Text

Creating text in Photoshop is a simple matter. Simply select the Type tool (see Figure 14.1) and click anywhere in the current image to bring up the Type Tool dialog box (see Figure 14.2).

FIGURE 14.1

The Toolbox with the Type tool flyout visible.

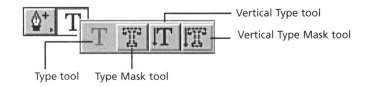

Vertical Type tool

Vertical Type Mask tool

Type tool   Type Mask tool

FIGURE 14.2

The Type Tool dialog box.

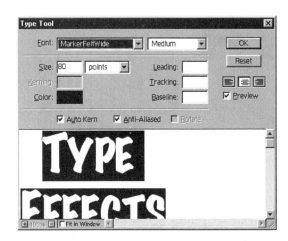

In the Type Tool dialog box, you can choose a font, the font's style, the size, and several other options that I'll describe later on. The following steps will walk you through adding type to an image:

1. Create a new image that is 500×300 pixels, has 72 dpi resolution, and the contents set to White.

2. Set the default colors by clicking on the small black and white squares to the lower left of the foreground/background color swatches.

3. Select the Type tool and click somewhere on the image to bring up the Type Tool dialog box.

4. Choose a font from the pull-down menu and set its size. I'm using MarkerFeltWide at 80 points, but you can select any font for the purposes of this exercise.

5. Click in the large window at the bottom of the dialog box and type some text. You'll notice, from Figure 14.2, that I've typed "Type Effects."

6. As you enter your text, you may notice that it appears in the image immediately. You can stop typing and move the text into a better position just by moving the mouse to the image window and moving the text. It's that simple to place the text. Give it a try. After typing your name, for example, center the text in the image by clicking-and-dragging it into position as I've done (see Figure 14.3).

FIGURE 14.3

Type in a new image.

TYPE EFFECTS

7. Click OK to set the text and clear the dialog box.

8. Take a look at the Layers palette. You'll notice that a new layer has been created and that there is a new symbol alongside the layer's name in the layer's title bar (see Figure 14.4).

9. You can save your image at this point, but it's not necessary.

FIGURE 14.4

New Type layer.

The uppercase "T" signifies that this is a type layer. Because this is a type layer, it is somewhat different than other layers. You can change this layer into a regular layer by choosing Layer, Type, Render. If you do so you won't be able to edit the text without re-creating it from scratch. With older versions of Photoshop, a text layer was like any

14

other layer. Once you exited the Type Tool dialog box, the text became a bitmap layer like any other. Now, however, the text layer remains a special text layer. You can edit the text by simply double-clicking on the layer's title bar in the Layers palette. Do that now, if you're following along, and you'll see that the Type Tool dialog box reappears instead of the Layers dialog box.

Selecting and Editing Text

As you can see, it's easy enough to add text to an image, but what do you do when you need to go back and edit it in some way? What if you misspelled a word? What if you want to change the font? Well, with Photoshop 5, it's easy to edit existing text. All you need to do is reopen the Type Tool dialog box.

For example, if you want to change the size of your type, you simply need to select the text at the bottom of the dialog box. If for some reason the text isn't already selected, all you have to do is click-and-drag to select the text. Now enter a different value into the Size box. I entered 100 to enlarge the text I had previously typed (see Figure 14.5).

FIGURE 14.5

Text enlarged by changing the Size value in the Type Tool dialog box.

TYPE
EFFECTS

You can just as easily edit the text. For example, you could correct a spelling error, add or remove words, and so on. With the Type Tool dialog box still open, I'll change the word Type to the word Text (see Figure 14.6).

FIGURE 14.6

Text edited by changing the text in the Type Tool dialog box.

TEXT
EFFECTS

You can also change the font and size of separate letters. This is something that was not possible with older versions, either.

Try it! Double-click the text layer's title bar to bring up the Type Tool dialog box. Then, select a single letter and change its size by entering a new value in the Size box.

I've enlarged the first letter of each word to 120 points. After doing so (you'll find that you can't select both first letters at once and that you must do so in two steps), I noticed that the words weren't quite centered. Of course, all I had to do was drag the text layer around until I was satisfied with the placement.

Now that you have the text you want, what if you decide to change the color of the type? No problem! Just click the Color swatch in the Type Tool dialog box. This will bring up the Color Picker dialog box, where you can select a new color. The change will take place immediately (see Figure 14.7).

FIGURE 14.7

Text with enlarged first letters and colored blue.

If you're sure that the text is the way you want it, you can render the layer by choosing Layer, Type, Render. You can still change the text by deleting the layer and starting over. If there is a lot of text on your image, though (if you're creating a brochure, for example), you might want to leave the layer as a text layer. This will make it easy to go in and change dates, names, places, and so on.

Photoshop's Built-In Effects

Photoshop 5 comes with some new built-in filters that, while not specifically designed for text, work really well on your type. To see the various effects available, choose Layer, Effects and select one of the available options. I'll choose Drop Shadow. This will bring up the Effects dialog box (see Figure 14.8).

14

FIGURE 14.8

Effects dialog box for Drop Shadow effect.

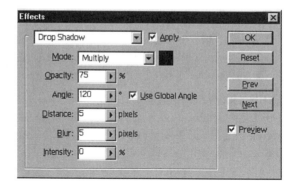

If the Apply box has a check mark in it, you'll notice the changes on the text in your image (see Figure 14.9).

FIGURE 14.9

Drop Shadow effect applied to text.

The other effects are demonstrated in Figures 14.10–14.16.

FIGURE 14.10

Inner Shadow effect applied to text.

FIGURE 14.11

Outer Glow effect applied to text.

FIGURE 14.12

Inner Glow effect applied to text.

FIGURE 14.13

Bevel and Emboss effect (Inner bevel) applied to text.

FIGURE 14.14

Bevel and Emboss effect (Outer bevel) applied to text.

FIGURE 14.15

Bevel and Emboss effect (Emboss) applied to text.

FIGURE 14.16

Bevel and Emboss effect (Pillow Emboss) applied to text.

14

For the most part, I've used the default settings to arrive at the effects in the different figures. As you can see from the different options available, though, your choices are
almost limitless. There are certainly far too many for me to demonstrate them all in this
chapter. However, I invite you to play around with the different effects and their options
to see what you can come up with.

Advanced Type Tricks

I call these advanced type tricks, but they are really not hard to accomplish. I'll walk you
through them step-by-step, and you'll see for yourself how easy it is to create some
pretty awesome effects with type in Photoshop. In the following sections, you'll learn to
create patterned text and work with the leading and kerning.

You've already seen how you can select an image, or a portion of an image, and define a
pattern with it. You've also seen how easy it is to subsequently fill a selected area with
the pattern. The one problem you may have noticed with this process, though, is how
you have no real control over the pattern and how it's placed within your selection. The
following techniques demonstrate how you can add a pattern to type and have complete
control over where the pattern is placed within the text.

If you'd like to play along, open the sunset.psd file from the day14 folder on the
CD-ROM.

1. Hold the mouse button down over the Type tool until the flyout menu appears.
   Select the second tool, the Type Mask tool.

2. Click somewhere on the image to bring up the Type Tool dialog box.

3. Choose a font and a size. This is a little more difficult than with the Type tool
   because the type doesn't show up on the image, so you may have to play around
   until you get something that fits and looks right.

4. When you click OK to exit the dialog box, you'll see your type. It won't be type,
   though, it'll just be the marching ants of a marquee. If the font and size you've
   chosen don't fit because the type is way too small or too large, choose Edit, Undo
   and click within the image to try again. I used the MarkerFeltWide at 85 points
   (see Figure 14.17).

5. With the type selection created, you can move the text around until you get exactly
   the area of the underlying image you want to see in the text. Simply drag the text
   around until it's in the right place. I moved the text around until I could see the sun
   through some of the letters (what would a sunset be without the sun?).

6. To capture the type and the pattern displayed below it, simply choose Edit, Copy.

7. Now choose File, New and click OK in the New dialog box to open a file that is
   sized to take the type you just created.

FIGURE **14.17**

Selected text created with the Type Mask tool.

8. Choose Edit, Paste and you'll have the patterned type or, as I like to call it, Image in Type in its own separate image.

9. At this point, you may want to enlarge the canvas to give you some breathing room. Choose Image, Canvas Size and enter values that are larger than the values showing. The values that are present represent the current size of your image. I added about 100 pixels to the width and the height.

10. With the foreground color set to black, I added a border around the text. To do this, you need to first Ctrl-click (Cmd-click) the layer that contains the text to select all non-transparent areas of a layer. Then choose Edit, Stroke and enter the width and the location. I entered 2 for the Width and Inside for the location (see Figure 14.18).

FIGURE **14.18**

Image in Type.

14

11. Now that you have the text on its own layer and filled with an image, you could easily copy and paste it onto another image. Simply choose Select, All then choose Edit, Copy. Make the image you want the type pasted to current by clicking on its title bar and choose Edit, Paste. This will paste the patterned text into a new layer in the image. Figure 14.19 shows the words Escape Winter pasted onto the sunset photo.

12. Once again, you can save your image at this point, but it's not necessary.

FIGURE 14.19

Image in Type in an image.

This might make a good start for a travel agency brochure. The addition of an agency logo and some text describing the vacations, advertising a sale, and so on would finish this image off nicely.

One thing you might notice with this text is how the two words seem to be much closer together than in the previous examples. This was accomplished by using the Leading option.

Leading, Kerning, and Tracking

Leading and kerning have to do with typesetting. Leading (pronounced like Redding) describes the amount of vertical space between lines. In Figure 14.20 the type has the leading set to 80. Figure 14.21 has the default leading (or, you might say, unleaded type). Figure 14.22 has the leading set to 170. The numbers you use will depend on the size of the text and the resolution you're working at. In any event, you'll be able to see the results of any changes in both the dialog box and the image in real time.

FIGURE 14.20

Leading type.

Leading &Kerning

FIGURE 14.21

Unleaded type.

Leading &Kerning

FIGURE 14.22

Leading type at 170.

Leading &Kerning

Leading options are great for when you need to fix the vertical spacing of your text, but what do you use to set the horizontal spacing? That's where kerning and tracking come in. Kerning determines the space between any two characters, whereas tracking controls the spacing between all of the letters. You can set both of these options in the Type Tool dialog box.

Figure 14.23 demonstrates text with the tracking set to 100, and Figure 14.24 shows text with the tracking set to 200. Again, these numbers will vary, depending on the resolution of your image and the size of your text.

14

FIGURE **14.23**

Tracking type at 100.

Leading &Kerning

FIGURE **14.24**

Tracking type at 200.

Leading &Kerning

One other important type feature to mention is baseline shift. The baseline, which is the imaginary line that all of your text sits on, describes how much space there is at the bottom of your text. With the Baseline option, you're able to create such effects as superscripting and subscripting. A positive value will bump the letter or character up from the baseline, and a negative value will bump the letter or character below the baseline. Figures 14.25–14.27 demonstrate the default setting, a setting of 50, and a setting of 100. Figure 14.28 demonstrates superscript and subscript, created with a baseline of 20 and −10, respectively.

You can play around with these values to get some cool effects, such as merging lines of text together as I did with Figure 14.19.

FIGURE **14.25**

Default baseline setting.

FIGURE **14.26**

Baseline setting of 50.

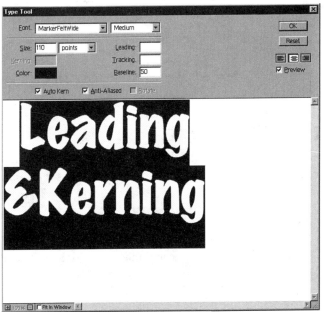

14

FIGURE 14.27

Baseline setting of 100.

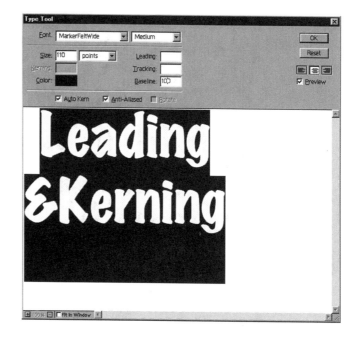

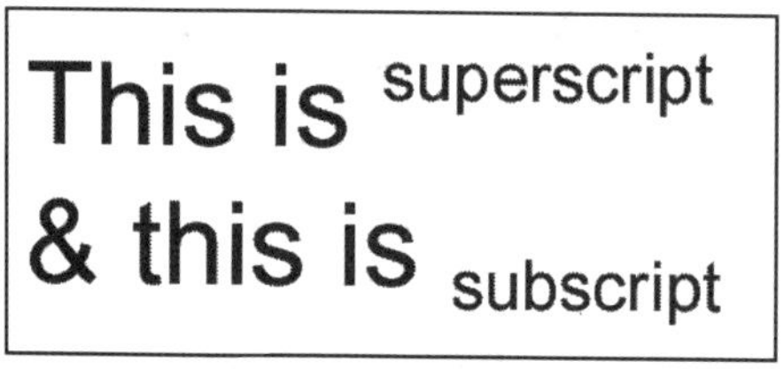

FIGURE 14.28

Superscript and subscript type, created using different baselines.

This is ^{superscript} — rendered as: This is superscript

& this is subscript

Rotating Your Text

There's one more trick I'd like to show you before I get into importing text from other programs. Photoshop 5 has added a feature that makes it possible to place text in a circle with relative ease.

1. Open a new 500×500 file at 72 dpi with the contents set to White.

2. Choose View, Show Grid. I have the Grid set to 1 inch and the subdivisions set to 4 (see Figure 14.29). You can set these values under File, Preferences, Guides & Grids.

FIGURE 14.29

New file with the grid on.

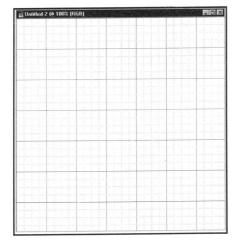

3. Create a new layer by clicking on the Create New Layer icon at the bottom of the Layers palette.

4. Select the Paintbrush tool and draw a small dot at the center of the image. You'll use this as a guide for positioning the individual letters.

5. Select the Type tool and enter some text. I entered the word Circle (ever the inventive one) at 110 points in MarkerFeltWide.

6. For this trick to work, you'll have to render the text to a layer. Choose Layer, Type, Render Layer.

   With the grid set up, the dot for a guide, and the text in place and rendered, you're ready to go (see Figure 14.30).

7. Select the Magic Wand and click it on the first letter in your word. In my case this would be the first C. The letter will now be selected, as you can verify by the marching ants.

8. Choose Edit, Transform, Rotate. So far none of this is really new (except that you had to render the type layer), but Adobe has added a center of rotation to the Transform feature.

9. Look closely at the bounding box around the letter and you'll see a small circular icon at its center (see Figure 14.31).

10. You can click and move this circular icon. Click on it and drag it into place over the dot you created. It should snap into place if you've set Snap to Grid. If not, choose View, Snap to Grid.

14

FIGURE 14.30

Text, grid, and guiding dot in place.

FIGURE 14.31

Text, grid, and guiding dot in place with a letter selected.

11. Move the cursor back into proximity with the letter until the cursor turns into a small curved arrow. You can now drag the letter into place, and it will move around the new center of rotation that you set (the dot at the center of the image).

12. Move the letter until it's roughly in the same place as the letter C in Figure 14.32.

13. With the letter in place, double-click it to get the marching ants back (you can't do anything else until you've "dropped" the letter in place by doing so).

14. Select the next letter by clicking on it (the Magic Wand should still be the active tool).

15. Choose Edit, Transform, Rotate.

16. Move the center of rotation to the dot you drew.

FIGURE 14.32

First letter moved into place.

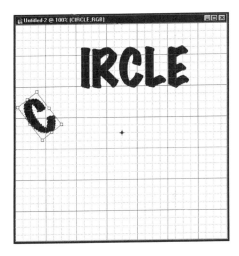

17. Move the cursor near the letter until it turns into a small curved arrow and drag the letter into place (see Figure 14.33).

FIGURE 14.33

Second letter moved into place.

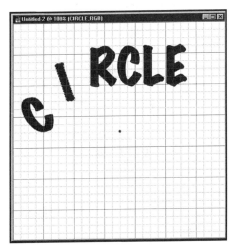

18. Continue on with the first half of the word. Once you've moved half of the word, start with the last letter in the word and work backwards until you've moved all of the letters into place.

19. You can discard the layer with the dot by dragging and dropping it onto the small garbage can icon (the Delete Current Layer icon). You should then end up with text that lays along a circular path (see Figure 14.34).

14

You could get a little more inventive, of course, and spin the letters on their own center of rotation. If you really want to create text on a path, though, you should use a vector program such as CorelDRAW or Adobe's Illustrator.

FIGURE 14.34

Text on a circular path.

Importing Text from Other Programs

Creating text on a path is a snap with vector-based drawing programs. I'll demonstrate how it's done with CorelDRAW and Illustrator. If you own another drawing program such as Xara or Freehand, the process should be somewhat similar.

Importing Text from CorelDRAW

To import text from CorelDRAW into Photoshop, simply follow along with the steps below.

1. Open CorelDRAW and open a new file.
2. Select the Ellipse tool and, while holding down the Ctrl key to constrain the ellipse to a circle, click-and-drag to draw a circle.
3. Select the Text tool and move the cursor over the circle you just drew.
4. Click on the circle and type in the text you want.
5. Select the Pick tool and click away from the circle and the text to deselect both.
6. Select the circle by clicking on it.
7. Press the Delete key to remove the circle.
8. Choose File, Export and export the file in the EPS format. You can now open this file in Photoshop (see Figure 14.35).

With the file in Photoshop, you can do anything you want with the text, including copying and pasting it onto another image. The text won't be editable, though.

FIGURE 14.35

Text on a circular path created in CorelDRAW.

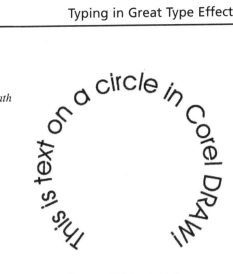

Importing Text from Illustrator

Importing text from Illustrator is even easier. Because Illustrator and Photoshop are both from Adobe, it's easy to transfer information back and forth between the two programs.

1. If you have Illustrator, open a new file.

2. Select the Ellipse tool and, while holding down the Shift key to constrain the ellipse to a circle, drag to draw a circle.

3. Select the Path Type tool and move the cursor over the circle you drew. Click on the circle and type in your text.

4. Click away from the text, and the circle and the path will disappear, leaving just the text.

5. With Photoshop open, shrink both Illustrator and Photoshop so that you can see both programs.

6. Create a new file in Photoshop.

7. Make Illustrator the active application.

8. Select the text you created and click and drag it to the image that you opened in Photoshop. It's as easy as that (see Figure 14.36)!

14

FIGURE 14.36

Text on a circular path created in Adobe's Illustrator.

Using just the built-in Photoshop options, there are an unlimited number of effects you can apply to your type to make it stand out. The next effect I'll demonstrate shows how you can create textured, beveled text using only the built-in features of Photoshop.

Textured Beveled Text

Sometimes you may find yourself in need of a simple logo. You don't necessarily want or need a fancy illustration, and you believe that if you could just fancy up some type, it would fit the bill.

This next example is just one way that you can spice up some type. You can use existing textures such as I'll be doing, or you could create a texture specifically for the type you have in mind. I'll be using a wooden texture thanks to Mother Nature. That is, I scanned in a portion of a plank from the fence being built by my next door neighbor. If you'd like to follow along, you'll find this texture on the CD-ROM.

1. To get started, open the wooden texture, or some other texture if you prefer (see Figure 14.37).
2. Select the Type Mask tool.
3. Place the cursor over the image and click to bring up the Type Tool dialog box.

Note

When using the Type Mask tool, you won't be able to see the size or placement of the type on your image, and you may have to try a couple of times to get the exact size you want. Don't worry about the placement, though, because you'll be able to move the mask into place after exiting the Type Tool dialog box.

FIGURE 14.37

Wooden texture courtesy of Mother Nature.

4. Choose a font and a size and enter your text. I chose the Benguiat Bk BT set at bold and at 140 points. I also left Auto Kern and Anti-Aliasing on.

 Note

This particular font is thick and has a nice serif. I chose it because I want the resulting type to appear as though it is actually carved out of wood.

5. Enter your text and click OK. You'll now see that your text is visible on the textured image, but only as a marquee (see Figure 14.38).

FIGURE 14.38

Wooden texture with text marquee visible.

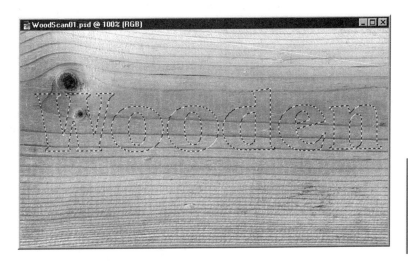

14

6. You can move the marquee around the image by simply clicking and dragging it with the mouse. Move the marquee around until you get a good view of the wood texture beneath it. I moved the marquee around and made sure that the small knot is visible in the marquee (no mistaking the fact that this is a wood texture this way).

7. With the marquee in a suitable place, choose Edit, Copy.

8. Choose File, New and click OK to accept the default size that comes up.

Note   When you cut or copy a section of an image and then open a new file, Photoshop automatically sets the size, resolution, and mode to match that of the selected area.

9. Choose Edit, Paste to paste the text into the new image. You'll notice that you now have your textured text nicely placed in the center of a new image (see Figure 14.39). You'll also notice that the text takes up the entire image. You can get a little breathing room by choosing Image, Canvas Size.

FIGURE 14.39

Wooden textured text in new image.

10. With an image of these dimensions, you can easily add about 100 to both the height and width. To do so, just change the values in the Canvas Size dialog box. You can leave the default positioning so that the text remains in the center of the image. I enlarged the canvas to 700×200 (see Figure 14.40).

Tip   To make sure that when the canvas is enlarged it fills in the new area with the same color as the current background, you must change the current background color. To do so, click the background color swatch and set the color appropriately.

FIGURE 14.40

Wooden textured text with enlarged canvas.

Not bad, but this image needs a little more. A bevel would do nicely. There are several ways (many ways actually) that this can be accomplished. You could use the new layer effects feature available in Photoshop 5. To do so, choose Layer, Effects, Bevel and Emboss, and set the Style to Inner Bevel. The result should be similar to Figure 14.41.

FIGURE 14.41

Wooden textured text with Photoshop's Inner Bevel effect applied.

Although this is nice, it's a bit subtle. Another choice would be to use Alien Skin's Eye Candy Inner Bevel filter. If you have Eye Candy, this filter provides many choices, and you can see the effects in real time as you apply them. An example of applying the Eye Candy Inner Bevel effect can be seen in Figure 14.42.

FIGURE 14.42

Wooden textured text with Eye Candy's Inner Bevel effect applied.

14

What if you don't want the subtlety of Photoshop's filter and you don't own Eye Candy? Here's a solution that will enable you to create a nice bevel effect with the built-in tools available in Photoshop.

1. Ctrl-click (Command-click on a Mac) in the Layers palette on the layer that has the text. This selects only the text.

2. Create a new layer by clicking the Create New Layer icon at the bottom of the Layers palette.

3. Choose Select, Modify, Contract and enter 3 in the dialog box. Click OK.

4. Choose Select, Feather and enter the same value, 3, in the dialog box.

5. Set the foreground color to black (you can set the default foreground/background (black/white) colors by pressing "D").

6. Press Alt-Backspace (Option-Backspace on a Mac) to fill the selection with black.

7. Choose Filter, Stylize, Emboss. In the Emboss dialog box, set the Angle to 137 degrees, the Height to 9, and the Amount to 150%. You'll now have a nice grayscale bevel effect (see Figure 14.43).

FIGURE 14.43

Wooden textured text with beveled grayscale effect.

The problem is that the effect is covering the text. No problem! Layer modes to the rescue.

Change the mode of the new embossed text layer to Hard Light. The layer mode can be set for any current layer by choosing the new mode from the pull-down menu near the top of the Layers palette. Choose Select, Deselect and your finished textured, beveled text should resemble the image in Figure 14.44.

You could always add to this image further by changing the background color or by adding a drop shadow, and so on. Another idea is to use the Variations feature to change the overall color of the wood. You could make it look as if it were stained with a mahogany or cherry color, for example. Have some fun with it and see what you can come up with.

Creating Chrome Text

Chrome text must be one of the most sought-after looks on the Web. I imagine that it's also quite big with people doing brochures and advertisements. There are so many ways to achieve this look, because there are so many ways to describe chrome visually.

Have you ever looked at something that's chrome—I mean really looked? What did you see? What you see is a lot of highlights, some shadows, and a lot of middle gray areas. Depending on the chrome and where it was, you might also have seen the sky reflected along the upper areas and the ground reflected in the lower areas. Chrome doesn't really have its own color; it reflects its surroundings. This is why there are so many interpretations of chrome available. To create chrome text, do the following:

1. Open a new file at $500 \times 200 \times 72$ dpi with the contents set to white and the mode set to RGB.

2. Set the default black and white foreground/background colors by pressing the "D" key.

3. Select the Type tool.

4. Set the font to something fairly thick and with a nice serif. I chose the Benguiat Bk BT with the bold setting at 110 points. I also left Auto Kern and Anti-Aliasing on (see Figure 14.45).

FIGURE **14.45**

Black text on white.   **Chrome**

5. Choose Layer, Type, Render Layer to render the type layer.

6. Ctrl-click (Command-click on a Mac) the type layer to select just the type.

7. Choose Select, Modify, Contract and enter a value of 5 in the Contract dialog box. This leaves the center of the characters selected.

14

8. The foreground and background colors should be set at their defaults (black and white). If they aren't, press "D" to reset the defaults.

9. Select the Linear Gradient tool.

10. Set the Gradient to Foreground to Background.

11. Place the cursor near the top of the selected area in one of the tallest characters. With my text, this would be the "h."

12. Hold down the Shift key and drag the cursor to the bottom of the selected area. Holding down the Shift key restrains the movement and makes it easier to draw the gradient along a straight line (see Figure 4.46).

FIGURE 14.46

Black text on white with a marquee around the inner text and a gradient applied.

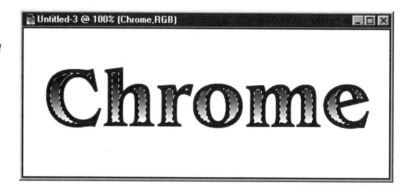

13. This next part is a little tricky. You'll want to select the outer part of the text and to do so, choose Select, Inverse. You'll now have the outer portion of the text selected, but you'll also have the background selected as well.

14. To get rid of the background, select the Magic Wand tool and Alt-click (Option-click on a Mac) the background area around the text. Make sure that you also Alt-click any areas inside of letters like "o," "e," and so on. When you're done, you should be left with the outer portion of the text selected.

15. Choose Select, Feather and enter a value of 1. This helps smooth out any jaggedness introduced by the other steps you've taken so far.

16. Click the small curved arrow just to the upper-right of the Foreground Color/Background Color swatches in the toolbox to reverse the default colors. Alternately, you can press the "X" key.

17. Select the Linear Gradient tool again and place the cursor near the top of one of the taller letters.

18. Hold down the Shift key and drag the mouse to the bottom of the letter. You should now have two gradient fills on your text (see Figure 14.47).

FIGURE **14.47**

*Text filled with two
opposing linear gradi-
ents.*

Wow! This text already looks pretty good. It can be better, though.

19. Choose Select, Deselect.

20. Choose Image, Adjust, Levels.

21. In the Levels dialog box, drag the right-most slider to the left until the value is
    about 180 and the preview of the text shows that the contrast has been elevated
    (see Figure 14.48).

FIGURE **14.48**

*Contrast changed
using levels.*

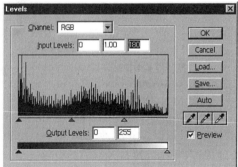

You want to get to the point where the whites are really white, but there's still some definition left along the top of the letters. In other words, you should still be able to make
out where the letters end and the white background layer begins. This text looks quite
good, but there's just one more step to add to the overall chrome look.

22. Ctrl-click (Command-click) the type layer to select all the text again.

14

23. Create a new layer by clicking the Create a New Layer icon at the bottom of the Layers palette.

24. Contract the selection by 1 pixel by choosing Select, Modify, Contract and entering a value of 1 in the Contract dialog box.

25. Feather the selection by 1 pixel by choosing Select, Feather and entering a value of 1 in the Feather dialog box. You may notice that this is a similar process to the one used with the previous textured, beveled text. This time, however, I want the bevel to be much closer to the edge of the text, which is why I'm using 1 pixel for the contraction and feathering instead of 3.

26. Set the default foreground/background colors by pressing "D."

27. Press Alt-Backspace (Option-Backspace on a Mac) to fill the new layer's selection with black.

28. Choose Filter, Stylize, Emboss and set the Angle to 137 degrees, the Height to 9, and the Amount to 150%. You'll now have an embossed layer above the chrome text. Time to combine the layers with a little blending magic.

29. Set the Blending mode of the embossed layer to Hard Light, and you should have text that resembles that shown in Figure 14.49.

FIGURE 14.49

Chrome text created with Photoshop 5.

As I stated earlier, there are countless ways to create a chrome effect. In fact, this is the sixth or seventh way that I've discovered myself. Play around with the various filters and options and see what you can come up with. More than just textured type and chrome type, though, you can create countless type effects with Photoshop and a little imagination. I hope you'll try to come up with some on your own and that you'll have fun while doing so.

Summary

In many ways I've only scratched the surface of what you can do with type in Photoshop. You can create chrome and gold textures, add all kinds of cool effects using some of the filters that ship with Photoshop, and more. You can pick up some tricks by visiting GrafX Design online at http:www.grafx-design.com. There are many other sites that contain type tricks such as fire text, ice text, and much, much more. One type of effects book that I strongly recommend is *Photoshop Type Magic*, written by David Lai and Greg Simsic and published by Hayden. This book is devoted solely to creating type effects with Photoshop.

Q&A

Q Why would I ever need to use the Type Mask tool?

A You can use the Type Mask tool to mask out text. An example of this was demonstrated in today's chapter. Using this tool, it is easy to place an image within your text.

Q I want to use a third-party filter for my text. How do I install it?

A You should follow the software installation instructions and install the filter into a folder under the main plug-ins folder. The main plug-ins folder is the folder pointed to in your Photoshop Preferences setup. Once installed in this folder, Photoshop should load your filters at runtime, and you can access them via Filters.

Workshop

This is a quick quiz about the chapter you have just read. If you have any problems answering any of the questions in the quiz, see the section directly following it for all of the answers.

Quiz

1. What is leading?
2. What is the difference between tracking and kerning?
3. What do you need to do to create new text?
4. How do you apply a filter effect to text?
5. Are there other effects that can be used for type?

Quiz Answers

1. Leading is the vertical space between lines of text.
2. Tracking refers to the space between all letters, whereas kerning refers to the space between any two letters.
3. Select the Text tool, and then click on the area of the image where you want to add text. When you do, the Type Tool dialog box appears, and you can choose the size, color, and font—and more—for your text.

14

4. Choose Effects from the Layer menu and then select the effect you want to apply.

5. Yes. Most plug-in filters will have some effect on type. In Photoshop 5, however, you must first render the type using Layer, Type, Render Layer.

WEEK 3

At a Glance

In this third and final week, you'll learn some of the more advanced aspects of Photoshop, and you'll put your creative juices to the test. This week covers the following topics:

- Applying artistic, brush stroke, and distortion filters
- Installing third-party filters
- Understanding what's behind color correction
- Fixing the effects of a flash on subjects at different distances
- Removing dust marks and scratches from old photos
- Automating your common tasks with the help of actions
- Creating a collage from three separate photos
- Creating a photo montage
- Creating brushed metal and wood textures
- Getting your work out and onto the great World Wide Web

DAY 15

Applying Filter Effects

Plug-ins and filters are external programs you can access through the menus in Photoshop. These plug-ins can import and export images, and they can help you add certain special effects to your images. Some of these filters are built-in and others are available from third parties. In this chapter, I'll cover each of the following:

- Working with Import and Export filters
- Applying Artistic, Brush Stroke, and Distortion filters
- Installing third-party filters
- Using multiple filters to create special effects

I'll use the terms filters and plug-ins interchangeably in this and other chapters. As a rule of thumb, a filter is an action applied to an image that can be "undone" and is a subset of a plug-in. Therefore, all filters are plug-ins, but not all plug-ins are filters.

Built-in Filters Versus Add-on Filters

As I stated earlier, Photoshop comes with several filters, such as Stained Glass or Charcoal, and plug-ins, such as GIF89a export, already built-in. Some of these filters are woven into Photoshop so well that they don't seem to be plug-ins. The Variations option, for example, is really a plug-in.

Working with Import and Export Filters

Photoshop uses certain filters to enable you to import and export your images. Importing images via scanners and digital cameras is done through the use of the TWAIN module. This module, which you run by choosing File, Import, TWAIN (or TWAIN32), runs the external program for your scanner or camera. These modules are installed automatically when you install Photoshop.

A couple of export filters are installed as well. The GIF89a filter and the Paths to Illustrator are both installed when you install Photoshop. The GIF89a filter enables you to save Web-ready artwork in the GIF format. The GIF89a format enables you to use transparency in your GIF images. I'll demonstrate this process on Day 21, "Preparing Your Art for the Web."

Photoshop also includes the Paths to Illustrator filter. This filter enables you to export paths, which can be opened in Illustrator. This is helpful, for example, if you wish to add text to a path on a Photoshop image. To accomplish this, you create a path in Photoshop, export the path, and open it in Illustrator. Then you create the text along the path and cut and paste the text back into Photoshop. The following example demonstrates how this can be accomplished:

1. To begin, open a file in Photoshop and make a selection. I used the following image and made a selection around the iris of the person's eye (see Figure 15.1).

2. Next change the selection into a path (see Figure 15.2) by using the Paths pull-down menu (accessed via the small arrow next to the Paths tab in the Paths palette).

FIGURE 15.1

A selection around the iris.

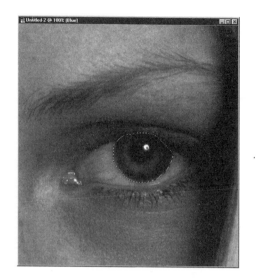

FIGURE 15.2

A path created from a selection.

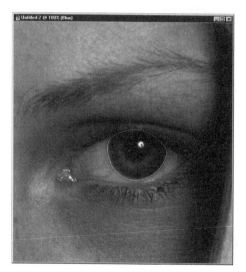

3. Choose File, Export, Path to Illustrator to export the path. Keep the Photoshop image open.

4. Open the AI file you exported to Illustrator and add some text on a path (see Figure 15.3).

FIGURE 15.3
FIGURE **15.3**

Text added to a path in Illustrator.

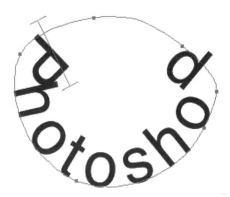

5. With both Photoshop and Illustrator open, click and drag the text from Illustrator onto the image in Photoshop. The text comes in as a new layer and is easily repositioned (see Figure 15.4).

FIGURE **15.4**

Text on a path dragged and dropped from Illustrator to the image in Photoshop.

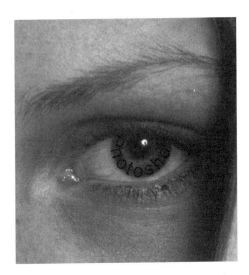

This process, which can be used to create some pretty cool effects, is impossible, or would be very tedious, using Photoshop alone. The Import and Export filters, however, aren't the only ones that enable you to create great effects, as you'll see in the following section.

Artistic Filters

What used to be separately available as the Gallery Effects plug-ins started shipping with Photoshop 4. These plug-ins were a collection of filters that made it easy to create many different artistic effects. I'll describe and demonstrate a couple of them here and include some images that compare the effects that these filters have on an image. Due to the number of filters (and their almost infinite settings and options), I won't be able to demonstrate them all, but I do encourage you to take an image or two and play with the various possibilities yourself.

Under Filters, Artistic, you'll find a number of filters. Fifteen of them are available, in fact, ranging from Colored Pencil to Watercolor. To apply any of these filters to an image, simply choose the filter you wish to apply.

Note

There may be occasions where you'll find that the filters you decide to use are "grayed out" and are not available. Usually the reason for this is that you're trying to apply a filter to an image with an incompatible mode. This will happen, for example, if you try to use filters on an Indexed Color image. When this happens, check the mode and adjust it as necessary. Most filters require you to be in RGB mode. You can, of course, switch modes, apply the filter, and switch the mode back.

To test these filters out, we'll need a volunteer from the audience. Ah, the basket of fruit in the second row will do nicely. Open the image, fruit.psd, from the day15 folder on the CD-ROM if you'd like to follow along (see Figure 15.5).

FIGURE 15.5

Fruit.psd.

1. Choose Filter, Artistic, Colored Pencil to bring up the Colored Pencil dialog box (see Figure 15.6).

FIGURE **15.6**

Colored Pencil dialog box.

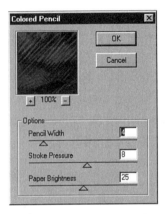

2. In the Colored Pencil dialog box, you can see that you're able to set the Pencil Width, the Stroke Pressure, and the Paper Brightness. Rather than have me explain these options, you can easily see for yourself the effect that changing any of them has on your image in the real-time preview window. This preview window, seen in the upper-left hand corner of the dialog box, is available in most, if not all, of the built-in filters. You can change the Zoom level by clicking the plus or minus sign below the preview window. You can click and drag within the preview window to move the view around as well.

Once you see a setting that appeals to you, click OK. I've kept the default settings to change the still-life of the fruit into the image you see in Figure 15.7.

Tip

If you've played around with the settings in any of the filter-related dialog boxes and are not sure you like the changes you've made, you can get back to the default settings by holding down the Alt key (Option key on a Mac). This changes the Cancel button to a Reset button. It is available in any of the filter's dialog boxes.

The next filter under the Artistic menu is the Cutout filter. This filter can turn your image into an illustration (see Figure 15.8). And I'll bet you thought it took years of training to become an illustrator.

FIGURE 15.7

The Colored Pencil fil-
ter applied to a still-
life image.

FIGURE 15.8

The Cutout filter
applied to a still-life
image.

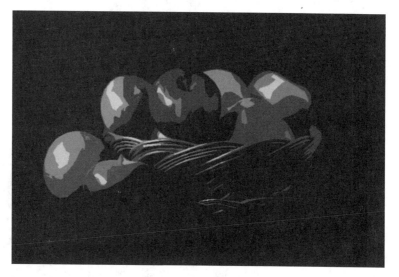

One thing you may notice when you access the Filter menu is that the most recently used
filter appears at the top of the menu. This makes it easy to reapply the effect without
going through the process of choosing the filter and clicking the OK button in the dialog
box. You can also access this feature by pressing Ctrl+F (Control+F on a Mac). You may
notice, after using a filter, that a Fade option is available. You can use this option to
change the amount of the effect that the most recently applied filter will have. When you

choose this option from the menu (or by pressing Shift-Ctrl+F, or Shift-Command+F on a Mac), a small dialog box appears (see Figure 15.9). The shortcut Alt-click (Option-click on a Mac) also opens the dialog box of the most recently used filter.

Tip

You may be asking yourself why you'd want to reapply a filter. You could have several images open that you want to apply the same effect to, or you may want to experiment with multiple applications of the same filter on one image or portions of an image. I've discovered some pretty remarkable effects through the multiple applications of one filter to a single image. I invite you to play around with the various filters available to get a feel for the effects they have and to not necessarily stop at one or even two applications.

FIGURE 15.9

The Fade dialog box.

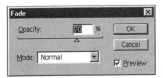

From within the Fade dialog box, you can set the Opacity and the Blending mode. By setting the Opacity to 70%, for example, I brought a little of the detail back into the fruit (see Figure 15.10).

FIGURE 15.10

The Cutout filter faded to 70%.

> **Note**
>
> You should note that you do not need to undo the original filter effect to use the Fade command. Photoshop keeps an entire copy of the previously unaltered image in the clipboard. This copy is only discarded after another step is executed. With the Fade command, Photoshop combines the copy in the clipboard with the desired opacity of the Filter effect.

Again, there are 15 different filters under this menu choice, and I encourage you to try them out. Choose an image and apply each filter in succession to see what the different effects are. Play with the brush settings and the other options that each filter gives you. You'll be surprised at the results you can get from these built-in filters.

Brush Strokes

In addition to the Artistic filters, a couple of more "painterly" effects are available with the built-in filters. You can find them under the Brush Strokes menu choice.

The Brush Strokes filters offer other artistic effects grouped together as eight different types of brush strokes, ranging from Accented Edges to Sumi-e. To see how these filters affect an image, we'll need another volunteer. I think the image of the dandelions (Dandelions.psd in the Day15 folder of the CD-ROM) will do nicely. If you'd like to follow along, open the image in Photoshop (see Figure 15.11).

FIGURE 15.11

Dandelions.

Figure 15.12 is the dandelions with the Crosshatch filter applied and Figure 15.13 is the same image with the Ink Outlines filter applied.

FIGURE 15.12

Dandelions with the Crosshatch filter applied.

FIGURE 15.13

Dandelions with the Ink Outlines filter applied.

As you can see, these filters provide even more artistic effects. But the fun doesn't stop there. In the next section, we'll try out the Distortion filters.

Distortion Filters

The Distortion filters distort an image, or a selected area of an image, in some weird and wonderful ways. You can, for instance, wrap an image around a sphere (see Figure 15.14).

15

FIGURE 15.14

*Dandelions globe
accomplished with the
Spherize filter.*

To achieve this effect, I made a circular selection using the Elliptical Marquee tool. I copied and pasted the selection to a new layer, and then chose Filter, Distort, Spherize. This left me with an image of the dandelions that appears to be in a glass sphere.

Note

> If you plan to run the Spherize filter on an image, you should be aware that the result may not be what you expect. For a true spherical effect, the area you want to affect should be centered in the image. To get around this, I generally make a circular selection around the area I want to run the filter on.

You can use some of these filters to get some really different effects, too. For example, I've had many people ask me how they can get text to appear as though it were typed on an old typewriter. This is how:

1. Open a new image at 500×200, at 72 dpi, and in the RGB mode with the contents set to white.

2. Set the default foreground/background colors (black foreground and white background). You can do this quickly by pressing the D key.

3. Select the Type tool and click the image to bring up the Type Tool dialog box.

4. Select Courier New as the font, select Bold, set the size to 80 points, and click OK (see Figure 15.15).

FIGURE **15.15**

Hmmm, typewriter fonts on a computer.

Typewriter

5. Position the text in the middle of the image.

6. Choose Layer, Type, Render Layer so that you can apply the effect.

7. Choose Filter, Distort, Ripple, and in the Ripple dialog box set the Amount to 50 and the Size to Medium. Click OK and you should get something like Figure 15.16.

FIGURE **15.16**

Old typewriter text created with the Ripple filter.

Typewriter

Now supposing you still can't get the effect you want with an Artistic, Brush Stroke, or Distortion filter. Don't worry, you can combine one or more of these filters to get some great and unusual effects.

Combining Filters

So many built-in filters exist that you could literally play with them for days at a time and still not see all the combinations. And although I can't cover all the combinations here, I can show you an example to spark your creativity.

In the next example, I combine the Emboss and Gaussian Blur filters and a Blending mode to get a woodcarving effect. To begin, I opened a wood texture file and an image of a stylized bird that I created in CorelDRAW. I copied the bird and pasted it onto the wood texture image (see Figure 15.17).

FIGURE 15.17

The stylized bird in a layer above a background layer with a wood texture.

15

With the bird on a separate layer, it's a simple exercise to apply a filter to it without affecting the wood texture below. I chose Filters, Stylize, Emboss to give some height to the bird by getting a highlight and shadow edge (see Figure 15.18). I set the Direction to 135 degrees, the Height to 8, and the Amount to 200.

FIGURE 15.18

The Emboss filter applied to the stylized bird.

At this point I want the bird itself to disappear, leaving behind only the highlight and shadow. To do so, I set the Layer mode to Soft Light. The nice thing about this mode is that not only does it get rid of the gray bird, but it makes the highlight and the shadow somewhat transparent (see Figure 15.19). Having the highlight and shadow partially transparent adds to the effect that this is a woodcarving.

FIGURE 15.19

The Layer mode changed to Soft Light.

The last filter I applied was Gaussian Blur (Filter, Blur, Gaussian Blur). This softened the transition between the wood texture and the edges of the highlights and shadows (see Figure 15.20). To prevent the edges from being too soft, I applied the Gaussian Blur with a setting of only 1 pixel for the radius.

FIGURE 15.20

The woodcarving created in Photoshop with the Emboss filter.

This is only one of the many kinds of effects you can achieve by playing with some of Photoshop's built-in filters; I've only scratched the surface here. A number of filters with virtually unlimited options are available. As well as the built-in filters that come with Photoshop, you can add third-party plug-ins.

Third-Party Plug-ins

There are so many third-party plug-ins available that I couldn't even start to make a list of what's available. I instead will discuss and demonstrate some of the ones that I use on a daily basis, including filters from Auto F/X, Alien Skin, Kai's Power Tools, Ulead, and Digimarc.

Installing Third-Party Plug-ins

Before you get started using any of the plug-ins that you purchase, you must install them. The simplest thing to do is to install your plug-ins in a separate folder under the Plug-ins folder on your hard drive. Most filter installation programs will ask you where you want to install the plug-ins. By keeping all your plug-ins in separate folders under the plug-ins folder, you can easily make them accessible to any other programs you have that are capable of using Photoshop-compatible plug-ins. After Photoshop has been installed, there should be a Plug-ins folder. Simply point your plug-in installation programs to that folder.

Once you've installed your filters, you should be able to access them from within Photoshop. Your new filters should appear at the bottom of the Filter menu. If you had Photoshop running when you installed your filters, you have to exit and restart Photoshop. If the filters still don't appear, choose File, Preferences, Plug-Ins & Scratch Disks. Make sure that the folder points to where you stored your filters.

 Note

> Although it's never a good practice to install new software with other programs running, you will find, if you install a new filter with Photoshop already running, that it won't be available until you restart Photoshop.

Auto F/X

Auto F/X makes a number of plug-ins, and you can learn about their products by visiting their Web site at http://www.autofx.com. Several volumes are available, each with a large collection of edges you can use to spruce up your images. One of my favorites is their Photo/Graphic Edges.

You may recall how I used a feathered layer mask to create a vignette effect on a photo on Day 11, or how I created an edge effect by creating a new brush on Day 10. Well, the Photo/Graphic Edges filter makes creating these effects simple. Not only that, you get a whole library of edges to choose from.

When you run the Auto/FX filters (choose Filter, Auto F/X, Photo/Graphic Edges), you are presented with a colorful dialog box (see Figure 15.21).

FIGURE 15.21

*The Auto F/X
Photo/Graphic Edges
dialog box.*

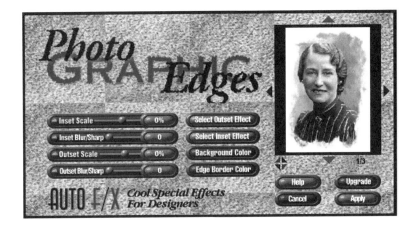

After choosing Outset and Inset effects, you can set the colors, the scale, and the blur/sharpness. The effects are stored on the CD-ROM that comes with the program and there are quite a number to choose from. I applied one to the old photo you see in Figure 15.22 to add some character to the image.

FIGURE 15.22

*The Auto F/X
Photo/Graphic Edges
filter applied to an old
photo.*

This filter set also ships with a printed catalog of the available effects to make choosing them a little easier.

Alien Skin

Another one of my favorite plug-ins is Alien Skin's Eye Candy 3. This is a collection of 21 different effects, including Chrome, Inner and Outer Bevels, Fire, Fur, and more. Eye Candy's dialog box (see Figure 15.23) enables you to view the result of the effect in a real-time preview window.

FIGURE 15.23

Eye Candy dialog box.

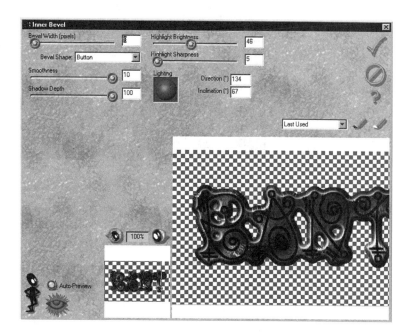

You get to control a number of variables that pertain to the particular filter as well. You can even start off with one of the preset values and modify it to your liking.

I created the following effect by placing text on a layer, selecting the text, and creating a new layer with the selection active. I then filled the selected area with a texture created in KPT (Kai's Power Tools). This resulted in the image you see in Figure 15.24.

I then applied the Fur filter followed by the Inner Bevel filter to arrive at the final image you see in Figure 15.25.

FIGURE 15.24

KPT Texture applied to a selected area.

FIGURE 15.25

Eye Candy Fur and Inner Bevel applied to create the final effect.

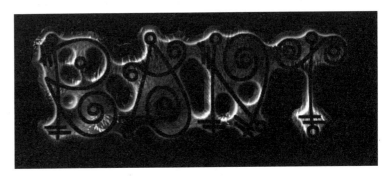

Actually, I applied the Inner Bevel filter twice, which just goes to show the power of play. I almost always experiment with images and filters and don't often stop after just one application. This can result in some strange and unusual effects that others will find hard to copy.

You might also want to explore the possibilities of using third-party filters in conjunction with the built-in filters that come with Photoshop. Anything that you think will create really cool effects or give you an edge over another digital artist is worth exploring.

Note   For more information on Alien Skin's Eye Candy, visit Alien Skin's Web site at `http://www.alienskin.com`.

Kai's Power Tools

Kai's Power Tools is a collection of eclectic filters. They include a Gradient Designer, a Texture Generator (which was used to create the fiery texture in Figure 15.24), a Spheroid Designer, Page Curl, and more. Included with Power Tools is a set of tools that perform effects similar to those available in Photoshop. These tools give you access to sharpening, blurring, and more. The interesting part of these tools lies in the interface (see Figure 15.26).

This interface can be moved around the image, giving you a view of the image through the lens in the interface. You can change the settings, modes, and other options and see how this affects certain portions of the image.

The other interfaces that come with the different filters are equally as stunning visually as the lens interface. Figure 15.27 shows the Spheroid Designer interface.

15

FIGURE 15.26

KPT Edge Effects being applied to an image in Photoshop.

FIGURE 15.27

KPT Spheroid Designer interface.

There are so many filters and so many options available in Kai's Power Tools that whole books have been written about this collection. One such book is *Kai's Power Tools: Filters and Effects*, including a CD-ROM, written by Heinz Schuller and published by New Riders.

Note For more information on Kai's Power Tools, visit MetaCreation's Web site at http://www.metacreations.com.

Ulead

Ulead makes a number of Photoshop plug-ins. The one that I use most, and really couldn't live without, is their SmartSaver plug-in. This program is an export plug-in and, once installed, is accessed via File, Export, Ulead SmartSaver.

When you run SmartSaver, you'll be presented with a dialog box that enables you to choose which file format you'd like to export your image to (see Figure 15.28).

FIGURE 15.28

Ulead SmartSaver dialog box.

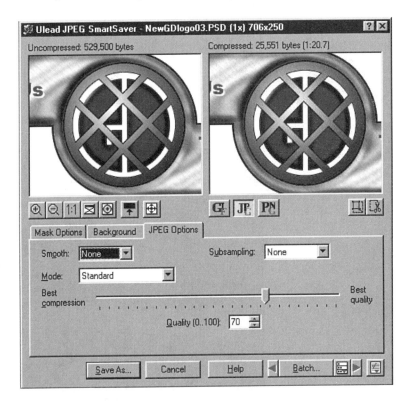

Within the dialog box you can see a real-time preview of what your image will look like once exported to the format of your choice. As well you can change various file format settings, such as the number of colors for GIF files and the compression level for JPEGs. When you make a change, the preview window on the right updates immediately to reflect how the change affects the file. This option can be extremely helpful when you're faced with making the decision whether to use GIF or JPEG for saving your images for Web use.

As well as the preview, you get to see how much disk space will be used by the exported file. This, coupled with the real-time preview, is indispensable in helping with the decision of which file format to use. If you create Web graphics more than occasionally, you'll find this tool to be a necessity.

Note
> For more information on Ulead's SmartSaver, visit Ulead's Web site at
> http://www.ulead.com.

Digimarc

With the advent of the Web, it has become too easy for people to willingly, or unwittingly, "borrow" your images. If you pour a lot of time and effort into creating your work, it can be quite a shock to find that someone else is using your images.

Although not a solution to the actual theft of your work, digital watermarking makes it possible to store a copyright invisibly within each image. Thereafter, if you find an image of yours being used, you can at least prove ownership.

Digital watermarking is provided with Photoshop via the Digimarc plug-in. The service requires you to register, but this registration has two levels. The first level, which enables you to embed your copyright information, is free. The second has a yearly charge involved, but it enables you to track your images on the Web. The tracking process is accomplished via a Web spider. The spider, a type of program that can traverse the Web searching for information embedded in HTML files and in image files, reports back to you if it finds any of your copyrighted images being used without your permission.

Although this is not a perfect solution, it can help you keep track of your all too easily copied digital images.

> **Note** For more information on Digimarc's digital watermarking filter, visit their Web site at http://www.digimarc.com.

Summary

Hopefully you've seen how filters can be used as time-savers and how they can help you produce different effects with your images. To help you get started, we've included a number of demos of some of the different packages on the CD-ROM that accompanies this book.

Q&A

Q You say that filters and plug-ins are similar, some filters are plug-ins, and some plug-ins are filters. What exactly is the difference between the two?

A It's really more semantics than anything else. However, one would usually refer to effects plug-ins as filters and import/export plug-ins as plug-ins or modules.

Q Are there any memory considerations that I need to take into account when working with filters?

A Not really. No more than with any other options applied against large images.

Workshop

The next section is a quick quiz about the chapter you have just read. If you have any problems answering any of the questions in the quiz, see the section directly following it for all the answers.

Quiz

1. Which filter enables you to import images from scanners and digital cameras?
2. How do you export a path to Adobe Illustrator?
3. How do you apply one of the Artistic filters?
4. What is a Distortion filter?
5. What is a digital watermark?

Quiz Answers

15

1. The TWAIN module enables you to import images from digital cameras and scanners.

2. After the path has been created, choose File, Export, Paths to Illustrator.

3. Choose Filter, Artistic and select one of the filters from the drop-down menu.

4. A Distortion filter distorts the image in some way. This can be a spherical distortion (almost like a fish-eye lens effect), a ripple effect, or one of several others.

5. A digital watermark is a code hidden in the image (invisible to the naked eye). This code holds a key that can prove the copyright of the image.

WEEK 3

DAY 16

Correcting the Color

Color is a bit subjective. If you send the same negative to two different labs, you'll probably get two fairly different prints back. At one time or another, you probably wished that you could adjust the prints to your own liking. Well now you can!

Photoshop includes many great tools and features to help you adjust the color of your photographs. In this chapter I'll demonstrate how to use the Variations feature to set the color and brightness of the entire image. In addition, I'll show you how to use the Color Balance and the Curves features to adjust certain color levels within your images.

Using Variations

Depending on how bad your initial print is and what the scan looks like, you may be able to even out the problems before getting down to the serious work. Take a look at Figure 16.1.

FIGURE **16.1**

The original scan of Marianne.

Note

In a black-and-white book, it's extremely difficult to discuss color without being able to show it. Therefore, I've included a copy of this image, called Marianne01.psd, on the CD-ROM so that you can easily follow along. In addition to placing this image on the CD-ROM, I've also reproduced the steps of this technique in the color section of this book.

Although this photograph of Marianne is a pretty good image, there are some obvious problems. The scan itself is a little dark, and the original print, while quite good, leans a little too far into the green for my taste.

I think, though, that it's a good candidate for the Variations feature. I believe this because it's a pretty good image. It's quite even in brightness and contrast, and the green color cast is evident throughout the image.

The Variations feature is nice because it gives you a real-time view of the changes and possible changes that you can make to an image. This makes it fairly easy to correct a photograph. Let's see how.

1. Open the Marianne01.psd file from folder Day16. Notice the problems I discussed earlier. The image is too dark, and it's a little greenish.

2. To get an idea of the changes you're making and how they affect the original image, you can create a copy of the original and perform all of the changes on it. This way you'll have a constant comparison to the original. To create the duplicate, choose Image, Duplicate and press the Enter key to leave the default name.

3. Open the Variations dialog box by choosing Image, Adjust, Variations (see Figure 16.2). In the Variations dialog box, you can see the effect that making changes on your image will have.

FIGURE 16.2

The Variations dialog box.

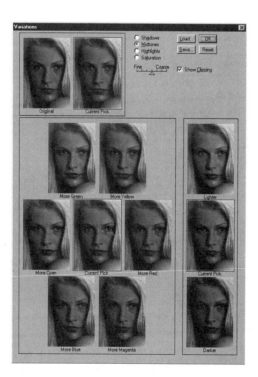

4. You can choose whether the changes will affect the Shadow, Midtones, Highlights, or Saturation. Also, you can add Green, Yellow, Cyan, Red, Blue, and Magenta and you can change the overall brightness of the image. I've chosen to add More Yellow, Lighten, add More Blue, and Lighten once more. The result is Figure 16.3.

Note

While it's true that adding yellow and then adding blue results in no change, these are the steps I took as a result of viewing the thumbnails and making decisions based on what was displayed in them. You may often find that making one change and then another leaves you with a result that should be changed back. Having the preview thumbnails help you make these decisions.

FIGURE 16.3

Image with more yellow, lighter, more blue, and lighter again adjustments.

If you are following along, you'll notice a big change in the image already. The image is obviously brighter, and you can see more detail in the shadows. There hasn't been any loss of detail in the highlights, though.

If you look at the hair in the upper-right corner, you'll see that the detail is still evident. Now look at the lower-left corner. A lot more detail has been added. The overall color cast is much better now than in the original scan.

It's still not quite right, though. Even though the color is better, it still needs some work. The skin is a little too red, and the hair still seems a little too green.

Adjusting the Color Balance

You can make some more exacting changes by using the Color Balance feature.

The Color Balance feature enables you to fine-tune your color changes with more precision than the Variations option. Using the Color Balance option, you can make adjustments to a particular color rather than just add an overall color shift as with the Variations option. Choose Image, Adjust, Color Balance. This will bring up the Color Balance dialog box (see Figure 16.4).

Note   If the thought of making these changes makes you a little nervous, remember that you can use Adjustment layers, which are easily reversed, you can use Undo to undo the last step taken, and you can step backwards through the History palette to reverse any or all of the steps you've taken.

FIGURE 16.4

The Color Balance dialog box.

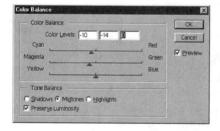

In Figure 16.4, you can see that I've added some cyan (which tones down the red a little) and some magenta (which tones down the green) to the midtones, and I've left the yellow/blue alone. At this point, you'll probably want to choose values similar to mine, but because color is so subjective, these values needn't be identical to produce a pleasing effect.

Note   While you're making these changes, you can see the difference you're making by toggling the Preview option on and off. If you enter the values I did and click the Preview on and off, you'll notice that the changes are quite subtle.

The image as it stands now can be seen in Figure 16.5. You may notice that we've been fine-tuning more and more by selecting options that are less general in scope. The first correction was made with the Variations option. It's a general change that affects the entire image, although it can be run on a selection. In fact, I used the Variations option to change the model's eyes to green in another version of this scan that I played around with.

The next change, which was the adjustment to the color balance, was less global and affected the separate color's balances. Now we'll go one step further and fine-tune the image by adjusting the curves.

FIGURE 16.5

The color balance adjusted by adding a little more cyan and magenta.

Adjusting the Color Curves

The Curves feature enables you to really zero in on the colors present in an image. For example, I now find that the changes that have been made have done a pretty good job overall, but I still find that there's a little too much red in the model's face. Luckily, the Curves option allows me to fix this without affecting the rest of the image too much. The following steps show how you can use this amazing feature to take some of the red out of Marianne's cheeks without affecting the rest of the image.

16

1. Open the Curves dialog box by choosing Image, Adjust Curves (see Figure 16.6).

FIGURE 16.6

The Curves dialog box.

2. Move the cursor over the portion of the image that you want to change. In this case it's the redder areas of Marianne's cheeks.

3. Now, left-click the mouse (that would just be "click the mouse" on a Macintosh). With the mouse button down, look over at the dialog box and you'll see a circle appear on the line in the main window of the dialog box. This is the area that you want to target.

4. When I clicked I got the numbers 138 and 138 as the Input and Output values. More importantly, I made a mental note of where the circle was on the line. In my case it was just a hair above the center. Now that I know where I want to change the curve, I can do so.

   To follow along, you can place the cursor just above the center of the line and drag it into the position you see in Figure 16.7. This will lighten the image a little and take a lot of the red out of the portrait without affecting the overall color (see Figure 16.8).

FIGURE 16.7

The new curve set in the Curves dialog box.

FIGURE 16.8

The final photo of Marianne.

At this point, we're done with color correction. You can save your work if you want, but it's not necessary.

If you created a copy to work on, as I suggested earlier, you can see the side-by-side comparison of the original scan and the adjusted version.

Considering the small amount of effort that went into the changes, they are quite remarkable. The image has much more detail and a better tone for the hair, the eyes, and the skin. Overall, this is substantially better than the original scan, and it's even a fair bit better than the print I got back from the film processors.

16

Wrapping It Up

You can use these tools and some of the others, such as Hue/Saturation, to adjust your own images. I suggest that you work in much the same way with your own photographs as you did in this exercise. Start with fairly global changes, take stock of the changes, make a decision about which direction to go in, and work down towards fixing smaller and smaller details.

 Hue and Saturation: I didn't discuss Hue/Saturation in the preceding exercise because I didn't have need for this particular adjustment. Hue/Saturation affects the overall hue, or color, and saturation, or amount of color, in an image. I suggest you open an image and play with the settings available to you in the Hue/Saturation dialog box. You'll find that changing the Hue setting has a profound effect on the overall color cast of your image and that the Saturation setting can produce some startling results, as well. You can, for example, take most of (or all of) the color out of your image by reducing the saturation.

Remember that you can use Adjustment layers, Undo, and/or the History feature to undo any changes that don't quite work out. You might also want to save various versions of the image at different stages so that you can always fall back on that one version that was almost right just before you turned it into mud. It's quite easy to spend many hours getting an image just right only to turn around and make one last change that really doesn't work.

The most important thing to remember is that you should have fun. If you do, it will show up in your work. Color correction is serious business, but not that serious. Enjoy it.

Testing Your Color Output

On Day 7, we discussed the basics of calibrating your system and setting color modes. Digital imaging and Photoshop present many challenges when you finally decide to output your image to a device besides your monitor. Every output device has its own color gamut—that is, a range of colors that it is capable of reproducing. Depending on the range of that gamut, your output may look very different from what you see on your monitor. Although several options for color management exist on both the Mac and PC desktop computers, there has yet to be an easily configurable, cross-platform and system-wide implementation of such an option. Until now, that is.

As we have already seen, Photoshop 5.0 comes with the Adobe Gamma control panel, which is an easy and effective way to create an ICC profile for your monitor that is compatible with the Apple ColorSync system and Windows ICM 2.0. These color profiles convert colors from other sources to match as closely as possible to the gamut of your monitor. Photoshop 5 allows you to specify how to handle profile mismatches with the Color Settings menu. However, most consumer-grade input and output devices, like flatbed scanners and high-resolution inkjet printers, do not calibrate as easily as monitors.

Some day soon, all input and output devices will come with improved color profile support. Theoretically, if every designer, photographer, illustrator, and printer (to name just a few professions involved with image production) uses embedded profiles with images, then the system will take care of color correction for us, but unfortunately, not everyone is using ICC color profiles. This section will introduce you to one method of controlling color output more efficiently within Photoshop. Using some simple deductive observation, you will learn how to manage your image output.

Note | ICM 2.0 is rumored to be fully integrated into the Windows 98 release. Currently, Photoshop 5 for Windows installs its own system additions to control color. Macintosh systems with ColorSync 2.2 or higher will have more ICC profiles available than Windows systems.

Because the steps involved in the following sections are a bit lengthy, here's a brief outline of the exercise you'll use to gain better control over your color output:

1. You'll need to take two images that are reflective of the type of work you do and place them into an empty Photoshop document, which serves as a template.

2. Within that template, you'll create color bars to function as gamut indicators.

3. You'll output the file to your preferred print device or to a variety of output devices.

4. Next, you'll compare the results—under correct lighting—to the image on your monitor.

5. Then, you'll create a new profile for your monitor that will match the output.

6. You'll use adjustment layers on the Photoshop template to color-correct the image.

7. Finally, you'll output the file once again and compare the results to the image on your screen.

16

Note

> Most likely, you'll need to repeat steps 5-7 until the image output is satisfactory. And to check output with additional output devices, you'll need to repeat steps 3-7 with your original monitor profile.

Sound easy enough? It is, but you may want to take some time thinking about the task at hand. Color output has become relatively inexpensive in recent years, but it still costs more than a black-and-white laser print. If you're using an inkjet printer, be prepared to use quite a bit of ink. All right then, let's get started.

Making an Image Output Template

The first thing you need to do when creating your template is choose two images that best represent your photographic or image style. Take into consideration the lighting, subject matter, and how the image was acquired. Try finding some photos that are full of different colors. If the image was scanned from a color print, then most of the colors the scanner sees will probably print with a CMYK device like an inkjet. If the scan was made from a slide, some vibrant colors may be out of the inkjet's gamut. Why? Because a print is reflective, it most likely has colors that ink dyes can't reproduce. Scans from transparent materials such as slides may have some beautiful colors, but it is likely that they will appear dull in a printed piece. For this exercise, two different styles of photography were used, as seen in Figures 16.9 and 16.10.

Tip

When you're looking at your images in Photoshop, use Select, Color Range and set the Select drop-down menu to Out Of Gamut. By default, the preview pane will show white for the colors in the image that fall outside of the CMYK gamut.

FIGURE 16.9

Image of Ivan, a shop owner, behind his counter.

1. Open the two images in Photoshop, if you haven't already, and choose File, New to create an 8" × 10" document at 300 ppi in RGB mode with a transparent background. (In pixels, this same document is 2400 pixels wide by 3000 pixels tall.) Give it a name like "Image Output Template." This new image will be the template for what you output. See Figure 16.11 for the new file settings.

Note

Make sure your machine can handle an image this size. As a rule of thumb, multiply the image file size (in MB) by 2 or 3 to see how much RAM you should have installed on your machine. For this color output test, you should have at least 64MB of physical RAM to use in Photoshop. If you don't have that much RAM or if you have a slow hard drive, feel free to reduce the image size in step 2 accordingly.

FIGURE 16.10

The Badlands National Park near Wall, South Dakota.

16

FIGURE 16.11

The Image Output Template image settings.

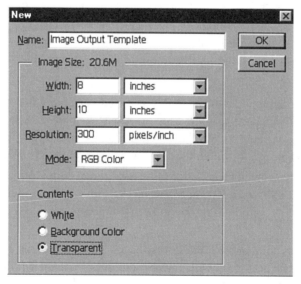

2. In the new image called Image Output Template, rename Layer 1 to "50% Gray."
(To rename the layer, double-click the layer name in the Layers palette to rename a
layer.) Choose Edit, Fill and for the Contents drop-down menu select 50% Gray.
Leave the other settings at their defaults. See Figure 16.12 for the Fill settings.

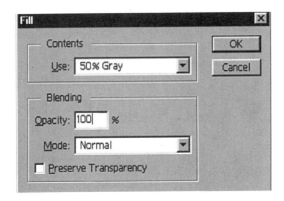

3. Go back to the two images you selected for the output test. If you already have
Adjustment layers for each image, you can choose one of two steps.

You can choose Select, All and Edit, Copy Merged and then paste the copied
image—with Adjustment layers combined with it—into the Image Output
Template.

or

You can highlight the image layer, use the Move tool to drag it into the Image
Output template, and then redo the Adjustment layers there. If you simply have an
image scanned directly from your flatbed (or an image with a Background layer
only), use the Move tool to drag a copy of it into the template image area.

4. If either copied image is too large for the area of the Image Output template, use
the Edit, Free Transform command to resize the image. Remember to hold down
the Shift key while resizing to keep the image dimensions proportionate to one
another.

At this point in the exercise, resize each image to the extent that both fit on the
template neatly. We will come back to these images later. Refer to Figure 16.13 for
an example using the two sample images.

FIGURE 16.13

The Image Output template with the Ivan and the Badlands images copied to it.

5. After each image has been copied and resized to the template, hide every layer except the 50% Gray layer.

6. Create five new layers. To make a new layer, click the Create New Layer icon at the bottom of the Layers palette, or choose Layer, New, Layer. Give the following names to the five new layers: Red, Green, Blue, Spectrum, and Grayscale. You should now have a Layers palette similar to the one shown in Figure 16.14.

7. Choose File, Preferences, Guides & Grids and then change the Grid values to the following: Gridline every 100 pixels and Subdivisions 1. Also, change the Grid color to Custom. If the Color Picker dialog box doesn't show up when you switch to Custom, double-click the color chip in the Gridline settings area. Type 50 for the Red (R), Green (G), and Blue (B) fields in the Color Picker dialog box. Compare your Guides & Grid settings shown in Figure 16.15. Click OK to close the Preferences box.

FIGURE 16.14

The Layers Palettes should look like this after you complete step 6.

FIGURE 16.15

The Guides and Grid dialog box.

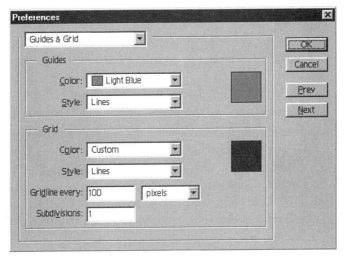

8. Show the grid by choosing View, Show Grid and make sure the Snap to Grid feature is checked in the View menu. If there's already a check next to it, do not choose it again. This turns it off. You should have a template similar to that shown in Figure 16.16.

FIGURE 16.16

The Image Output template with the grid turned on.

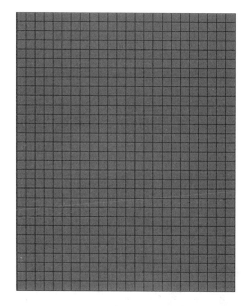

9. Highlight the Red layer. Click the Rectangular Marquee tool or choose the letter M on the keyboard. Starting 100 pixels from the left and 100 pixels down from the top (the first upper-left intersection on the grid), draw a long width-wise selection similar to that shown in Figure 16.17.

FIGURE 16.17

A rectangular selection at the top of the template.

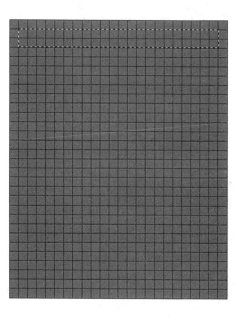

16

10. On the toolbar, select the default Foreground and Background Colors icon or press D on the keyboard. Flip the colors using the curved arrow on the toolbar or typing X on the keyboard, so that white is now the foreground color.

11. Double-click the white color chip on the toolbar. In the Color Picker dialog box, select pure red in the upper-right of the Color palette. If your Color palette is showing another section of the spectrum or if you want to be sure that pure red is selected, type 255 in the R text field and 0 (zero) in both the G and B fields (see Figure 16.18).

FIGURE 16.18

The Color Picker dialog box for RGB values for pure red.

 12. Choose the Line Gradient tool on the toolbar. Bring up your Options palette by choosing Window, Show Options and set the Gradient to Foreground to Background. Compare your Options palette to the one shown in Figure 16.19.

FIGURE 16.19

The Gradient tool options.

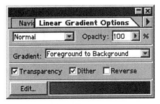

13. Inside the selection you drew in step 9, click and drag with the Gradient tool. Start at the left end of the selection about 100 pixels (which equals one gridline) right of the selection border. End the line about one gridline left of the right end of the selection border. Holding the Shift key while drawing constrains the line to a 180

degree line. For proper cursor placement, see Figure 16.20. When you finish, you should have a Red layer that looks like Figure 16.21.

FIGURE 16.20

Drawing a line with the Gradient tool.

FIGURE 16.21

The template with a red-to-black gradient on the Red layer.

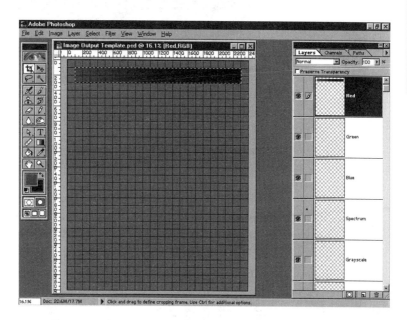

14. This is a good time to save your Image Output template image as a Photoshop (PSD) file, so go ahead and save it now.

15. Highlight the Green layer and change the foreground color chip to a pure green in the Color Picker dialog box (refer to step 11). Again, typing 255 in the G field and 0 (zero) in the R and B fields ensures that you have selected pure green.

16. Choose the Rectangular Marquee tool. If the selection is still active, then click and drag inside the selection, moving it below the gradient. If you lost your selection, draw a new one exactly like the previous selection. It shouldn't be difficult because the selection will snap to the gridlines. Leave a 100 pixel (1 gridline) border between the selection and the Red gradient.

17. Repeat step 13. You should now have a template similar to the one shown in Figure 16.22. Save your template file.

FIGURE **16.22**

The template with a new green-to-black gradient on the Green layer.

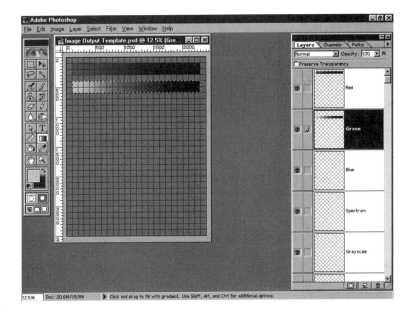

18. Highlight the Blue layer and change the foreground color chip to a pure blue. In the Color Picker dialog box, type 255 in the B field and 0 (zero) in the R and G fields to make sure a true blue has been chosen.

19. Repeat steps 16-17. You should have an image like the one shown in Figure 16.23.

FIGURE **16.23**

A blue-to-black gradient is added to the Blue layer.

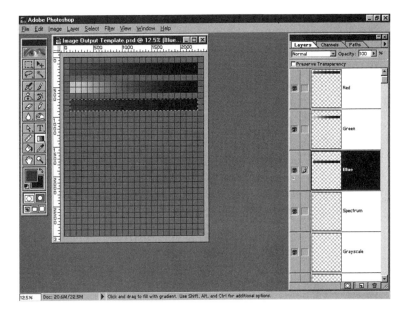

20. Highlight the Spectrum layer. Choose the Gradient tool and go back to your Options palette. Change the gradient to Spectrum. See Figure 16.24 for the new setting.

FIGURE 16.24

The Gradient tool options set to Spectrum.

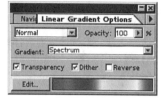

21. Repeat steps 16-17. You should now have an image similar to Figure 16.25.

FIGURE 16.25

The Spectrum layer with a spectrum gradient.

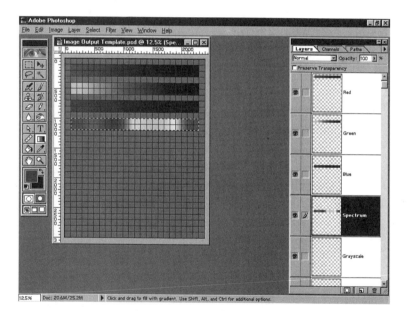

22. Highlight the Grayscale layer and make sure the Gradient tool is active. Again, go to your Options palette and change the gradient to Black, White.

23. Repeat steps 16-17, except this time, while you drag the gradient line across the selection, go from right to left. See Figure 16.26 for the current state of the template.

FIGURE 16.26

The template with a white-to-black gradient on the Grayscale layer.

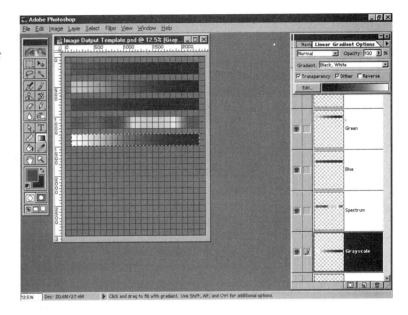

24. Now save the image template as a Photoshop (PSD) file. Your image template is almost complete.

25. Show the two layers that contain the images you opened at the beginning of this exercise. Most likely, the color bars overlap the images. Deselect the current selection if it is still active by choosing Select, Deselect. Resize each image with the Edit, Free Transform command. Remember to hold down the Shift key to avoid distortion. When you are done, you may want to turn off the gridlines (View, Hide Grid). The sample template with the images resized and repositioned can be seen in Figure 16.27.

26. Resave the image template as a Photoshop (PSD) file. It's not necessary to save different versions of this file because everything is on its own layer.

Whew! Now that you've created your template, you're probably ready for a break. Take as long as you need. When you come back, the steps will still be here, and you'll be ready to prepare the template you created for output.

Preparing the Template for Output

Okay, you're now ready to output your personalized image template to your printer or preferred output device. Before you output it, use Photoshop's CMYK Preview mode (Ctrl-Y on a PC; Cmd-Y on a Mac) to get an idea of what the image will look like. Notice that our vibrant colors become dull and washed out. That's because these colors fall outside of the CMYK color gamut.

FIGURE 16.27

The complete Image Output template.

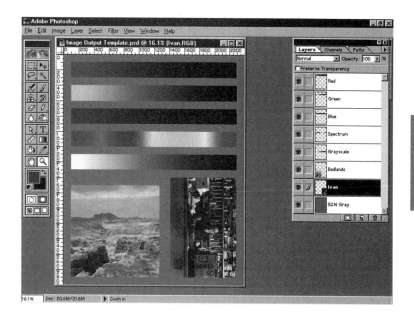

16

What can you do about this color loss? Unfortunately, you can't do much unless you use a print process with more than four inks, or you output the image to film (a RGB process). One step you may want to take right away is the addition of Adjustment layers to your image. Follow these general steps to prepare the image template for output:

1. Change the View mode in Photoshop to CMYK Preview by choosing View, Preview, CMYK or by choosing Ctrl+Y (Cmd+Y on a Mac).

2. Add a new Adjustment layer by choosing Layer, New, Adjustment Layer and then choose a type that you prefer.

3. Try to increase the contrast in areas where the template appears dull. You may want to make selective Adjustment layer masks for your smaller images (refer to Day 11 for more details on selective Adjustment layer masks). Make sure you don't change the appearance of the 50% Gray layer.

4. Resave the template as a Photoshop (PSD) file. You can overwrite your existing file if you like, because we have only added an Adjustment layer.

Printing at a Service Bureau

If you take this file to a service bureau, then save a copy of the template as a TIF file or a format that they can accept. When you submit the order for output, specify that the file be printed "as is," or that no color correction be applied to the image.

At this point, some may argue that the image should be changed to CMYK mode for output. This all depends on how you want to handle image output. Most people are not commercial printers who know to optimize CMYK ink preferences in Photoshop. If your service bureau has recommendations for the type of paper stock that you need to use, you may want to prepare a specific CMYK-converted copy of the image template. For most purposes, though, keep your image in RGB mode to retain the widest possible gamut for a variety of output devices.

Printing to Your Personal Printer

If you have your own inkjet printer, then you simply print the template from Photoshop. Because printer software utilities and drivers differ widely, here are some general guidelines for the setup of your inkjet printer:

- Leave the color settings at their defaults. If you decide to experiment with different values, then be consistent with all subsequent outputs. This is much like a science experiment where we want to have control over all of the variables and change as few as possible.

- In the Print dialog box for Photoshop, you might be able to access a specific ICC or ICM profile for your printer. For example, Epson Stylus Color inkjets automatically install profiles that Photoshop can use. These profiles should automatically appear in the Space drop-down menu of the Print dialog box. If you do use a printer-specific profile, make sure the Printer Color Management option is checked.

- If you do not have an ICC or ICM profile for your output device, simply choose CMYK Color for the Space in the Print dialog box. Deselect, or uncheck, Printer Color Management to let Photoshop control the ink percentages.

Consider what kind of paper stock (or transparency) to use for these output tests. For best results, use a glossy coated stock. Because this is not a digital prepress book (and there's plenty of them), we will not go into issues such as dot grain and screen frequency. Do keep in mind, though, that different paper stocks can produce drastically different results. Be consistent with whatever you decide to use.

When you're ready, go ahead and print the template. While it's printing, start reading the next section.

Changing Your Monitor Profile

Before you compare the output to the monitor image, you need to have adequate lighting to view the output. Using an ordinary desktop lamp is not recommended for viewing reflective artwork of any kind—that is, artwork like what appears on your monitor. Because most computers are set up away from brightly-lit windows to avoid glare, you should set up a small halogen lamp to view your output.

Why? The color from ordinary household lamps is usually too warm for viewing purposes. We need to look at output under a cooler light source, like halogen. Set up the halogen lamp somewhere close to your monitor. Compare the printed output under the halogen lamp to the template as it appears on your monitor. Chances are high that they don't match each other very well. If you're lucky, you may be satisfied with your output, but if you're not, the following steps show you what to do next.

Note

> Keep your Image Output template in CMYK Preview mode for the remainder of the exercise.

1. To begin, find your original monitor profile. In Windows, you will find the ICM file in the C:\WINDOWS\SYTEM\COLOR directory. In the Mac OS, ColorSync ICC profiles can be found in the ColorSync Profiles folder of the System folder. After you've located your profile file, copy it into another folder.

Note

> Before changing your ColorSync ICC profile, you should make a copy of it just in case you overwrite the existing profile in the next steps. That way, you always have the original to go back to.

2. Go to the Adobe Gamma control panel. In Windows, this is in your Control Panel window, accessible from the Start menu, Settings menu. In Windows, you'll want to view the Adobe Gamma control panel while viewing your template in the background. Make sure Photoshop is showing behind the control panel. (On a Mac, you'll find the Adobe Gamma control panel in the Apple menu, Control Panels sub-menu.)

3. In the Adobe Gamma dialog box, select the Control Panel version instead of the Step-by-Step Wizard or Assistant that you may have used to create your original monitor profile. See Figure 16.28 for a sample Adobe Gamma dialog box. Choose Next to proceed to the next dialog box.

FIGURE 16.28

The Adobe Gamma control panel.

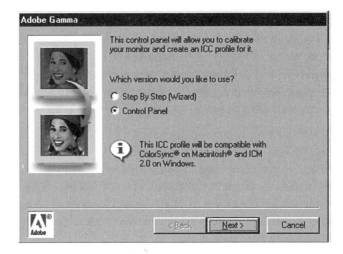

4. If View Single Gamma is checked, uncheck it. You want to control each individual gamma. Now move the Red, Green, and Blue gamma sliders to match the output as closely as possible. If necessary, change the Desired numeric Gamma value to brighten or darken the monitor. Lower numbers increase the whiteness, whereas higher numbers decrease it. Do not expect to match the output exactly; you want to get it as close as the control panel will allow you. For a sample configuration, see Figure 16.29.

5. Although it's generally not recommended, you may want to try adjusting the monitor's controls to match the output. This should be avoided if possible and should be done only if you have digital onscreen controls. Dials and buttons that do not report any value to the monitor are not very reliable for consistent calibration.

6. Change the ICC Profile name at the top of the dialog box. You'll want to be able to go back to the previous settings after this exercise is complete. Give the new profile a name that describes the output device and stock used, such as Monitor-to-EPSON STYLUS 600 Glossy. "Monitor" was inserted in the name so that it wouldn't be confused with any profiles used by the printer itself.

7. Click OK and save the new profile. The screen should still be showing the new gamma corrections.

This may seem like a lot of work, but you'll be glad you took the time to optimize your work to your preferred output device. We're almost done—there's only one section left to the exercise.

FIGURE 16.29

FIGURE 16.29

The real control panel for Adobe Gamma. These settings are specific to the monitor used for this exercise. Do not replicate these values in your control panel.

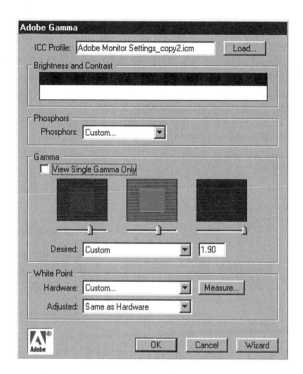

16

Changing the Image Output Template

Back in Photoshop, keep the template in CMYK Preview mode and add any necessary Adjustment layers to the image. Usually, for color calibration, you need only to add Color Balance, Curves, or Hue/Saturation Adjustment layers. Remember to highlight the topmost layer before adding any Adjustment layers. At first, try to use Adjustment layers that affect the entire template. If necessary, select an individual area or load a selection from a layer that appears to be out of sync, and apply an Adjustment layer to it. Output the image template once again and compare the results.

Keep repeating the preceding two sections of this exercise until you achieve satisfactory results, and save a new profile every time you use the Adobe Gamma control panel. When you've finished this exercise, go back and select your original monitor profile. Also, resave your final Image Output template complete with new Adjustment layers as a Photoshop (PSD) file. Remember to turn off CMYK preview for other images in Photoshop. Only use CMYK preview when you want to see Photoshop replace out-of-gamut RGB values with CMYK equivalents.

So now what do you do with the profile you spent so much time creating? Whenever you're ready for output again, simply load the last profile you made from this exercise. Most importantly, copy the values from any Adjustment layers you used on the Image Output template to new Adjustment layers on future images that you plan to output. It's just as important to keep any original Adjustment layers intact, so don't be afraid to stack Adjustment layers on top of one another.

In this exercise, you calibrated your images to look good on the monitor, adding any Adjustment levels necessary. Then you created a profile to accurately preview your images in CMYK mode and added more Adjustment levels specific to the output device you are using. Now, whether you're printing to a personal printer or to an output device at your local service bureau, what you see as the end result should be pretty close to what you see on your monitor.

Summary

Today was the first really serious day. You learned how to use some of the more powerful features that Photoshop has to offer to help you adjust and correct the color of an image.

Don't think, though, that these skills can be attained in just one day and after working with one image. To become really skilled at adjusting and correcting color photographs requires a great deal of time and effort. It'll be worth it, though, when you can look at an image and almost immediately spot what's wrong with it, and even more when you can decide what needs to be done to correct it.

Q&A

Q Are there other factors that affect color balance?

A Yes. Every monitor will display colors differently. Even monitors from the same manufacturer will be different. Also, ambient light will affect the colors you see on your monitor. An image that is color corrected on one machine may look different on another. Adobe has taken steps to reduce the differences with Photoshop 5, though. They've included features that enable an image to carry along its specific color information. When you open an image in Photoshop 5, this image will be read and applied, along with your monitor's settings, to help make sure that you're seeing the image as it was intended to be seen by the person who adjusted it.

Q **Is it always necessary to create an image output template?**

A An image output template will help you calibrate your work in Photoshop to the output devices you prefer to work with. Because not everyone uses ICC or ICM profiles with his/her image files, it's difficult to swap images back and forth consistently. With your own work and output, though, using an image template will minimize the chance of getting poor output results. It will also reveal the limitations of your output device.

16

Workshop

The following section is a quick quiz about the chapter you have just read. If you have any problems answering any of the questions in the quiz, see the section directly following it for all of the answers.

Quiz

1. What do you need to do to access the Variations dialog box?
2. How do you access the Color Balance dialog box?
3. Of Shadows, Midtones, and Highlights, which ones can you correct to produce changes in the color balance?
4. How do you preview real-time changes within the Color Balance dialog box?
5. What do you need to do in order to change the color curves?
6. How do you preview your image for CMYK output?

Quiz Answers

1. You can access the Variations option by choosing Image, Adjust, Variations.
2. To access the Color Balance dialog box, choose Image, Adjust, Color Balance.
3. All three can be corrected in the Color Balance dialog box.
4. You can preview the changes in real time in the Color Balance dialog box by placing a check mark in the Preview option.
5. You can change the color curves of an image by choosing Image, Adjust, Curves.
6. Choose View, Preview, CMYK or use the Ctrl+Y (Cmd+Y on a Mac) shortcut.

DAY 17

Retouching and Repairing Images

Do you have a collection of old family photos? We all do, right? Have you ever wished that you could fix some of those old photographs up a little? Well with Photoshop you can! With Photoshop it's possible to remove scratches and dust marks, fix the contrast and the brightness, and even make some corrections to add some life to those old family photos. In this chapter, I'll demonstrate how you can use some of your new skills to

- Fix the effects of a flash on subjects at different distances
- Fix the brightness and contrast of an old black-and-white photo
- Remove dust marks and scratches

Evening Out the Brightness

When you take a look at the image in Figure 17.1, the first thing you may notice is that the lighting is not even. The gentleman on the left received much more light from the flash than the other two did. You'll also notice that the overall brightness and contrast aren't that good.

FIGURE 17.1

The original scan of the fishermen.

If you try to fix the contrast and brightness so that, for example, you can see more detail in the person on the right, you'll probably wash out the guy on the left. Figure 17.2 shows how, when the brightness is adjusted by +46 and the contrast is adjusted by +37, the gentleman on the right has much more detail but the gentleman on the left is almost completely washed out.

FIGURE 17.2

Adjusted brightness by +46 and contrast by +37.

What can be done in a situation like this? Why use a mask, of course. If you mask out the gentleman on the left, you can adjust the rest of the photo without making any changes to the fisherman on the left. Because there is quite a bit of contrast between the man on the left and his surroundings, it will be an easy matter to use the Magnetic Lasso.

1. If you haven't opened this file, do so now. It's in folder Day17 and it's called fishermen.psd.

2. Select the Magnetic Lasso tool and click-and-drag it around the shirt and face of the gentleman on the left. You should be able to use the default settings of 0 for the Feather, Anti-alias on, Lasso Width 10 pixels, Frequency 57, and an Edge Contrast of 10%. Because the shirt and the face are the most problematic areas, you should just draw around them.

3. Once you get all the way back around to your starting point, let go of the mouse button to close the selected area. You may notice, like I did, that the selection, while good, is not perfect (see Figure 17.3).

FIGURE 17.3

Selection made with the Magnetic Lasso tool.

4. At this point I decided to go into Quick Mask mode and make the necessary adjustments to the selection. Click the Quick Mask Mode icon at the bottom of the toolbox (it's the button on the right, second row up from the bottom). With the Quick Mask active, it's easy to see where the mask needs some touch-ups (see Figure 17.4).

Of course, it's hard to see here in black and white, but if you're following along you'll see where the mask needs work. All-in-all I'd say that it's a pretty good mask, though.

FIGURE 17.4

Quick Mask mode active.

You can add to and subtract from the mask by painting with the paintbrush.

5. Select the Paintbrush tool and set the foreground color to white to remove the red portions of the mask, and set the foreground color to black to add to the red portions.

6. You should probably zoom in to the area that you want to work on to help you make a more accurate mask. Paint the areas of the mask that need correcting.

7. Once you're satisfied with the mask, set the editing mode back to Standard mode by clicking the button to the left of the Quick Mask Mode button (it's the one on the left in the second row from the bottom on the toolbox). You should now see the finished mask outlined by the marquee. What you actually want is the rest of the image to be selected, though, so choose Select, Inverse to invert the selection.

8. At this point it would be prudent to save this selection, so choose Select, Save Selection. Even though it was created without too much work, it would still be awful to start over from the beginning. Also, you'll want to turn this mask on and off several times before you're finished.

9. In the Save Selection dialog box, keep the file's name and the default channel. In the Name field enter a name for the channel and click OK.

With the mask active it's time to try to adjust the brightness and contrast again.

10. Choose Image, Adjust, Brightness/Contrast and set the Brightness to 46 and the contrast to 20. Click OK, and then save your image, which should now resemble Figure 17.5.

> **Note**
>
> You can toggle the visibility of the selection on and off to get a better view of the image. Press Ctrl+H (Command+H) to toggle the marquee on and off.

FIGURE 17.5

Brightness and contrast adjusted on the unmasked portion of the image.

17

This is much better. You can see more detail in all three of the fishermen now. The mask has protected the gentleman on the left from any change while allowing the brightness and contrast to bring detail back into the other men.

Adjusting the Shadows, Gray Levels, and Highlights Using Levels

Now that the brightness in the image is more even, it's time to make a final brightness/contrast adjustment. You can use the Levels feature to bring out detail in the highlights and shadows of an image.

1. If the image you were working with in the preceding section is not open, open it now to continue.

2. Choose Image, Adjust Levels to bring up the Levels dialog box (see Figure 17.6).

FIGURE 17.6

Levels dialog box.

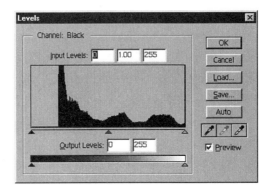

Notice how there is a space between the black level indicator (it's the first small black arrow at the bottom of the input window) and the actual start of the shadows histogram in the input window? Drag the arrow over until it lines up with the start of the graphed data. It should be at about 44 or so. If you have a check mark in the Preview check box, you'll notice that the image gets a little darker and there's more contrast. This is because moving the black arrow increases the shadows in the image.

3. Now drag the middle arrow (the Gray Levels indicator) over towards the left until the middle input window reads 1.44 (optionally, you could change the value in the window). In other words, you've changed its value by the same amount as the black.

4. You can punch up the highlights a little, as well. Drag the rightmost arrow to the left until its value is 240 or so.

5. Click OK to apply the changes, and then save the image.

To see how far the image has come, compare this version (see Figure 17.7) with the original Figure 17.1.

FIGURE 17.7

Brightness/contrast and shadows/high-lights adjusted.

17

You can see at a glance how much more detail there is in Figure 17.7. Take a look at the buildings in the background and you'll see that there are details present that weren't even visible in the original scan. All that's left now is to clean up the dust marks.

Cleaning the Dust & Scratches

Although Photoshop has a built-in Dust & Scratches filter, I'd recommend against using it on a photo of this quality. Doing so would only soften the image and cause a fair loss of the detail you worked so hard to get back. Instead, I'd suggest that you remove the dust marks and scratches using a combination of the Paintbrush tool and the Rubber Stamp tool.

On smaller scratches and dust marks you can simply sample a nearby color (shade of gray, actually) using the Eyedropper tool and then use the Paintbrush to fill in the offending area. The close-up in Figure 17.8 shows a good selection of some of the not-so-bad and some of the worst marks.

1. If the image you were working with in the preceding section is not open, open it now to continue.
2. To clean up these marks, zoom in and select the Eyedropper tool.

FIGURE **17.8**

*Dust marks and
scratches.*

3. Click next to one of the smaller dust marks to choose a similar color to what the spot should be.

4. Select the Paintbrush, set the tool to a small soft brush, and simply paint over the dust mark.

   You may find that because many of the marks are in similarly shaded areas, you don't have to select a new color for each dust mark. You can actually fill in quite a number of the marks before moving on to another area and another shade of gray. I made the corrections you see in Figure 17.9 and selected the Eyedropper tool only two or three times.

FIGURE **17.9**

*Smaller dust marks
cleaned up.*

After you've eliminated the smaller marks, it's time to remove the scratches and the larger dust marks.

5. Select the Rubber Stamp tool and move the cursor near an area that needs correction.

6. Alt-click (Option-click on a Mac) on an area nearby that closely matches the offending area, and then move the cursor over the area that needs correcting.

7. Mix short and long strokes and reset the tool as necessary by Alt-clicking (or Option-clicking on a Mac) a different area. This is really more an art than a science, and practice will go a long way to honing your retouching skills.

Figure 17.10 shows the same enlarged area as Figure 17.8.

FIGURE 17.10

Larger dust marks and scratches cleaned up.

17

Only a couple hundred more dust marks to go and this photo will have cleaned up quite nicely (see Figure 17.11).

8. Save your image.

Cleaning Up with the Unsharp Mask

With the final dust marks and scratches gone, it's time for one final adjustment. I feel that the image is still a little soft. A quick application of the Unsharp mask should fix that.

To clean it, choose Filter, Sharpen, Unsharp Mask and enter 200% for the Amount, 3.0 for the Radius, and 36 for the Threshold to arrive at the final image you see in Figure 17.12.

FIGURE 17.11

All of the dust marks and scratches cleaned up.

FIGURE 17.12

Final corrected image.

I chose these values for this image by moving the sliders around and alternately clicking the preview setting on and off until I was satisfied with the results. If you're working on another image, you may have to play with the settings until you get something that appeals to your artistic sense.

Note

> Here are a couple of clues to get you started, though. The Amount controls how much the contrast between pixels will be affected by the mask. The Radius determines the number of pixels around the edge that will be affected, and the Threshold determines how different the brightness between two adjacent pixels must be before they are considered an edge.

Summary

17

Well, today was more practice than theory, but I think you covered a lot of ground nonetheless. You learned how to employ some of the tools that were discussed in earlier chapters, and you saw the results of applying these tools firsthand.

You also learned how to use a Quick Mask to create a selection that enabled you to adjust a portion of an image while leaving another area untouched. You got firsthand experience with dust and scratch removal, and you learned how to apply the Levels feature to boost the detail in the shadows and highlights of a photo.

I think it's time to haul out that old family album and go through it with a more critical eye—aimed at how you could restore some of those great old photographs.

Q&A

Q I don't really understand all of the graphs and such in the Levels dialog box. What does all of this information mean?

A The Levels sliders let you make gradual changes to the brightness, contrast and midtones in an image. You can, for example, adjust the midtones without affecting the highlight and shadows too much. You can use the input sliders, directly below the histogram, to increase the contrast of your image, and you can use the output sliders to decrease the contrast. Level adjustments can be made on the entire image at once or on separate channels and groups of channels. To select a separate channel, simply choose the channel from the drop-down menu. To select a group of channels, you can Shift-select them from the Channels palette (to do so, hold down the Shift key and click the title bar of the channels you wish to select). These groups will show up in the pull-down with the first letter combinations of the selected channels. For example, a group with the red and blue channels will show as RB.

Q **My old photograph got folded in half and now has a wrinkle running across the middle of it. What's the best way to restore this photo?**

A You can restore this photo using some of the techniques used in this chapter. You can use the Rubber Stamp tool to help remove the crease, for example. You can also select a nearby area and copy and paste it over the crease. You may need to soften or smudge the edges of the selection to help it blend in.

Q **I have a new photograph that I want to look old. Is there a way I can add an aged or sepiatone effect?**

A Yes. If the photo is in color, you should first change its mode to grayscale by choosing Image, Mode, Grayscale. Next, change its mode to Duotone. In the Duotone Options dialog box set the Type to Duotone. Select a color for the second tone (the first should remain as the default black) by clicking the small swatch for Ink 2. This will bring up the Custom Colors dialog box. Choose a warm medium brown such as PANTONE 716 CVC. Click OK in the Custom Colors dialog box and again in the Duotone Options dialog to finish the process.

Workshop

The following section is a quick quiz about the chapter you have just read. If you have any problems answering any of the questions in the quiz, see the section directly following it for all of the answers.

Quiz

1. How do you set the brightness and contrast of an image?
2. How do you access Photoshop's Levels feature?
3. How do you increase the shadows in an image?
4. How do you apply the Unsharp mask?
5. What are the three options available with the Unsharp mask?

Quiz Answers

1. You can do so by choosing Image, Adjust, Brightness/Contrast.
2. You access the Levels feature with Image, Adjust, Levels.
3. You can increase the details in the shadows in an image by adjusting the contrast though Image, Adjust, Brightness/Contrast or through Image, Adjust, Levels.
4. Choose Filter, Sharpen, Unsharp Mask.
5. Amount, Radius, and Threshold.

DAY **18**

Saving Time with Actions

Actions, a way of automating a series of steps, were a welcome addition to Photoshop 4. In Photoshop 5, they have been refined and now support many more palettes (for example, the Paths palette and the Layers palette) and tools (such as the Gradient tool, the Marquee tool, the Line tool, and the Crop tool to name just a few) than the previous version. Actions are great time-savers, and today we'll highlight many examples of their power:

- Understanding what an action is
- Working with the Actions palette
- Running built-in actions
- Creating your own actions

What Are Actions?

Using actions you can record a series of steps and processes. Once recorded, this action can be saved and reused again. This automation of certain tasks can save you lots of time. You can also share your action files with others, saving them lots of times as well. In fact, actions are becoming widely available.

Note

You can purchase Metacreation's Kai's Power Actions and there are bound to be others. A number of Web sites also offer free collections of actions. Some of the online tutorials that I offer at GrafX Design (http://www.grafx-design.com) have associated actions that you can download and apply to create your own effects.

Actions can also be applied against whole folders of files. This means that once you've created and tested an action you can use it to batch process large numbers of files. All of these can be fully automated, freeing you to do other work while Photoshop prepares your images. Pretty slick.

Understanding the Actions Palette

Photoshop comes with a number of built-in actions to get you started. These include a sepia tone, clear embossed text, button creation, cast shadows, and more. Actions, both built-in and any you create or acquire, are run from the Actions palette (see Figure 18.1). To access the Actions palette, choose Window, Show Actions.

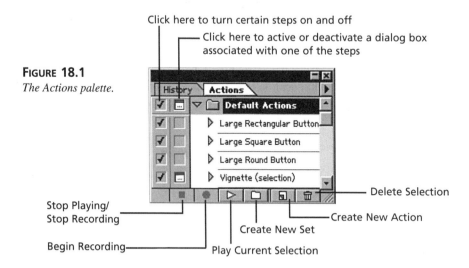

FIGURE 18.1
The Actions palette.

The Actions palette is similar to the other Photoshop palettes. You'll see a list of the available actions. Down the left side of the palette you'll see a series of checkmarks. These icons enable you to toggle the steps of an action on and off. This can be useful for debugging your actions. By excluding certain steps, you can try to pinpoint problems or make small adjustments to your own or existing actions.

> **Note**   Debugging is a computerese term meaning to find and correct problems with a program or a script, such as a Photoshop action.

The next column to the right enables you to activate/deactivate a dialog box that may be associated with a step in an action. By having the dialog box activate during the running of an action, you can change the settings in that dialog box.

Next comes the list of the actions. You can see a small triangle icon next to each action or step. If the arrow icon is pointing to the right, you see only the title of the action or step. You can click the arrow, which then points down, to see the entire set of steps in the action or the settings of a particular step. Let's try it.

1. Open the Actions palette by choosing Window, Show Actions. The default action palette should contain a list of the built-in actions that come with Photoshop. The top entry should say "Default Actions" and the arrow to the left of the title should be pointing downward. There should also be a listing of actions below this entry.

2. Click the arrow next to the Default Actions folder. It should now point to the right and the only visible entry will be the Default Actions entry.

3. Click the arrow again so that the actions below the top entry are visible.

4. Click the arrow icon next to the Large Rectangular Button action. You should now see a list of the actual steps that make up this action. A number of steps are involved in this action and they won't all be visible in the palette. There is a scrollbar to the right, however, that can be used to scroll down through the steps.

Along the bottom is a row of icons that enable you to control an action. Starting at the left, you have the Stop Playing/Recording, Begin Recording, Play Current Selection, Create New Set, Create New Action, and Delete Selection icons. I'll demonstrate these in turn as they come up today.

Running Built-in Actions

To see how an action works, open the baloons.psd file in folder day18 (see Figure 18.2). You're going to add some clear text over the photo. This is a cool effect that would take a number of steps to complete by hand.

FIGURE 18.2

Hot air balloons.

1. If the Actions palette is not visible, choose Windows, Show Actions.

2. Scroll down the palette until you see the entry called Clear Emboss (Type). The word Type in parentheses means that this action works on a layer with type in it, so you'll need to add some type to the image.

3. Select the Vertical Type tool (available from the Type tool flyout) and click the image to bring up the Type dialog box.

4. In the Type Tool dialog box, set the Font to Arial Black and the Size to 40 points.

5. Enter the word Balloons and position it along the left-hand side of the image (see Figure 18.3).

6. For the action to work, the text must be rendered first. To render the text, choose Layer, Type, Render Layer.

Now everything is in place and you're ready to create clear embossed text. All that's left is to click the play icon and the Photoshop action takes care of all the necessary steps.

Figure 18.3

Hot air balloons with text added.

7. Highlight the Clear Emboss (Type) action by clicking its title in the actions palette.

8. Click the Play Current Selection icon. You should see a bit of activity going on in the Layers palette and on the image. Once the action has finished running, you should have a result similar to Figure 18.4.

To see the exact steps that were taken by this action, click the small arrow next to the entry for the action. You'll see the following list of steps:

*Make Snapshot

Make Layer

Merge Layers

*Set Current Layer

*Fill

*Set Layer Effects of Current Layer (you may need to expand the palette horizontally to see all of this title)

*Set Current Layer

FIGURE **18.4**

*Hot air balloons with
clear embossed text
added via a Photoshop
action.*

The entries in the list marked with an asterisk have additional steps or settings (on the
Photoshop screen these entries have a small arrow icon). You can view the settings or
additional steps by clicking the small arrow icon next to the entry. For example, clicking
the arrow icon next to the Set Layer Effects of Current Layer shows you the following
sub-steps involved in this step:

> To: Layer Effects
>
> Bevel and Emboss: bevel and emboss
>
> Highlight Mode: color dodge
>
> Shadow Mode: color burn
>
> Style: inner bevel

As you can see, there would be a fair amount of work involved in creating this effect by
hand. As it is, with the action provided, all you need to do is place the text, render it, and
start the action. You can see how nice it is to have actions available that enable you to
perform multiple steps on an image with a simple mouse click.

Another nice thing about an action is that you can see exactly how someone created a certain effect. You can even view the numbers used for the different values in the dialog boxes by the person who created the effect. This can help you understand how certain effects can be achieved. You can then use this knowledge in creating your own actions or in your work with Photoshop.

Installing Third-Party Actions

As I stated earlier, you can buy actions and even find free ones on the Internet. I've included a couple on the CD-ROM that accompanies this book. Steven (Alex) Alexander II created these actions. If you'd like to get more of the incredible actions that Alex has created, stop by his Web site, Alexander's Creative Conundrum at `http://www.intertech.net.alex/index.html`.

All of Alex's actions are free, and they are some of the coolest actions around. In fact, his Chromium action, which creates a really neat chrome effect with text or any other object on a separate layer, is the best chrome effect I've seen.

To add any actions that you buy or download you should first store them somewhere so that Photoshop can access them. I recommend creating an action folder under your main Photoshop folder, if one doesn't already exist, and then simply copying your new actions to this folder:

18

1. From within Photoshop, access the Actions menu. This is accomplished by clicking the small black arrow to the right of the Actions tab in the Actions palette.

2. From the menu, choose Load Actions.

3. Using the Load dialog box, point Photoshop to the action that you want to load. Your new actions will now be accessible.

Creating Your Own Actions

Creating your own actions is as simple as performing the steps involved in creating a particular effect. This next exercise demonstrates just how simple by having you create a drop shadow action.

1. Open a new 500×300 72 dpi image with the content set to white and the mode set to RGB.

2. Choose a foreground color.

3. Select the Type tool and enter some text in the dialog box. The settings aren't that important as long as your text fits in your image.

4. Position the text in your image and click OK in the Type Tool dialog box.

5. Render the type by choosing Layer, Type, Render Layer. You're ready to record your very first action.

6. Choose New Action from the Actions palette menu. This brings up the New Action dialog box (see Figure 18.5).

FIGURE 18.5

New Action dialog

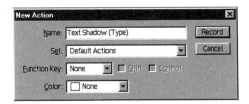

You can name the action, as I've done, Text Shadow (Type) and leave Set at Default Actions. You also have the option of selecting a Function key that runs the action, and you can color code the action as well. It's not necessary to set these options, but you can if you like. If you select a function key, you can run your new action in the future by pressing the key you've chosen. The color coding changes the colors used for the title bar of your action in the Actions palette.

Both of these options can be changed at a later date by double-clicking the title of the action in the Actions palette. For now, just leave the defaults and click Record to start recording your action.

Note

The color that you set for an action only affects the display of the actions when you choose Button Mode. You can set Button Mode via the Actions pull-down menu, which is accessed via the Actions palette menu.

Every step you make is now recorded into your action. After you're done, you need to click the Stop Playing/Recording icon. It's the first icon on the left at the bottom of the Actions palette. For now, though, you've got an action to create.

1. To create a drop shadow, you first need to duplicate the text layer. Do so by dragging the current text layer onto the Create New Layer icon at the bottom of the Layers palette. Doing so records this step in your new action.

2. Now click the Preserve Transparency option in the Layers palette so you can color the new text without touching the surrounding areas. This, too, will be recorded.

3. Press the D key to set the default foreground/background colors.

4. Press Alt-Backspace (Option-Delete on a Mac) to fill the new text with black.

5. Click Preserve Transparency once again to deselect it. This is necessary because you're going to blur the black text so that it resembles a soft shadow.

6. Choose Filter, Blur, Gaussian Blur and set Radius to 3.0 pixels (remember that these values can be reset by you or someone else as the action is being run later).

7. Click OK to apply the filter and store the step in your action file.

8. Click and drag the shadow layer so that it's below the original text layer in the Layers palette.

9. Press Ctrl-Down Arrow (Cmd-Down Arrow on a Mac) three times.

10. Press Ctrl-Right Arrow (Cmd-Right Arrow on a Mac) three times.

11. Click the Stop Playing/Recording icon to end your action.

That's it! You've just created a new action. Now let's test that new action.

1. Open a new 500×300 72 dpi file with the contents set to white and the mode set to RGB.

2. Enter some text and render the type layer.

3. Highlight the Drop Shadow action you just created and click the Play button. You should see a drop shadow created right before your eyes. You can modify your action at a later date as well.

4. From the Actions palette menu, you can choose to insert steps and also choose to set a stop. For example, you can set a stop that gives the user some information. You can use this option to stop the action before it runs and have it display your name and email address. You'll see this on many of the actions you download from the Net.

5. To personalize your new action, Click the action title to make it current and choose Insert Stop from the Actions palette menu. This brings up the Record Stop dialog box as seen in Figure 18.6.

6. Type a message into the dialog box as I have done and make sure that you place a check mark in the Allow Continue option. This allows the user to continue on with the action after viewing your message. Click OK.

18

FIGURE 18.6

Record Stop dialog box.

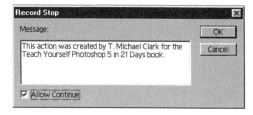

You may find that the stop was not positioned exactly where you wanted it. This is easy to fix. You can simply click and drag the stop into place as you would drag a layer in the Layers palette. With your stop in place, run the action again and you'll see that it now stops at the beginning and displays your message before continuing on. Now everyone that uses your action will know that you created it.

Batch Processing with Actions

If you have a folder filled with files that you need to perform a certain effect on, you can choose to have the effect performed on every file in the folder. All you need is to have the effect set up as an action.

To run any action against every file in a particular folder, choose File, Batch to bring up the Batch dialog box (see Figure 18.7). Within this dialog box, you can choose the action set, the particular action from that set, the source folder (where the files you want to run the action against are stored) and the destination folder (where the affected files are stored).

FIGURE 18.7

Use the Batch dialog box to run an action on multiple files.

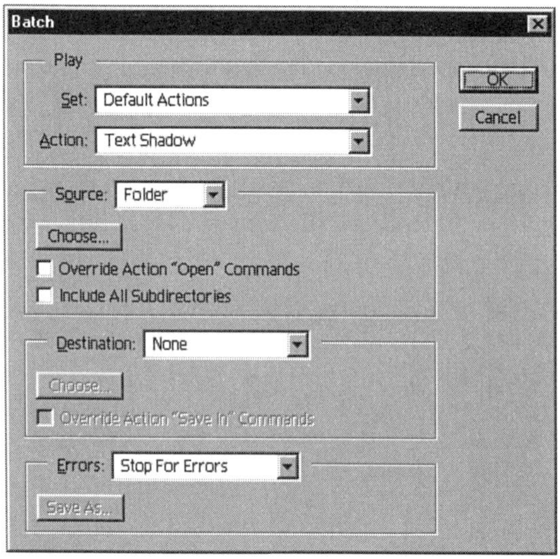

Running an action against a whole folder of files is an extremely powerful option. You can set the process up and take a break. Imagine your boss's surprise when you come back from that extended lunch hour and you still have all the changes made to the files as he requested. Just don't tell him how it was done, lest he decide to replace you with a LAN running Photoshop.

Summary

Today's work was certainly worthwhile. You just found out how to get Photoshop to work on its own for you. From now on you can put your feet up and let Photoshop handle the grunt work. Of course, this requires that you write a whole lot of actions to get the job done, but you'll never have to repeatedly run the same processes over and over. Freedom from the drudgery is at your fingertips.

Q&A

Q Help! I'm trying to run an action, but it's not running all the way through. What could I be doing wrong?

A There could be any number of problems. You might be trying, for example, to run an action against an image that's in a mode that doesn't support the steps the action is trying to execute. You should walk through the action with the dialogs turned on or place stops along the way to help you debug the action.

Q What do I need to do to save an action I've created?

A Choose Save Actions from the Actions palette menu.

Q Is it possible to edit actions? If so, how?

A Yes. You can insert and remove steps from an action. To insert steps, choose Insert Menu Item from the Actions palette menu. To delete a step, simply drag it onto the small trash can icon at the bottom of the Actions palette.

18

Workshop

The next section is a quick quiz about the chapter you have just read. If you have any problems answering any of the questions in the quiz, see the section directly following it for all the answers.

Quiz

1. What is an action?

2. How do you access the Actions palette?

3. How do you install an action?

4. How do you name an action?

5. How do you run a batch-processing action?

Quiz Answers

1. An action is a recorded set of steps that can be applied against an image to create an effect or change the image in some way.

2. Choose Window, Show Actions.

3. Place the action in a folder on your hard drive and choose Load Actions from the Actions palette menu. From within the dialog box, browse to the location of the action file and click Load.

4. You can name an action anything you'd like. You should choose something descriptive, of course. When you first start the recording process for a new action, Photoshop asks you to name the action.

5. Choose File, Automate, Batch, and, in the Batch dialog box, select the action and the folder you'd like to run it against.

DAY 19

Compositing Two or More Images into One

One of Photoshop's biggest strengths is its capability to combine two or more images into a single image. This chapter will show you a couple of techniques that you can put to use. You'll be able to create beautiful collages from your photographs, and you'll be able to create believable photo-montage images that can only be done with the help of digital processing. This chapter covers the following:

- Understanding the difference between a collage and a montage
- Creating a collage from three separate photos
- Creating a photo montage

Collages and Montages—What's the Difference?

Although the two terms, collage and montage, have been somewhat blurred together by people discussing the subject as it relates to digital art, they really are separate and quite different.

Collages refer to a collection of items from different sources. Remember when you were in school and the teacher had you create a collage out of bits of paper, scraps of cloth and string, and maybe some shells? What you were creating was a collage. When I discuss collages in this chapter, I'll be discussing the process of compositing, or layering, several images with the intent that the images will still look as if they were meant to be separate. They may share a common theme (or not), but the viewer won't think that the image is anything other than a composition.

A montage, on the other hand, is created in such a way as to fool the viewer into believing that the composite image was not manipulated in any way. In other words, a montage is a digitally altered set of photographs that looks as though it was not created or manipulated. For example, you may have always wanted a photo of yourself in front of the Eiffel Tower. Well, now you can have it without visiting France. I'll show you how to accomplish this effect later in this chapter. In other words, a digitally altered set of photographs that looks as though it is a result of a single exposure could be a considered a montage.

Creating a Collage

To create the following collage, or any collage for that matter, with Photoshop, you'll need to exercise some of the skills you learned in the previous chapters. You'll need to make and feather selections, create and manipulate layers, and maybe even add a mask or two.

If you want to follow along, open up the image Flowers.psd from the day19 folder on the CD-ROM that accompanies this book (see Figure 19.1). You also need to open the Wedding1.psd and Wedding2.psd files from the same folder, as shown in Figures 19.2 and 19.3.

FIGURE 19.1

Flowers.psd.

FIGURE 19.2

Wedding1.psd.

19

Figure 19.1 is a photograph I took of the flowers that my Mom made for my baby sister's wedding. Figures 19.2 and 19.3 are photographs from my wife's and my tenth wedding anniversary (our original wedding photos were accidentally destroyed when the photographer opened the camera without rewinding the film).

FIGURE 19.3

Wedding2.psd.

Notice how there is a good amount of space available in the corners of the photo of the flowers. This space can be put to good use. It's quite easy to squeeze a couple of images into the corners and still have the flowers remain visible.

1. To get started, select the Lasso tool and drag a selection around the figures in the photo, Wedding1 (see Figure 19.4). It doesn't have to be perfect or exclude the background. It just has to include the figures. If you want to save time, the selection has already been made and saved with the PSD image.

2. To see the selection, open the Channels palette. To load the selection, choose Select, Load Selection and click OK in the dialog box that pops up.

3. After you've made the selection, choose Select, Feather and enter 10 for the Feather Radius value in the Feather dialog box.

4. Choose Edit, Copy to copy the selection.

5. Make the Flowers image current by clicking its title bar.

6. Choose Edit, Paste to paste the figures from Wedding1 into the Flowers photo.

FIGURE 19.4

Wedding1.psd with a selection.

7. Use Ctrl (or Command on a Mac) and the mouse to move the copied figures into the lower left corner of the Flowers photo (see Figure 19.5).

FIGURE 19.5

Copied selection from Wedding1.psd pasted into Flowers.psd.

19

The figures are a little large and they're covering more of the flowers than I like. This is easy to correct, though.

8. Choose Edit, Transform, Scale. You'll see a bounding box appear as in Figure 19.6.

FIGURE **19.6**

Composite image with the Scale bounding box visible.

9. Move the mouse over one of the corners of the bounding box and you'll be able to click and drag the bounding box to resize the image. You'll know you're in position when the mouse cursor changes to a small diagonal line with arrows at both ends.

   When you're satisfied with the new size, you can press the Enter key (the Return key on a Mac) or double-click with the mouse inside the bounding box to finalize the resizing process. If during the process you change your mind, you can abort by pressing the Esc key.

Tip

> You can constrain the resizing to keep the proper ratio of height to width by holding down the Shift key as you move the mouse.

10. Once you've got the size right, you may want to reposition the image. To do so, simply press the Ctrl key (Command key on a Mac) and click and drag the figures into position. You can see my result in Figure 19.7.

Adding a Selection from the Second Photo

You can repeat the process with the second wedding photo. Again I've saved the selection along with the image to save you time. You can, if you choose, make your own selection, though. My selection is visible in Figure 19.8.

FIGURE 19.7

First wedding image in place.

FIGURE 19.8

Selection made on second wedding image.

19

You may notice that I'm not being overly careful with my selections. There's no need to be because you can make any adjustments you'll need once the images are pasted, resized, and properly placed.

1. With the selection made, choose Select, Feather and enter 10 for the Feather Radius value.

2. Choose Edit, Copy to make the flowers image current and choose Edit, Paste to paste the second wedding photo onto the flowers photo.

3. Choose Edit, Transform, Scale and scale the image to fit in with the rest of the collage.

4. When you're satisfied with the size, press Enter (Return on a Mac) and move the layer into place by pressing and holding the Ctrl key (the Command key on a Mac) while click and dragging the layer into position with the mouse. As you can see from Figure 19.9, we're almost done.

FIGURE 19.9

Second wedding image in place.

Smoothing the Selections

There is a little cleanup that needs to be done, though. If you used my selections instead of making your own (and even with your own), you'll notice some small white marks along the bottom of the first wedding photo. To get rid of these, follow the steps below:

1. Select the Eraser tool, and in the Eraser Options palette set the tool to Paintbrush. This enables you to use feathered brushes.

2. Make sure that you're working on the proper layer by selecting it in the Layers palette (click the layer title in the Layers palette).

> **Note**
>
> Another method for selecting specific layers is to right-click the area of the image with the Move tool active (or Ctrl-right-clicking the area). This displays a menu of all layers showing in that area, and the name can be selected and made active. On the Mac, Ctrl-Command-clicking the image area accomplishes the same thing.

3. Select a small feathered brush and move the cursor over the small white marks until they disappear.

4. At the same time, you might want to have a little more of the pink flower show up behind my shoulder. Again, to do so just erase the area you want to have the lower layer show through.

   Remember you don't have to be too exact. This is a collage and you expect people to know that there are several composited images here. The results of my working on the layer with the first wedding photo are seen in Figure 19.10.

FIGURE 19.10

First wedding image touched up.

19

4. To complete the work on the second pasted image, make its layer current by clicking its title in the Layers palette, and use the Eraser tool to remove some of the excess image.

Remove only what you think is necessary to balance the whole image. Again, you don't have to be exact, just get a pleasing look and composition. Mostly I just wanted to smooth out the rougher edges of the original selection and allow a little more of the white flower to show through as seen in Figure 18.11.

FIGURE 19.11

Second wedding image touched up.

5. Now decrease the opacity of the Eraser tool to around 80% (you can adjust this setting in the Eraser Options palette). This adds a bit of a softer look in the areas that I worked on, although I had to go over a couple of areas more than once to erase enough of the layer.

Adding Text to the Image

As a final touch, let's add some text to the composited image.

1. Select the Type tool and click anywhere in the image to bring up the Type Tool dialog box.

2. Set the text color to white (because this is a fairly dark image and you want the text to show up well).

3. Select a script font like Brush Script MT or, if it's available, the font I chose, which is Bradley Hand ITC.

4. Set the size to 30 points and type in Our Wedding.

5. Move the type into position in the upper-left corner and click OK to clear the dialog box.

6. You should have a finished collage that resembles the one shown in Figure 19.12.

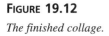

FIGURE 19.12

The finished collage.

With the skills you've learned so far, you should now be able to easily create your own collages. The necessary skills include selections, layers, masks (which I didn't use on this image), and color correction (if you want the images to blend a little more).

Creating believable montages is a little trickier and more demanding of your skills as well, but it is well within your grasp at this point. In the next section I'll demonstrate how to create a montage.

Creating a Montage

When working with montages, as opposed to collages, there are more things to be aware of if your montage is to be believable. You must consider at the very least film grain, lighting, focus, color, and scale.

If you're trying to create special effects, you might also need to consider camera angles and other variables that will help your final image, no matter how fantastic, be believable. The example I'll demonstrate is fairly simple but still requires some attention to detail.

You'll need to create a much more exacting selection here than with the collage exercise. The placement of the figure and its scale in regards to the background are more crucial to the effect in this exercise. The final result, though, will be worth the extra effort.

In this exercise, you'll take a studio portrait and turn it into a location shot. All you'll need, besides your newly-found Photoshop skills, are the two photos ToughGuy.psd and Graffiti.psd, both of which are included on the CD-ROM in the folder day19.

19

To get started, open both of these images in Photoshop. Figure 19.13 is a self-portrait of yours truly created for a darkroom exercise, and Figure 19.14 was shot on location in downtown Montreal. I've been wanting to composite these two images for some time and finally dug them out of hiding for this very chapter.

FIGURE **19.13**

Tough Guy.

To create the illusion that these two images were actually shot as one photo, it is necessary to make a good selection around the photo of the dude in the leather jacket. Because this was originally a studio shot with a solid colored background, this won't be too difficult.

I've saved the image as a layered PSD file with two selections saved in two separate channels. If you'd like to re-create these selections, though, you can do as I did.

1. To create the initial selection, use the Magic Wand tool set at its defaults (Tolerance 32 and Anti-aliased on).

2. Click the background to get a selection similar to the one you see in Figure 19.15.

FIGURE 19.14
Graffiti.

FIGURE 19.15

The initial selection of Tough Guy made with the default Magic Wand tool.

19

3. With this selection made, switch to Quick Mask mode by clicking the Quick Mask Mode icon on the toolbox.

4. In Quick Mask mode, it's quite easy to clean up the selection made by the Magic Wand.

Note — I suggest leaving the shadow selected with the figure because you may want to use both elements in another composition.

Some areas to watch out for with the selections in this photo are around the ears and between the legs. You might also want to check around the hair, as this can always be a problem area. Fortunately, I was having a decent hair day when I took that shot.

You'll notice that the area between the legs wasn't selected along with the rest of the background. Neither were the areas between the arms and the body. You can select the area between the legs when in Quick Mask mode because, with the shadows, the areas between the arms and the body weren't going to matter too much in this particular composition.

In Quick Mask mode, you can paint with white to add to the selection and paint with black to remove from the selection. It's easy to go back and forth between the two colors as you create and refine the mask. Once you're satisfied, you can switch back to Standard editing mode.

5. With the figure and the shadow selected, save the selection by choosing Select, Save Selection. I saved the figure and the shadow selection as Me and Shadow.

   Next go back to Quick Mask mode and remove the shadow from the selection and save it. I saved this second selection (me without the shadow) as Me.

   These two selections stay with the file as long as it's saved as a native PSD file.

   With the second selection completed, create a new layer and copy the selection from the original layer and paste it in into its own layer. This isn't necessary, but it makes it much quicker to grab the selection. All you need to do is Ctrl-click (Command-click on a Mac) the layer title to get the whole selection in one quick move. This adds to the final size of the image, though, so you might want to discard this layer when you're done. It can be re-created quickly due to the fact that the selection is saved in a channel.

6. With the figure selected (not with the shadow added), choose Select, Feather and enter a value of 3 for the Feather Radius. If you're following along but with your own images, you may need to adjust this value. The two images I'm using for this exercise are at 300 dpi. If you're using smaller resolution images, you may need to choose a smaller radius.

7. Click OK and choose Edit, Copy.

8. Make the Graffiti image current by clicking its title bar and choose Edit Paste. This pastes the figure into the Graffiti image (see Figure 19.16).

FIGURE 19.16

Tough Guy selection pasted into Graffiti image.

9. You'll notice, of course, that this has pasted me smack in the middle of the Graffiti image. It's a simple matter to move me (or rather the figure) into place. To do so, hold down the Ctrl key (the Command key on a Mac) and then click and drag the figure into place.

10. You'll want to hide the fact that the legs don't reach the bottom of the image by moving the figure down. You should also go for a good composition by moving the figure towards one side of the center. I chose the left side of the photo for no particular reason (see Figure 19.17).

19

It's not as though I was trying to make sure that the Eiffel Tower showed up well behind the figure. This particular composition leaves a lot of leeway for you the artist. In fact, you may find that the composition makes more sense to you by placing the figure towards the right. Heck, with the image saved in the PSD format and preserving the layers, you can always change your mind and go back anyway.

Adding Realism to the Montage

To help with the illusion, it's possible to partially blur a portion of the background. This gives the illusion that the photo was taken with a longer lens. The foreground and the figure are in focus, while the wall, being further away, is slightly out of focus.

FIGURE 19.17

Tough Guy selection moved into a better position compositionally.

To accomplish this, make the background layer current and draw a loose selection around the foreground, which should contain the bricks to the right and some of the foreground at the left. Inverse the selection with Select, Inverse to select the wall (see Figure 19.18).

FIGURE 19.18

Wall selected from the background.

You'll notice that I turned off the layer that contains the figure. This was done to make creating the selection easier. You might want to save this selection because you may need it still. To do so, choose Select, Save Selection and name the selection Wall.

You can now apply a light blur. Choose Filter, Blur, Gaussian Blur and enter a value of 2 for the radius.

There's still some work to be done with this image. Because it's a black-and-white composite, there's no need for color correction, but I find that the figure seems a little pasted-in. I think that some brightness and contrast adjustments are called for:

1. Make the figure layer active by clicking its title bar in the Layers palette.
2. Choose Image, Adjust, Brightness/Contrast. I set the brightness to +12 and the contrast to –21 to get the image you see in Figure 19.19.

Note

> Note that the Levels option gives you much more control of the brightness and contrast adjustments. For this image, it's fairly easy to make the adjustments using the Brightness/Contrast option, but you should play around with the Levels option as well to become more accustomed to how it works. The Curve option can also be used to adjust the contrast of specific portions of an image. Although more complex than Levels, this feature is even more powerful. For more on Levels and Curves, refer back to Day 16, "Correcting the Color."

FIGURE 19.19

Brightness and contrast adjusted on the figure to help it blend more realistically with the background.

19

Looks pretty good. Just one more thing. I hope you took my advice and saved the wall selection. I think that the foreground needs a little blur as well.

1. Load the selection by choosing Select, Load Selection and choosing the Wall selection from the dialog box.

2. Because this is a selection of the wall and you want the foreground, choose Select, Inverse.

3. Apply a Gaussian blur (choose Filter, Blur, Gaussian Blur) of 1.0.

That should do it. The final result is shown in Figure 19.20. What do you think?

FIGURE 19.20

Final "Tough Guy on Location" composite.

This was a fairly easy example. There were no major lighting problems, the images were in black and white (actually the studio portrait was in black and white and I converted the color Graffiti image into black and white for this composition), and the scale of the two images matched up pretty well. Of course, I had this composition in mind when I originally shot these images. Just as working in a darkroom makes you view things differently through your viewfinder, you may find that the digital darkroom of Photoshop can do the same.

Summary

Believe it or not, you've just learned some of the tricks and techniques that are used to create some of the most spectacular effects you see on television and in the movies. The techniques used in today's exercises are just the beginning of what you can accomplish with Photoshop. You can use your new skills to create collages, compositions, and montages that can bring your level of digital art skills to a new high.

I recommend you practice the basics of selection and image correction to the point where you won't even believe what your own eyes see after you've created a composite. With a little practice you'll be able to create almost any image you can imagine.

Q&A

Q Is it necessary to consider image resolution when compositing images? Why?

A Yes, because a monitor runs at a fixed resolution. Any difference in resolution between images results in size differences when you lay one image over another.

Q What can you do if the shadows are different on the images you're compositing?

q This depends on what the differences are and how extensive they are. If the shadow is on one side in one image and on the other side in the other, you might consider flipping one image horizontally. An alternative would be to use masks and adjust the images, but this can be a long and tedious process. This might be the only option available if the shadows are too different.

Workshop

The next section is a quick quiz about the chapter you have just read. If you have any problems answering any of the questions in the quiz, see the section directly following it for all the answers.

19

Quiz

1. What is a collage?
2. What is a montage?
3. How do you keep the selection proportional when resizing it?
4. How do you apply a Gaussian blur to an image?
5. How do you adjust the brightness and contrast of an image?

Quiz Answers

1. A collage is a collection of varying images combined into one final image.
2. A montage is a collection of images intended to fool the viewer into believing that the image was created with a single exposure.

3. Hold down the Shift key to keep the scaling constrained.

4. Choose Filter, Blur, Gaussian Blur.

5. You can use the Brightness/Contrast option (choose Image, Adjust, Brightness/Contrast), the Levels option (choose Image, Adjust, Levels), or the Curves option (choose Image, Adjust, Curves).

WEEK 3

DAY 20

Adding All Kinds of Special Effects

By now you're well aware of the power Photoshop has when it comes to correcting and manipulating photographs. What you may, or may not, be aware of, though, is the fact that Photoshop is capable of creating all kinds of special effects. Everything from the ubiquitous drop shadow to natural and maybe even unnatural textures. Today I'll demonstrate how you can use Photoshop to add some neat effects to your images and cover the following topics:

- Creating wood textures
- Creating brush metal textures and buttons
- Adding drop shadows and variations thereof
- Applying Glow filters

Creating a Wooden Texture

I'll bet you weren't aware that Photoshop could create wooden textures, right? Actually it's quite easy to do. There are a couple of tricks out there for creating a wooden texture, and this is the one I came up with. It uses a couple of the built-in filters (no extras needed) and creates a pretty good simulated wood texture.

1. Open a new 400×200, 72 dpi, RGB image with the contents set to white.
2. Set the default foreground/background colors by pressing the D key.
3. Choose Filter, Texture, Craquelure.
4. Set the Crack Spacing to 15, the Crack Depth to 6, the Crack Brightness to 6, and click OK. You should end up with something similar to Figure 20.1.

FIGURE 20.1

Craquelure texture added to a new image.

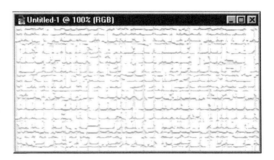

5. Choose Select, All and then choose Edit, Cut. You'll be left with the original white image.
6. Open the Channels palette and add a new channel by clicking the Create a New Channel icon at the bottom of the channel.
7. Choose Edit, Paste to paste the texture into the new channel.
8. Choose Select, Deselect.
9. Choose Filter, Blur, Motion Blur and set the direction to 0 and the Distance to 10 pixels. This gives you a texture that starts to resemble wood (see Figure 20.2).

This texture is actually used as a Bump map for the Lighting filter. To get a better effect, you should change the contrast. As it is now, the contrast is a little too low.

10. Choose Image, Adjust, Brightness/Contrast. You can bump the contrast up quite high. I used a value of +80 to get the image you see in Figure 20.3. You can really see the texture coming through now.

FIGURE 20.2

The texture with the Motion blur effect added.

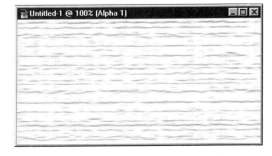

FIGURE 20.3

The texture with contrast adjusted.

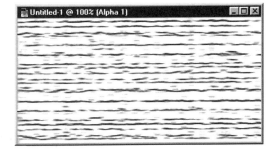

11. Open the Layers palette and click the layer's title bar to activate the layer.

12. Click the foreground color swatch to bring up the Color Picker.

13. Choose a nice medium brown color. The color I chose is R:164, G:108, and B:0.

14. Click OK.

15. Press Ctrl+Backspace (Command+Backspace on a Mac) to fill the layer with the brown color.

16. Choose Filter, Render, Lighting Effects to bring up the Lighting Effects dialog box (see Figure 20.4).

17. You'll notice an oval in the preview window on the left. This oval signifies the light that's shining on your image. You can change the shape and the direction of the light by dragging the handles that you see on the oval. You should first reposition the light so that is shines from the upper left.

18. Drag the handle that has a line connecting it to the center of the image up towards the upper-left corner of the preview window. You should also drag the oval outwards a little so that the light covers the whole image as well (see Figure 20.5).

20

FIGURE 20.4

Lighting Effects dialog box.

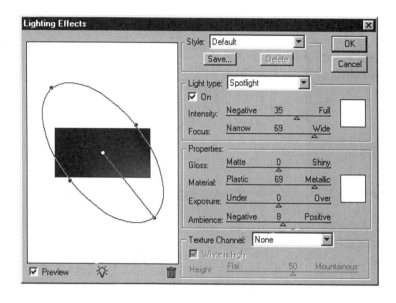

FIGURE 20.5

Lighting Effects dialog box with the light direction and size adjusted.

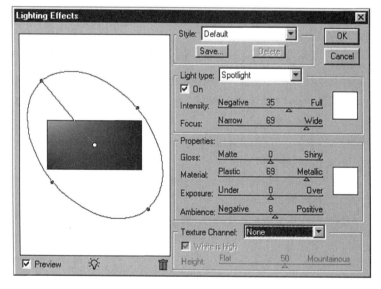

19. Click the pulldown menu next to the Texture channel and select the alpha channel you created. The other settings are not too important, and you can probably get away with the defaults for now (use the settings you see in Figure 20.5). Later on, when creating your own effects, you might want to experiment with these different settings because they can really change the effects you get.

20. Click OK to apply the Lighting filter and you should end up with something that resembles Figure 20.6.

FIGURE 20.6

Wooden texture.

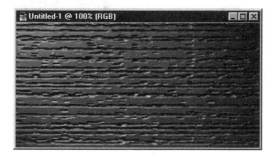

You may find that this texture still needs some adjusting. For example, I lowered the contrast to –30 by choosing Image, Adjust, Brightness/Contrast and entering –30 for the Contrast.

You can also change the color using the Variations option (Image, Adjust, Variations). I added blue twice and Darker once to get the image you see in Figure 20.7.

FIGURE 20.7

Wooden texture with the contrast, brightness, and color cast adjusted.

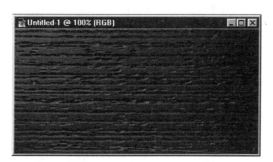

If you feel that the actual texture is not quite right, you can still change it a little as well. In Figure 20.8, I applied the Ripple filter (Filters, Distort, Ripple) with an Amount of 100 and a Size of Medium.

It's as easy as that to create a wooden texture. Now by playing with the variations, the brightness, and contrast, and maybe adding a Ripple effect, you can get dozens of different wood textures.

20

FIGURE 20.8

*Wooden texture with a
slight ripple added.*

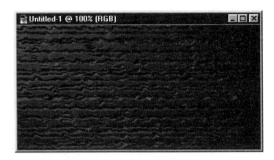

Creating Brushed Metal

This is one of the first effects I ever played with in Photoshop. I have seen it done several other ways, including one variation by Kai Krause, the founder of Metatools and legendary Mac Photoshop guru. I couldn't get his version to work the first time I tried it and I chalked it up to the fact that we were using different versions of Photoshop on different platforms.

At one point, I later decided I needed a brushed metal effect for an image I was working on and I came up with this method. I subsequently wrote an online tutorial that demonstrates how to use this method to create a metal plate with screws in the corners. It has quickly become one of the most popular online tutorials I've written.

1. To create the brushed metal, open a new 400x200, 72 dpi, RGB image with the content set to white.
2. Choose Filter, Noise, Add Noise.
3. In the Add Noise dialog box, set the Amount to 150, the Distribution to Gaussian, and place a check mark in the Monochrome option.
4. Click OK to fill the image with the monochrome noise (see Figure 20.9).

FIGURE 20.9

*Monochromatic,
Gaussian noise added
to a new image.*

5. Choose Filter, Blur, Motion Blur and set Direction to –45 and Distance to 15 pixels or so. This gives you a nice brushed metal texture as seen in Figure 20.10.

FIGURE 20.10

Brushed metal texture.

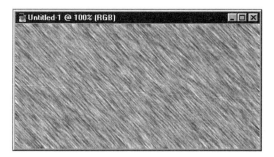

At first glance, this texture may seem a little simple, but it is a great basis for all kinds of great metal textures. By laying this very texture (with the opacity lowered) over a chrome effect created with Eye Candy, I created the metallic texture for the current image map at my Web site, GrafX Design (see Figure 20.11).

FIGURE 20.11

Brushed metal texture used on the GrafX Design navigational image map.

This image has sparked a lot of interest from visitors to the site, and I've received many emails asking how it was done. Now you know.

Creating Brushed Metal Buttons

This texture would also be great for buttons on a Web site. It's easy to cut different sections out and use them as buttons. Using the built-in Layer effects, this can be accomplished in mere minutes. Try this:

1. Select the Rectangular Marquee tool and crop a rectangle out of the texture image.
2. Choose Edit, Copy.
3. Choose File, New and click OK in the New dialog box.
4. Choose Edit, Paste to paste the selection into the new image.
5. Choose Layer, Effects, Bevel and Emboss.

20

6. Set the Style to Inner Bevel and the Depth to 15.

7. Click OK.

Voila! Instant metallic button (see Figure 20.12).

FIGURE 20.12

*Brushed metal texture
used to create a
button.*

This button can be used for all sorts of things. It can, of course, be used on a Web page, but it could also be used for multimedia presentations or for navigating a PDF file. All you need to do is add some text.

Creating Drop Shadows

Ah, the ubiquitous shadow. When I first started writing online tutorials for imaging programs, I saw dozens of requests for this effect daily. The requests have died down some but not disappeared. This effect is still so popular that Adobe shipped an action for it in version 4 and has now added a built-in filter to create it in version 5.

That aside, if you'd like to know how to create this effect yourself, this is how it's done. I'll demonstrate how to accomplish this effect with text, but it can be done with any object on a layer.

1. Open a new 400×200, 72 dpi, RGB image with the contents set to White.

2. Add some text to the image using any color but black.

3. Choose Layer, Type, Render Layer to render the text.

4. Drag the Text layer (by dragging its title bar in the Layers palette) onto the Create New Layer icon at the bottom of the Layers palette. You'll now have two copies of the text as well as a bottom layer.

5. Click the bottom most layer to make it active.

6. Press the D key to set the default black-and-white foreground/background colors.

7. Click the Preserve Transparency option in the Layers palette.

8. Press Ctrl+Backspace (Command+Backspace on a Mac) to fill the bottom text with black.

9. Click the Preserve Transparency to toggle it off.

10. Choose Filter, Blur, Gaussian Blur and set the Radius to 3 or so.

11. Press Ctrl+down arrow three times (Command+down arrow on a Mac) and Ctrl+right arrow three times (Command+right arrow on a Mac). You should have text with a nice soft drop shadow as in Figure 20.13.

FIGURE 20.13

Text with a drop shadow.

Creating a Variation of the Drop Shadow

If you, like many other artists, feel that the drop shadow has been overused (or even abused), you can try this variation. The following look has become popular in magazines and television ads lately.

1. With the file still open from the previous drop shadow exercise, make the actual Text layer active.
2. Ctrl+click (Command+click on a Mac) to select all the text.
3. Press D to set the default black/white foreground/background colors.
4. Press Ctrl+Backspace (Command+Backspace on a Mac) to fill the text with white. Now you'll have ghostly white text visible only because of its drop shadow (see Figure 20.14).

FIGURE 20.14

White text on white with a drop shadow.

Creating Perspective (Cast) Shadows

There are other alternatives to drop shadows that help lend a little dimensionality to your images without overusing the drop shadow. With Photoshop, it's relatively easy to create cast shadows as well. This technique makes use of the Transform options in Photoshop.

1. Open a new 400×200 RGB image at 72 dpi with the contents set to white.
2. Choose a foreground color other than black and use the Type tool to enter some text. The text should fit in the lower left-hand corner of the image (see Figure 20.15).

20

FIGURE 20.15

Text on a white background.

3. Render the type by choosing Layer, Type, Render Layer.

4. Drag the Type layer (by its title bar in the Layers palette) and drop it onto the Create New Layer icon at the bottom of the Layers palette.

5. Click the first Type layer's title bar in the Layers palette to make it current (it's the first one above the Background layer, in other words, the first Type layer you created).

6. Place a check mark in the Preserve Transparency option.

7. Press D to set the default white/black foreground/background colors.

8. Press Alt+Backspace (Option+Backspace on a Mac) to fill the text with black.

9. Choose Edit, Transform, Skew. This draws a bounding box around the text (see Figure 20.16).

FIGURE 20.16

Transform bounding box surrounding the text.

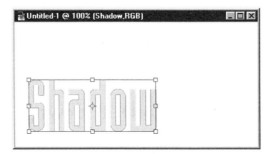

10. Click and drag the small square in the middle of the top of the bounding box way over to the right (see Figure 20.17). When you're satisfied with the placement of the shadow, press Enter (Return on a Mac) to complete the transformation.

11. You might want to scale the shadow down a little. To do so, choose Edit, Transform, Scale and drag the top-center square down a little (see Figure 20.18). Again, when you're satisfied with the change, press Enter (Return) or double-click within the bounding box to complete the transformation.

FIGURE 20.17

Text shadow skewed to appear as a cast shadow.

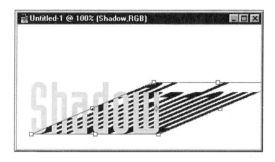

FIGURE 20.18

The text shadow scaled down a little.

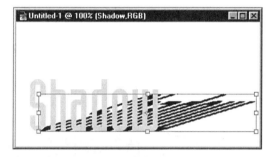

For the final touch, the shadow should fade as it retreats. To have it do so, add a Layer mask.

12. Choose Layer, Add Layer Mask, Reveal All.

13. Press D to set the default black/white foreground/background colors.

14. Select the Linear Gradient tool and, in the Linear Gradient Options palette, set the Gradient to Foreground to Background, the Opacity to 100%, and the Blend mode to Normal.

15. Place the cursor near the top of the shadow text and, while holding the Shift key, click and drag the mouse down until the cursor is at the bottom of the text. You'll now have a nice blending effect with the shadow appearing to disappear (see Figure 20.19).

Glowing Effects

As a change to the drop shadow, you might want to have a Glow effect.

1. Open a new 400×200 RGB image at 72 dpi with the contents set to White.

2. Press D to set the default black/white foreground/background colors.

20

FIGURE 20.19

Shadow blending into the background in the distance.

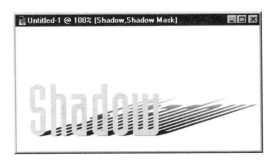

3. Press Alt+Backspace (Option+Backspace on a Mac) to fill the image with black.

4. Set the foreground color to a bright green. To do so, click the foreground color swatch in the toolbox to bring up the Color Picker dialog box. From there you can select a color.

5. Select the Type tool and enter some text. As a bit of a parody on a popular television show, I entered the text X-filters (see Figure 20.20).

FIGURE 20.20

Green text on black.

6. Render the Text layer by choosing Layer, Type, Render, Layer.

7. To add a little variety, and to further the parody, choose Filter, Distort, Ripple.

8. Set the Amount to 100, the Size to medium, and click OK. The text will now be all rippled (see Figure 20.21).

9. Click and drag the Type layer onto the Create a New Layer icon to duplicate the Type layer.

10. Ctrl+click (Command+click on a Mac) the new layer to select the text.

11. Press D to set the default foreground/background colors.

12. Press Alt+Backspace (Option+Backspace on a Mac) to fill the top layer of text with black.

FIGURE 20.21

Rippled green text on black.

13. Choose Select, Deselect.

14. Make the lower layer of text current by clicking its title bar in the Layers palette.

15. Choose Filter, Blur, Gaussian Blur and enter 6.0 or so for the Radius. You should end up with text that resembles Figure 20.22 (and the title screen of a certain television show).

FIGURE 20.22

Glowing-green text on black.

Summary

The techniques demonstrated in this chapter don't even begin to scratch the surface of what can be done with Photoshop. Many online tutorials can further show you how to create lightning, flaming text, interfaces, and much more. There is also a steadily growing list of Photoshop books that demonstrate many of these same techniques as well as others. Once you've completed this book and you feel comfortable working with Photoshop, you might want to check out some of the Web sites and books devoted to Photoshop.

20

Q&A

Q Is there a "Glow filter" out there somewhere that I can use in place of the Ripple and Gaussian Blur filters?

A Yes. In fact, one is included in the Layer Effects, and Alien Skin's Eye Candy has a good one as well.

Q What exactly does rendering do to an image?

A If you mean the Render, Lighting Effects, it enables you to add Lighting effects to an image. This filter can be used to give your images a 3D appearance.

Workshop

The next section is a quick quiz about the chapter you have just read. If you have any problems answering any of the questions in the quiz, see the section directly following it for all the answers.

Quiz

1. How do you access the Lighting Effects dialog box?
2. How do you bevel and emboss an image?
3. How do you render type?
4. How do you create a perspective shadow?
5. How do you access the Ripple filter?

Quiz Answers

1. Choose Filter, Render, Lighting Effects.
2. Choose Layer, Effects, Bevel and Emboss.
3. After creating your type, choose Layer, Type, Render Layer.
4. There is an action included (Cast Shadow) with Photoshop 5 that adds a perspective shadow. Alternatively, if you own Alien Skin's Eye Candy, you can use the Perspective shadow filter, or you can follow the steps outlined in this chapter.
5. Choose Filter, Distort, Ripple.

WEEK 3

DAY 21

Preparing Your Art for the Web

Open any Photoshop or imaging software book today and you'll find at least one chapter devoted to Web graphics. Most, if not all, graphics programs have been updated to offer at least some Web-specific features, and Photoshop is no different. Photoshop is extremely good at helping you create awesome images for your Web pages. In this chapter, you'll learn how to use Photoshop to create great Web graphics and how to do the following:

- Understand the GIF and JPEG file formats
- Create seamless textures
- Create counters to record the number of visitors to your site

Understanding Web File Formats

For now, until PNG becomes available under most browsers, you can use two formats for your Web graphics. They are JPG (really JPEG, for Joint Photographic Experts Group) and GIF (Graphical Interchange Format). Both of these formats or compression methods have their strong and their weak points.

The JPG Format

The JPG format yields a really good compression ratio, but it does so at a cost. This cost is that it discards some of the information that makes up an image. At the lower compression ratios, this is hardly noticeable to the human eye. If, however, the compression ratio is set too high, the image quality deteriorates. An editing, resaving, re-editing, and resaving cycle also deteriorates the image quality, as more and more of the original image's information is discarded with each subsequent saving.

Used properly, though, the JPG format can give good results with great compression ratios. This format should be used mainly for real-world images such as photographs and for images with smooth, continuous tone gradients. JPGs support 24-bit color and 8-bit grayscale.

When you choose to save an image with the JPG format from within Photoshop, you'll get the JPEG Options dialog box (see Figure 21.1).

FIGURE 21.1

JPEG Options dialog box.

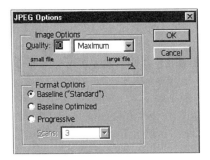

Within this dialog box, you can set the quality. A lower number gives you a higher compression and a poorer quality image, whereas the higher settings yield a larger image with better quality. You can also choose to select the Baseline ("Standard"), Optimized, or Progressive format. The Optimized baseline optimizes the color quality of the image over the Standard baseline. The Progressive format enables the image to be displayed progressively. What this means is that the entire image appears rather blurred an becomes more clear as it loads. This format is used sometimes on the Web to give viewers an idea of what the image will look like without having to wait for the entire image to download.

Exporting GIFs

Although a GIF image can contain only a maximum of 256 colors (less if you choose to use the browser-safe palettes), it has other attributes that make it a good choice for Web graphics. GIFs support transparency, which means that you can decide to have one specific color not display. This allows the background to show through your image and frees you from having all images display as rectangular.

Note   The only real way to get a handle on which settings provide you with the best size and quality options is to play around. Simply take an image and save it with different settings and options to see how these affect the overall size and quality of the image. Just remember that there will always be a trade-off between size and quality. For each image, you have to decide where to compromise.

GIF images also support multiple frames, which means that you can create animations and save them as GIF images. Virtually all browsers support animated GIFs, meaning that everyone will be able to see your animations without the use of special plug-ins. Animated GIFs are relatively easy to create as well and can be created with inexpensive software.

To save a Photoshop image as a GIF file, you can choose File, Export, GIF89a Export. If you attempt this without first converting the image to Indexed mode, however, you won't be able to use all the GIF89a features, such as transparency.

To properly export a GIF image, complete the following steps:

1. Choose Image, Mode, Indexed. If your image contains multiple layers or channels, you'll first be asked if Photoshop should flatten the image. If you want to save the layers and channels, you should first save a backup copy of the file in PSD format.

2. Once you've backed up the image, choose Image, Mode, Indexed again. This brings up the Indexed Color dialog box (see Figure 21.2). You can use the options in this dialog box to select the Palette and the Dithering options.

FIGURE 21.2

The Indexed Color dialog box

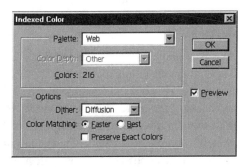

3. Choose File, Export, GIF89a Export to bring up the GIF89a Export Options dialog box (see Figure 21.3). Within this dialog box you can see the palette and a real-time preview of the image. Choose the interlace setting, and select a color that will be displayed as transparent. To choose a transparent color, select the Eyedropper tool and click the color in the Preview window.

21

FIGURE 21.3

*The GIF89a Export
Options dialog box.*

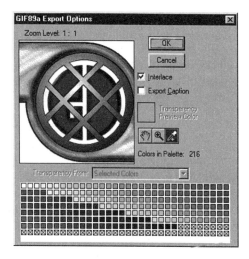

GIF images are good for line art and images with abrupt color changes or images with few colors. GIF is not a good choice for real-world images such as photographs and images with smooth continuous gradients.

Some Common Web Graphic Techniques

There are many types of Web graphics: buttons, bars, backgrounds, counters, and many more. In fact, there are so many techniques that several books have been written on this subject alone. Rather than try to cover all the ins-and-outs of Web graphics, I'll demonstrate a couple of useful techniques to get you started and point you toward a few Web sites where you can pick up a couple more hints.

Using Backgrounds

When I first started putting Web graphics tutorials online, I had an embossed background on the pages. I received several emails telling me that the text was hard to read because of the background. Subsequently, I lowered the contrast of the background image and I still received email. I then changed the background altogether, which seemed to work. When I moved the tutorials to their new virtual domain, however, I decided to get rid of the background and have never regretted the choice. This is not to say that backgrounds don't or can't work. I've seen backgrounds used to good effect on many Web sites.

Placing a background image on your Web pages is simply a matter of adding backg="filename.ext" to the <BODY> tag in your HTML. The keyword background uses the file "filename.ext," where "filename" is the name of your background image and "ext" is the file extension—which must be either GIF or JPG—as a background image on your page.

You can use any GIF or JPG image you'd like. There are some design-imposed rules you should consider, though. Like other images, you don't want the file size to be too large. You also don't want the background to detract from the content of your pages.

The Principles Behind Creating Seamless Tiles

One of the most basic rules of Web design is to keep the size of your graphics as small as possible, but when using a graphic for your background, a large file size is almost inevitable. Enter the seamless tile—a great way to create a beautiful background that takes up a small amount of K.

A seamless tile is an image that when tiled or repeated forms a seamless pattern. This means that you can use a relatively small image file that tiles itself on your Web page. Both Scott and Doc's background images are seamless tiles. The object, of course, is to get the sides to match up so that the smaller tile appears to be one large image when it's placed on your pages.

Before going on to show how to create a seamless tile with some of the various paint programs, I'll explain the basic principles involved. Demonstrating this is easier than trying to explain it, so bear with me a few paragraphs.

Suppose you have an image that you want to tile and suppose it's square (this works just as well if the image is a rectangle, but we'll use a square for demonstration purposes). What you want to do is swap the diagonal quarters of the image (I told you this was hard to explain). To get a better idea of what I'm talking about, let's look at a diagram (see Figure 21.4).

What we need to do is cut the image into quarters and swap the diagonal corners. Once we've moved the pieces, the image should resemble Figure 21.5. Moving the corners can be done in a variety of ways, depending on the program you're using.

The reason this works is kind of hard to see, but what's being done is that we're cutting the image and rearranging it so that the edges formed by the cutting process are all on the outside of the new image. Because the new edges were joined before we cut them, they match up when the image is tiled. Although this is hard to visualize, it does work.

21

FIGURE 21.4

Quartered image showing original placement of quarters.

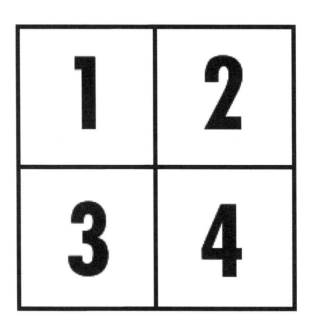

FIGURE 21.5

Quartered image with final placement of quarters.

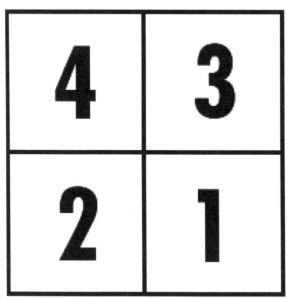

Here's a textured image created with Kai's Power Tool Texture Explorer (see Figure 21.6).

FIGURE 21.6

Texture image.

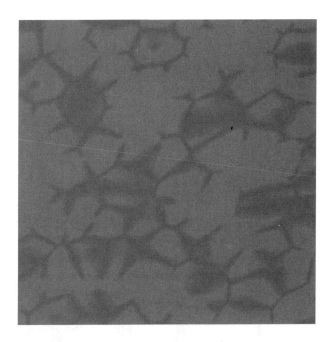

Figure 21.7 shows the same image with the corners numbered as in Figure 21.4.

FIGURE 21.7

Texture image showing numbered quarters.

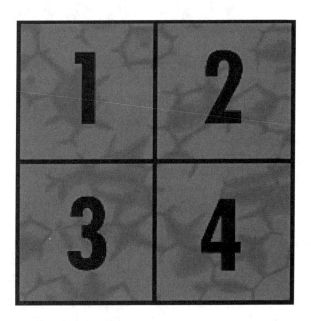

21

Of course, you don't have to draw the numbers in over the image; I've done it here to demonstrate the process more clearly.

Figure 21.8 is the image once the quarters have been swapped. Note that the numbers are still in place.

FIGURE 21.8

Texture image showing the numbered quarters with the corners swapped for tiling

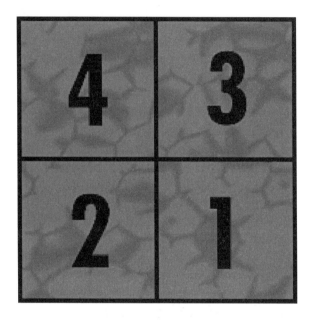

Figure 21.9 is the image with the quarters swapped and the numbers removed. This image will now tile seamlessly.

You may notice, however, that although the edges now match up, the center of the image has a vertical and a horizontal seam running through it. If we get rid of the vertical and horizontal seams, this image will be ready to tile, and there are a couple of ways to rid ourselves of the seam. Most paint programs have a Cloning tool, which copies one portion of the image over another. The cloning process is entirely under the control of the artist. Although it's a little difficult to master, it is very effective, as you'll see in the next section.

Creating Seamless Tiles with Photoshop

The swapping part of creating seamless tiles with Photoshop is relatively easy. Photoshop contains an Offset filter that does the swapping part for you. All you need to do is tell the Offset filter how much offset to use. The values you should use are exactly half of the width and half of the height of the texture image. To begin, open any Texture (see Figure 21.10).

FIGURE 21.9

Texture image with the quarters swapped for tiling.

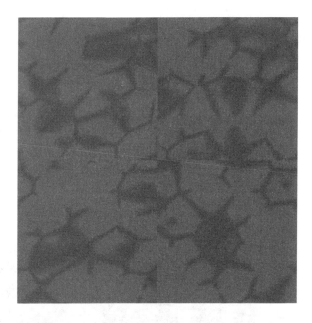

FIGURE 21.10

Texture image.

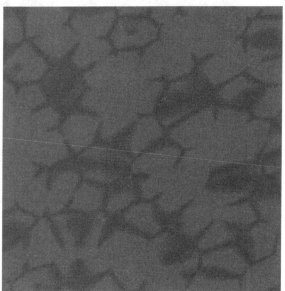

21

1. Choose Filter, Other, Offset.
2. In the Offset dialog box (see Figure 21.11), enter values for the Horizontal and Vertical offsets that are equal to half of the width and height, respectively, of your image.

FIGURE 21.11

Photoshop's Offset dialog box.

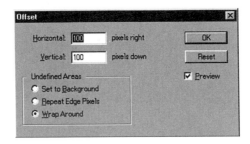

3. Because the original is a 200×200 texture image, enter 100 for both values as seen in Figure 21.11.

4. Click OK. Your image should look like Figure 21.12.

FIGURE 21.12

Texture image with quarters swapped for tiling.

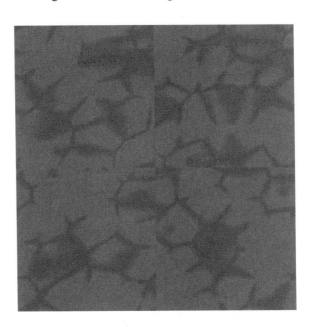

Now all that's left is to get rid of the seams that run through the middle of this image.

Note

Make sure that you don't make any changes to the edges of the graphic at this point. Doing so will mess up the seamless areas. You might want to save a backup copy of the image before you start the touch-up process. This will enable you to go back if you make a mistake that you can't undo.

Tip

You might find the touch-up will go a little more smoothly if you zoom in on the image.

There are a couple of ways to get rid of the seam. You can use the Rubber Stamp tool, you can draw into the seamed areas using the Pencil or Paintbrush tools, or you can use the Smudge tool.

The Clone tool takes a little getting used to but is a very effective tool for this type of work. The Clone tool enables you to copy one area of an image over another.

1. To begin, you must select an area using Alt-click. If you forget this step, you'll get an error message informing you that you must select a source point.

2. Once you select a source point, you can start to move the Rubber Stamp tool over an area. Doing so replaces the area under the Rubber Stamp with a small crosshair. You can change the area you're copying by pressing Alt-click (Option-click) again.

Tip

A couple of things you should do before and while using the Rubber Stamp tool include two steps. First, change the brush so that you see the brush size (choose File, Preferences, Display & Cursors) and set the Painting cursors to Brush Size. Second, vary the brush size as you work on the image.

3. Change the area several times as you work to avoid making large similar areas.

Once you've worked the seams over with the Clone tool, you should have something like Figure 21.13.

21

FIGURE 21.13

Texture image with quarters swapped for tiling after using the Rubber Stamp tool.

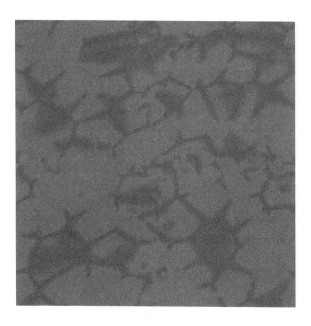

Before going any further, you might want to compare what the tile would have looked like on a Web page before it was made seamless and what it looks like now (see Figures 21.14 and 21.15).

FIGURE 21.14

A Web page example with a non-seamless background tile.

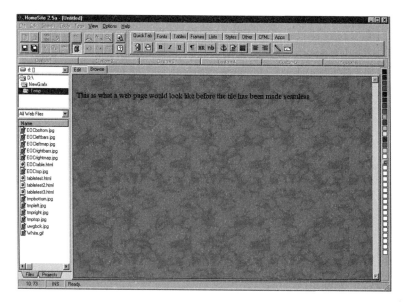

FIGURE 21.15

A Web page example with a seamless background tile.

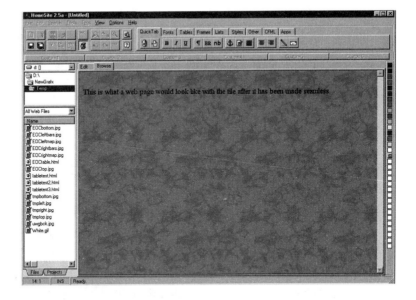

Even with this low-contrast pattern, the seam is quite evident in Figure 21.14. Seeing the finished tile in Figure 21.15, we can see that it doesn't really require any further touch-ups. If it did, however, you could use the Smudge tool, the Pencil tool, or the Paintbrush tool to make some fine adjustments.

Creating Web Page Counters

Counters seem to gather more interest than they're due. I'll admit to falling into the trap myself. I have at one time or another had counters on several of the pages at GrafX Design. I tend to use them more as a gauge than an actual indication of the traffic.

To see how much traffic I'm actually getting, I refer to the server logs. The server logs should be available from your ISP or the system administrator of the system where your Web pages are stored. A number of programs, both online and local, can help you decipher the large amounts of data that the log files gather.

21

Note

There are a couple of ways to implement a digital counter on your pages, and each of them involves running a CGI script. To learn how to implement counters, check with your ISP's technical support staff or consult *The CGI Book* by Bill Weinman (New Riders Publishing, 1997). After you've found out how to implement the counter, you should also be able to have it set up to display any digits you create.

There are sites that contain huge collections of digits, but if you're like me, you'll want to create your own that will go with the look and feel of your site.

Creating Counter Digits with Photoshop

You've seen those counter graphics that mimic automobile odometers, right? Maybe you've wondered how they're done. Here's a method you can use to create this look in Photoshop.

1. Open a new 400×100 RGB file (we'll shrink it down later).
2. Set the default black/white foreground/background colors by clicking the small black and white overlapping squares in the Foreground color, Background color swatch.
3. Select the Gradient tool and in the Gradient Tool Options palette choose Foreground to Background as the gradient.
4. Set the type to Linear and click the Edit button to bring up the Gradient Editor dialog box (see Figure 21.16).

FIGURE 21.16

Photoshop's Gradient Editor dialog box.

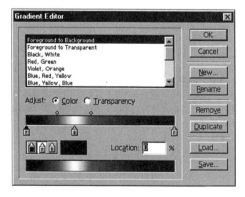

5. Set the two end colors to black.
6. Add another slider by clicking under the representation of the gradient.

7. Make the color of this slider white. The color can be adjusted by clicking the small color swatch near the lower-left corner of the dialog box.

8. Adjust the sliders above the gradient, so that you have something similar to Figure 21.16, and click OK.

9. Place the mouse near the top of the image and, while holding the Shift key, drag the mouse to the bottom of the image. You should get a gradient fill like the one in Figure 21.17. This will be the back of the numbers of the odometer.

FIGURE 21.17

Vertical linear black/white/black gradient.

10. Swap the background and foreground colors by clicking the small curved arrow in the Foreground/Background color swatch, so that the foreground color is white.

11. Select the Text tool.

12. Click anywhere in the image to bring up the Type Tool dialog box.

13. Choose a slim sans-serif font. I used Fujiyama, which you may not have. If that's the case, select something similar, such as Arial or Helvetica.

14. Change the size to 60 points and enter the digits 0,1,2,3,4,5,6,7,8,9, without the commas, of course. If you find that the digits don't quite fit, you can choose Edit, Undo and try using a different value for the size of the font. Once you're happy with the font you've chosen, you should have an image that resembles Figure 21.18.

FIGURE 21.18

Vertical linear black/white/black gradient with white digits.

21

Note

With Photoshop 5, the type will be on a separate layer. This layer will be active as well.

Here's a little trick to add the illusion of a real odometer. Have you ever noticed that the numbers never line up quite right on a mechanical odometer? To replicate this look, we'll select a couple of the digits and move them either up or down a couple of pixels.

1. Select the Marquee tool.
2. In the Marquee Options palette, set the Shape to Rectangular and the Style to Normal.
3. Make a selection around the 0 and, while holding down the Ctrl key (Command key on a Mac), press the down cursor key three times.
4. Select another digit, the 8 for example, and move it up three pixels.
5. Repeat this for another one of the digits. I moved the 4 up three pixels (see Figure 21.19).

FIGURE 21.19

A couple of digits moved vertically.

6. Select the Gradient tool again to color the digits.
7. In the Gradient Tool Options palette, click the Edit button to bring up the Gradient editor.
8. One at a time, click the black sliders, beginning with the ones at each end.
9. Click the color swatch, and in the Color Picker dialog box change the front slider's color from black to a fairly light gray.
10. Repeat the process for the end slider but make the gray a little darker.
11. You may want to add another slider next to the white, changing its color to white as well to widen the white area of the gradient. Place the cursor on the image above the numbers and, while holding the Shift key, drag the mouse a little past the bottom of the digits (see Figure 21.20).

FIGURE 21.20

The completed odometer image.

At this point, you should probably save the image. I'd recommend saving it as a Photoshop .PSD file, so that changes can be made to it later with a little more ease than if the layers aren't available.

If this image is going to be used with a counter program like Count, it must be cut into the individual digits. The next steps accomplish this.

1. Click the small black triangle icon at the top-right of the Layers palette and choose Flatten image.

2. Now resize the image to the appropriate or desired size, so that it fits nicely on the Web page.

3. Change the mode to Indexed Color. Select either Web palette (preferred) or Adaptive palette.

4. Turn the rulers on (Ctrl+R or Command+R), and drag guides out from the left rule onto the image, slicing the image into appropriate digit columns. This step ensures that no edge pixels are repeated or left out. If the guides need to be adjusted, use the Move tool to click and drag them.

5. Select the Rectangular Marquee tool and make sure Snap to Guides under the View menu is checked.

6. Extend the gray workspace around the image (this can be accomplished by dragging the outer edges or the corner of the image), so that you can start the selection outside the image, ensuring that all the edge pixels are selected. You don't see the "marching ants" of the selection, however, until the Marquee tool goes into the actual image space. Notice how the selection stops or snaps to the first guide that was created, separating the 0 digit from the 1 digit.

7. Choose Edit, Copy.

8. Choose File, New and click OK. Now choose Edit, Paste to copy the 0 into the new file. Change the foreground color to black.

9. Make the 0 the current image by clicking its title bar.

10. Choose Select, All and then choose Edit, Stroke.

11. Set the Width to 2 and the Location to Inside. Click OK. This draws a black border around the digit, helping complete the illusion of a real odometer when a series of digits is displayed.

12. Change the mode of the new 0 file to Indexed Color and choose Custom from the Palette drop-down menu. Photoshop automatically loads the Adaptive palette (or the specific colors from the Web palette) it creates from the entire odometer graphic. Click OK on the Custom Palette window. Then, using the File, Save As command, save the digit as a GIF image file.

21

13. Choose Image, Image Size. In the Image Size dialog box, there's a pull-down menu to the right of the Print Size Width. Choose this menu and select Percent. In the Width window, enter 40. This shrinks the digit down to a good size for the counter.

14. Choose File, Export, GIF89a Export. In the GIF89a Export Options dialog box, select Adaptive for the palette, 256 for the colors, and turn off the Interlaced option. Click OK. Give the file a name in the Export GIF89 dialog box and click Save to save the file.

15. Repeat this for each of the 10 digits. You may want to give the files names like odo0, odo1, odo2, and so on.

Your odometer digits that we created in this tutorial should look like the counter in Figure 21.21.

FIGURE 21.21

Completed counter digits displayed on a Web page.

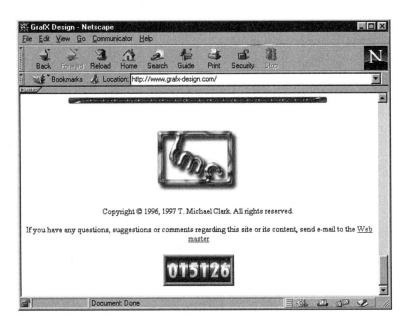

Summary

Again, many resources are available to you if you're creating Web graphics with Photoshop. You can visit the usenet discussion group at `comp.graphics.apps.photoshop`. You can also visit Web sites devoted to helping others use Photoshop for Web graphics. A few are:

- GrafX Design (my Web site) at `http://www.grafx-design.com`.

- i/us site at `http://www.i-us.com`.

Both of these sites contain links to other Photoshop Web sites. Also, Adobe's site at `http://www.adobe.com` includes tips, techniques, news, and links to other sites.

Q&A

Q Can you recommend any good books for creating Web graphics with Photoshop?

A I suggest you try *Photoshop Web Techniques* by J. Scott Hamlin or *Designing Web Graphics.2* by Lynda Weinman. Both contain excellent resources for creating great looking Web graphics that are optimized for use on the Web.

Q You mention the PNG format, but never really go into it. What exactly is it?

A The PNG format was created to replace the GIF format after the copyright holder of the GIF format decided to start charging developers for its use. As well, the PNG format has better transparency (it uses an 8-bit alpha channel) and allows 24-bit color as opposed to 8-bit.

Workshop

The following section is a quick quiz about the chapter you just read. If you have any problems answering any of the questions in the quiz, see the section directly following it for all the answers.

Quiz

1. Which types of images is the JPEG format best suited for?
2. Which types of images is the GIF format best suited for?
3. What is a seamless tile?
4. How do you get a seamless tile loaded on your Web page?
5. What does a counter do?

21

Quiz Answers

1. There are no hard-and-fast rules, but real-world images, such as photographs and images with continuous tone gradations, work best.

2. Line art and images with few colors are well suited to the GIF format.

3. An image that when tiled appears to be one large continuous image.

4. Use the HTML tag <body background="*filename.ext*">, where *filename* is the name of the file and *ext* is the file extension (either GIF or JPG).

5. A counter keeps track of the number of people who surf to your Web page. This isn't the most accurate method, but it is a fun way to keep track of the Web page impressions you serve up.

APPENDIX A

Keyboard Shortcuts and Tool Documentation

To start saving time by using Photoshop's tools, keyboard shortcuts, and palettes, turn the page…

The Photoshop 5 Toolbar

Rectangular Marquee
Elliptical Marquee
Single Row Marquee
Single Column Marquee
Crop (C)

Marquee tools (M)

Lasso
Polygonal Lasso
Magnetic Lasso

Lasso tools (L)

Rubber Stamp
Pattern Stamp

Stamp tools (S)

Blur
Sharpen
Smudge

Focus tools (R)

Pen
Magnetic Pen
Freeform Pen
Add Anchor Point (+)
Delete Anchor Point (–)
Direct Selection (A)
Convert Point

Pen tools (P)

Airbrush (J)

Eraser (E)

Measure (U)

Paint Bucket (K)

Hand (H)

Foreground Color

Default Foreground and
Background Colors (D)

Edit in Standard Mode (Q)

Standard Screen Mode (F)

Full Screen Mode with Menu Bar (F)

Adobe Online

Move (V)

Magic Wand (W)

Paintbrush (B)

History Brush (Y)

Pencil
Line

Drawing tools (N)

Dodge
Burn
Sponge

Tone tools (O)

Type
Type Mask
Vertical Type
Vertical Type Mask

Type tools (T)

Linear Gradient
Radial Gradient
Angle Gradient
Reflected Gradient
Diamond Gradient

Gradient tools (G)

Eyedropper
Color Sampler

Eyedropper tools (I)

Zoom (Z)

Switch Foreground and
Background Colors (X)

Background Color

Edit in Quick
Mask Mode (Q)

Full Screen Mode (F)

Photoshop 5 Keyboard Shortcut Quick Reference

The following tables list the myriad keyboard shortcuts for Photoshop's menu access and navigational needs. For all shortcuts, Windows users should use the Control key instead of Command—except where indicated—and use the Alt key instead of Option.

FILE MENU

New	Cmd+N
Open	Cmd+O
Open As (Windows only)	Alt+Cmd+O
Close	Cmd+W
Save	Cmd+S
Save As	Shift+Cmd+S
Save a Copy	Option+Cmd+S
Page Setup	Shift+Cmd+P
Print	Cmd+P
Preferences->General	Cmd+K

EDIT MENU

Undo	Cmd+Z
Cut	Cmd+X
Copy	Cmd+C
Copy Merged	Shift+Cmd+C
Paste	Cmd+V
Past Into	Shift+Cmd+V
Free Transform	Cmd+T
Transform->Again	Shift+Cmd+T

IMAGE MENU

Adjust->Levels	Cmd+L
Adjust->Auto Levels	Shift+Cmd+L
Adjust->Curves	Cmd+M
Adjust->Color Balance	Cmd+B
Adjust->Hue/Saturation	Cmd+U
Adjust->Desaturate	Shift+Cmd+U
Adjust->Invert	Cmd+I

LAYER MENU

New->Layer	Shift+Cmd+N
New->Layer Via Copy	Cmd+J
New->Layer Via Cut	Shift+Cmd+J
Group with Previous	Cmd+G
Ungroup	Shift+Cmd+G
Arrange->Bring to Front	Shift+Cmd+]
Arrange->Bring Forward	Cmd+]
Arrange->Send Backward	Cmd+[
Arrange->Send to Back	Shift+Cmd+[
Merge Down	Cmd+E
Merge Visible	Shift+Cmd+E

SELECT MENU

All	Cmd+A
Deselect	Cmd+D
Reselect	Shift+Cmd+D
Inverse	Shift+Cmd+I
Feather	Alt+Ctrl+D (Windows)
	Shift+Cmd+D (Macintosh)

FILTER MENU

Last Filter	Cmd+F
Fade	Shift+Cmd+F

VIEW MENU

Preview->CMYK	Cmd+Y
Gamut Warning	Shift+Cmd+Y
Zoom In	Cmd++
Zoom Out	Cmd+-
Fit on Screen	Cmd+0 (zero)
Actual Pixels	Shift+Ctrl+0 (zero) (Windows)
	Alt+Cmd+0 (zero) (Macintosh)
Hide Edges	Cmd+H
Hide Path	Shift+Cmd+H
Show Rulers	Cmd+R
Hide Guides	Cmd+;
Snap To Guides	Shift+Cmd+;
Lock Guides	Alt+Cmd+;
Show Grid	Cmd+"
Snap to Grid	Shift+Cmd+"

HELP MENU *(Windows only)*

Contents	F1

OTHER SHORTCUTS

Move view up/down 1 screen	Page Up/Down (W)
	Opt+PageUp/Down (M)
Nudge view up/down	Shift+Page Up/Down (W)
	Opt+Shift+PageUp/Down (M)
Move view left/right 1 screen	Ctrl+Page Up/Down (W)
	Cmd+PageUp/Down (M)
Nudge view left/right	Shift+Ctrl+Page Up/Down (W)
	Cmd+Shift+PageUp/Down (M)
Previous History Entry	Ctrl+Shift+Z
Next History Entry	Ctrl+Alt+Z
Scroll through Blending modes	Shift++ and Shift+-

The Photoshop 5 Palettes

The following pages break down the various Photoshop 5 palettes and their respective subpalettes and submenus. Those palettes that contain subpalettes and submenus use arrows to indicate where Photoshop will take you when you select a particular icon or flyout menu.

Navigator Palette

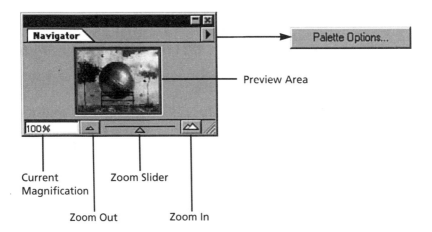

Info Palette

A

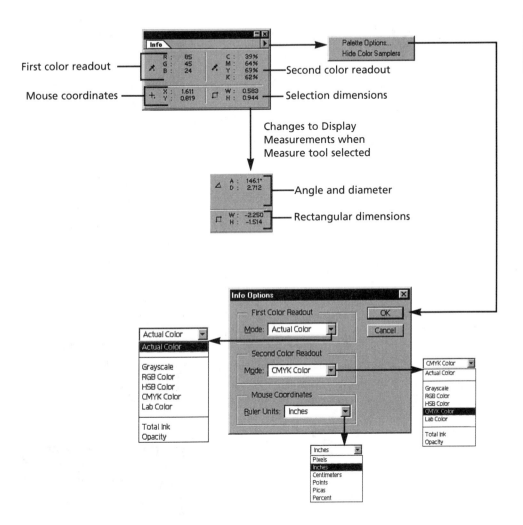

First color readout

Mouse coordinates

Second color readout

Selection dimensions

Changes to Display
Measurements when
Measure tool selected

Angle and diameter

Rectangular dimensions

Color Palette

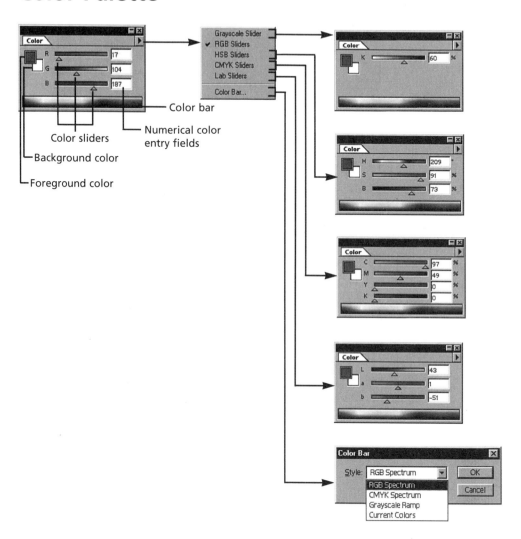

Color bar

Numerical color
entry fields

Color sliders

Background color

Foreground color

Swatches Palette

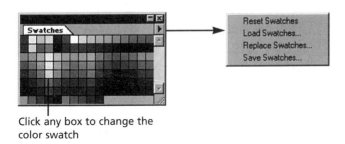

Click any box to change the
color swatch

A

Brushes Palette

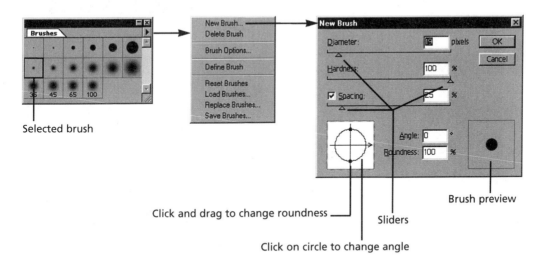

Selected brush

Click and drag to change roundness ⎯⎯⎯

Sliders

Brush preview

Click on circle to change angle

History Palette

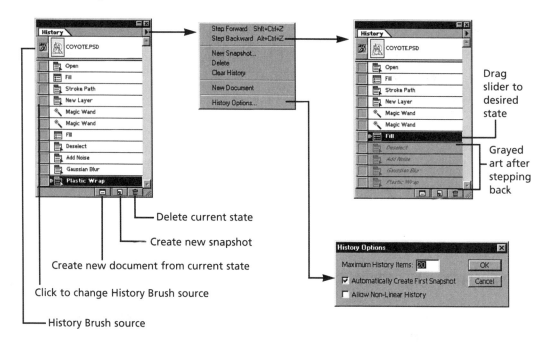

Drag slider to desired state

Grayed art after stepping back

Delete current state

Create new snapshot

Create new document from current state

Click to change History Brush source

History Brush source

Actions Palette

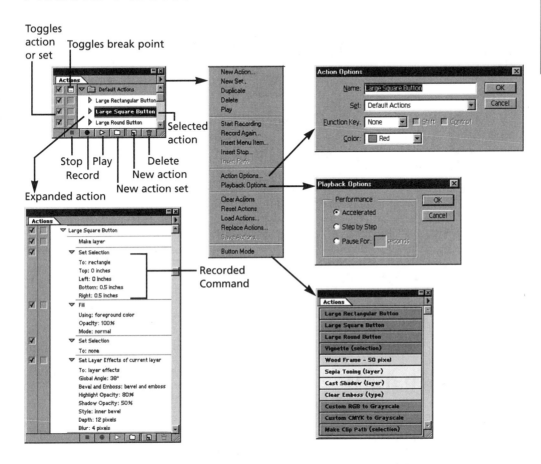

Toggles action or set

Toggles break point

Expanded action

Stop | Play
Record
New action
New action set
Delete

Selected action

Recorded Command

Layers Palette

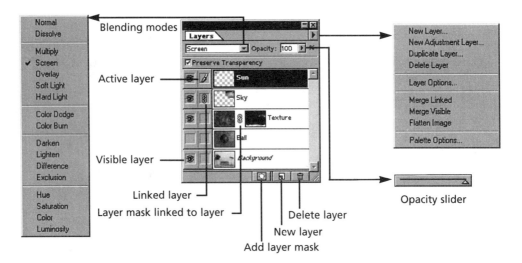

Channels Palette

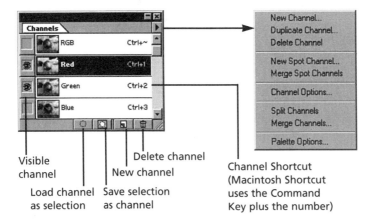

Paths Palette

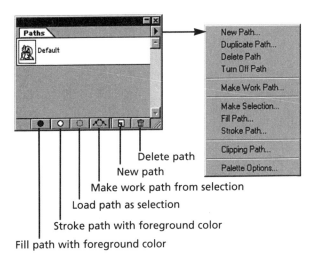

A

Delete path
New path
Make work path from selection
Load path as selection
Stroke path with foreground color
Fill path with foreground color

APPENDIX B

Troubleshooting Guide

Throughout your time using Photoshop 5.0, you are bound to experience a few problems. This appendix has been created to give you some basic troubleshooting information for a variety of different scenarios. This appendix is by no means a complete "how to fix everything that goes wrong" reference; however, it should give you helpful information on getting things sorted out. The troubleshooting information has been divided into a few key topics:

- Installation issues
- Problems with program operation
- Using tools
- Filter problems
- Working through actions and history
- Problems with input devices

Installation Issues

Experiencing problems installing Photoshop onto your workstation? This topic provides information on common installation problems.

The Photoshop Setup program tells me I've entered an Invalid or Incorrect Serial Number.

It is important that you enter the correct serial number for Photoshop 5.0 when prompted. A serial number for a previous version will not work with version 5.0. Make sure that you are entering the number that came with your software.

The Photoshop Setup program tells me I do not have enough disk space.

Photoshop requires approximately 67 megabytes for a complete installation. Always make sure that you have not only sufficient room for the program itself, but for your operating system swap files and Photoshop's own swap file.

The Photoshop Upgrade Setup program tells me that a qualifying version of Photoshop was not detected.

When upgrading from a previous release of Photoshop, you must either have the previous version (4.01 or lower) installed on your workstation or you must provide your original installation media. Make sure that you have a working copy of Photoshop 4.01 or lower installed or insert your original installation diskette or CD-ROM when prompted.

The Photoshop Setup program tells me a file is in use.

As with all installation programs, you should always make sure that you have exited any running programs before proceeding with the installation. If the Photoshop Setup program attempts to copy a file to your workstation that is already in use by another program, the Setup program will not be able to continue properly. Always close all running programs before beginning the installation.

Problems with Program Operation

If Photoshop itself is stubborn and refuses to work properly, this is the topic for you. Program errors and global issues are documented here.

My computer says that it cannot find PHOTOSHP.EXE when I choose the Photoshop icon from the Start menu.

If the Setup program did not properly complete its installation or files have been moved/removed from your workstation, the shortcut to the Photoshop program may not function properly. Make sure that you do indeed have a PHOTOSHP.EXE file on your workstation in the proper directory. If need be, reinstall Photoshop to re-create the necessary files and shortcuts.

I'm getting one of the following errors...

PHOTOSHP caused a General Protection Fault, PHOTOSHP caused an Invalid Page Fault, Application Error, Unhandled Exception detected, Illegal Instruction, or Segment load failure in...

Although a system error may appear to occur only in Photoshop, this does not necessarily mean that Photoshop is to blame. Memory conflicts between device drivers, software, and hardware can cause significant problems in many programs. Photoshop may just be the only application that is memory- or processor-intensive enough to cause the fundamental problem to manifest itself. One of the first things that you should do is exit all other programs and reduce the possibility of contention between resources. This may include disabling certain device drivers or system programs. Always make sure that Photoshop has enough free room with resources (RAM, physical hard disk, CPU) that it does not have to struggle to perform. Also, ensure that your system does not have any hardware conflicts that may cause such problems. Finally, you should uninstall Photoshop and reinstall it with your system in "Safe mode" to minimize conflicts. This insures that Photoshop is installed correctly.

I'm getting a "Scratch disk is full" error.

When working with large images, Photoshop uses a scratch disk to temporarily store data. The scratch disk requires suitable space to store this data. Make sure that the scratch disk you specified in the Preferences dialog box has enough free space to complete your action. If need be, clean up some space on the scratch disk or switch the scratch disk to another physical drive if possible.

My files of a certain image type are no longer recognized by Photoshop from the Explorer.

Often file extensions on Windows machines are shared between different file types. When a program is installed after Photoshop, sometimes these file types are associated with a different program for a different file type. You may need to re-create your file associations in the Windows Explorer. You can do so by selecting an affected file and right-clicking on it. Choose "Open With..." from the Context menu and select Photoshop from the dialog box.

B

I'm running out of memory. Operations are taking a long time and I'm getting error messages.

Photoshop is hardly a friendly beast when it comes to memory consumption. If you're finding you're running out of memory or the program slows down a lot after working for a certain amount of time, you can do two things: Use the Edit | Purge function to clear up Photoshop's RAM storage. Secondly, you can customize Photoshop's memory and scratch disk usage from the File | Preferences dialog box. You can also limit the History feature to minimize its rather blatant memory consumption (see Working through Actions and History).

I'm trying to save an image in a particular format, but the Save As... dialog box does not list that file type.

File types when saving a file are based on what mode you are working in. If you are working in RGB mode with layers, you will not see all available file types when saving your image. Make sure to flatten images before saving to a format other than Photoshop's own .PSD format. Additionally, make sure that the corresponding file format plug-in is located in the Photoshop Plug-ins directory. If you are in doubt, you may want to reinstall Photoshop to make sure that all required files are present.

When I try to open Photoshop, I'm getting a "Could not initialize Photoshop due to a disk error" message.

Sometimes Photoshop's Preferences file becomes corrupted, particularly with Macintoshes. You may need to delete the Photoshop Preferences file to get into Photoshop again. Unfortunately, deleting the Photoshop Preferences file restores Photoshop's default preferences and custom settings. This error might also indicate problems with your hard disk drive. You should use disk repair software, such as Scandisk under Windows or Norton Disk Doctor on a Macintosh to examine your hard drive and repair any errors.

When opening a file, I get an error that says "This document has been damaged by a disk error."

In the event of a disk problem, your images may be corrupted and unreadable by Photoshop. Photoshop does typically give the option to open the document anyway, but you may see screen artifacting or unreadable images. This typically happens due to a defective media (disk drive, hard disk drive, and so on), a defective SCSI cable, or incorrect SCSI termination. Make sure that your media is functioning properly before attempting to re-open the file.

Opening an image takes a REALLY long time.

Many images are simply too large to be loaded quickly by Photoshop. You can streamline the process by making sure that your images are a reasonable size. If this is not a possibility, make sure that Photoshop has ample resources available to it. Also, you can diminish Photoshop's redraw performance to improve speed in opening images. From the Preferences dialog box, select Image Cache. Enter "1" into the Cache Levels textbox and restart Photoshop. Additionally, some filters and plug-ins may cause extended load times. Consider removing plug-ins through process of elimination to make sure that they are not causing the problem.

Some menu items are missing from the menu bar!

On rare occasions, menu items may be missing due to multiple removable drives connected via SCSI on one machine. Remove any extra removable drives and restart Photoshop.

When trying to open an image I saved, I get an error "Could not open <filename> because the file-format module cannot parse the file."

If you changed an extension on a file but did not change to the corresponding file type when saving, the file is still saved as a Photoshop .PSD file with a different extension. Rename the file to a .PSD extension and try to open the file. It is possible that the file itself is corrupt however.

My familiar keyboard shortcuts don't work!

There have been some changes in Photoshop 5.0 to the keyboard shortcuts. Familiarize yourself with the new shortcuts.

Photoshop complains that an existing copy is in use on the network when I try to open it.

Photoshop 5.0 allows only one machine on a local area network with the same serial number to operate at one time. To use Photoshop 5.0 simultaneously on more than one machine, you need additional licenses for each copy.

Using Tools

Each Photoshop tool has its own quirks and oddities that may confound you. Here are some tips and troubleshooting notes on using individual tools in the program.

My painting tools don't work.

When working with painting tools, it is important to remember that they work only on the target layer and inside the current selection. Make sure that you are not painting outside of an active selection and that you are working on the correct layer.

I'm trying to use the History brush, but nothing seems to happen.

When painting with the History brush, make sure that you have made a selection in the History palette.

Not all type styles are available to me as they were in Photoshop 4.0.

Photoshop 5.0 has a new type engine and relies on the existing TrueType/ATM fonts installed on your system. Photoshop no longer "creates" the styles of italic or bold for all fonts. If you are looking for a particular style to apply to a font, you will need to locate a matching font file.

Filter Problems

With the power of filters can come the complexities and issues of add-ons. Familiarize yourself with filter troubleshooting to make sure that you get the result you want.

My plug-in filters are missing or dimmed in the Plug-ins menu.

If the Plug-in files are not located in the Plug-ins directory, they will not be available to Photoshop. Make sure that all Plug-in files are present in the proper directory. You may also have to change the Plug-ins directory in the File | Preferences dialog box. Finally, some filters can only be used on some images when they are in a particular mode (typically RGB). Make sure that you are in the proper mode when trying to apply a filter. On rare occasions, the Photoshop Preferences file does become corrupt and prevents Photoshop from using the Plug-in files. You may need to delete your Preferences file to correct this problem.

When applying a filter, I get an error "Could not complete your request because there is not enough memory (RAM)."

Many filters are very resource intensive. They not only require considerable CPU, but also a hefty amount of RAM. If your machine or Photoshop itself is low on RAM, you may not be able to carry out some actions. Make sure that you have allocated enough memory to Photoshop and that no other programs are competing with Photoshop for resources.

My filter doesn't work like I expected it to.

Filters can be stubborn animals, particularly when you are not familiar with them. A steadfast rule when working with filters is to make sure that you have the appropriate region of your image selected. Most filters work within a defined selection. Also take advantage of some filters' ability to real-time display how the effect will appear on your image. Finally, use History or Undo features to experiment with filters until you achieve the effect you desire.

Some of my old filters do not work properly with Photoshop 5.0.

Many older filters, particularly those from Photoshop 3.0, will not work properly with Photoshop 5.0. Seek out the vendor of the respective filter and see if they have a newer version compatible with Photoshop 5.0.

I have filters in several different directories on my hard disk drive. How do I let Photoshop use them all?

Unfortunately, all plug-ins must be located in the Photoshop Plug-ins directory. You must move your different files to the same physical location.

B

Working through Actions and History

Actions and History do not always work the way we would like them to. It is important to understand how to work through problems with these two features.

I ran an action and got an error. I fixed the problem, but now when I re-run the action I don't get the desired result.

Typically, if you know that the action in question works, this is because the action has created channels or layers but was stopped before it had a chance to delete them. When the action is run, it then goes to reuse the same layers and channels even though they were not created for that run. Before re-running any action that has been stopped, always check your Layers and Channels palettes to see if the action has created any new layers or channels. Delete them before continuing. As a general rule, you should always save before running an action so that you can revert, or use the History palette to step back.

My action fails when I try to perform a special effect or layer operation.

The most common cause for this is the mode the image is currently in. You may need to be in RGB mode, for example, for the action to be carried out.

When running an action, I get an error that says "the command 'set' is not currently available."

Some actions require an active selection. If a selection was not made before running the action, Photoshop does not have a selection to work with and tries to save it to a channel. Before running the action, make a selection.

When running an action, I get an error that says "the command 'hue/saturation' is not currently available."

Many actions expect you to have an image open in RGB mode. This error occurs when an image is in Grayscale mode and the action expects it to be in RGB.

The more I work on an image, the more Photoshop slows down.

The History feature in Photoshop 5.0 is a demanding one. The history is recorded in the enormous native Photoshop file format, which can cause considerable slowdown the more you work. Consider setting how far back the History setting goes from the History Options dialog box, found by clicking on the arrow tab of the History palette. The default is 20 steps; however, you may want to reduce that considerably. Also remember to purge Photoshop's RAM storage, including History, from the Edit | Purge function.

When I delete steps in the History palette, I lose all subsequent steps.

This is normal. The History palette is by default "linear." If you delete step two out of five steps, steps three through five are removed. However, you do have the option of making the History palette "non-linear" in the Palette Options. This can be incredibly confusing but very powerful. Consider it as more of a set of random image states that can be blended with the History brush.

Problems with Input Devices

Mice, tablets, scanners… all variety of input devices can cause problems in Photoshop. This last topic covers useful information when dealing with different devices.

My tablet doesn't seem to be working in Photoshop, but it is outside of it.

Make sure that you have the stylus size/opacity/color options checked in the Tool Option palette. Remember to turn them off when using a mouse, however, or you will get some strange non-pressure effects. Also keep in mind that some programs leave their tablet options running even after you leave the program, so you may need to restart your computer or reset your drivers for your tablet to work properly.

I'm not able to use my scanner or import from my digital camera directly into Photoshop.

Make sure that your scanner/camera software is properly installed and that you have selected the TWAIN source within Photoshop. Without the TWAIN source selected, Photoshop does not know how to speak to your device.

I can't get the level of control over my mouse that I'd like when drawing in Photoshop.

Keep in mind that not all mice are created equal. Many mice, especially those of the inexpensive variety, have a low resolution. If you want to work in high-resolution and detail, consider a higher quality mouse, trackball, or tablet.

B

APPENDIX C

What's on the Companion CD-ROM?

This appendix contains important information on the following topics:

- What's on the CD-ROM?
- How to run the CD-ROM
- System requirements
- Troubleshooting common problems

What's on the CD-ROM?

Within the companion CD-ROM, you'll find all sorts of goodies. The following sections break down the various folders and what you'll find within them.

Third-Party Software

The 3rdParty folder contains several different tools and utilities and is divided into Mac and PC folders. Be sure to use the utilities that match your operating system. Specific information about each item can be found in the folder for that item. The folders in the third-party directory include the following:

- Adobe—Including demos for several Adobe programs
- Earthlink—An easy access ISP
- Extensis—Demos of several Extensis tools
- Filters—From Alienskin, Andromeda, AutoFX, and Metatools
- Fonts—Packages of fonts to use in your creations
- Netscape—The complete Navigator 4.04 browser

Dstock

The Dstock folder contains images from Digital Stock. These images are sorted into folders for each category. To get an overview of the contents of each image folder, view the .pdf file that corresponds with that folder. You must have Adobe Acrobat Reader installed to view .pdf files. You can find Acrobat Reader in the 3rdParty\Adobe\ folder.

Examples

All the example files from the book are included in this folder. The examples are arranged by day (for example, Day4, Day5, and so on). Some days in the book do not have examples, thus you will not have 21 folders in the Examples directory.

Extras

In this folder you can find the Sample Chapter from *Inside Photoshop 5* in .pdf format. *Inside Photoshop 5* by Gary Bouton is a more extensive book on Photoshop and includes more details on the finer points of the program. You must have Adobe Acrobat Reader installed to view .pdf files. You can find Acrobat Reader in the 3rdParty\Adobe\ folder.

The ACE folder within the Extras directory contains the Adobe Certification Expert prep exam. This is a tutorial to help you prepare for the actual Adobe Certification Expert Exam given at Sylvan. The test is in HTML format and can be started by clicking on the Start.htm file. You will be asked 20 questions related to Photoshop, after which you will receive your score. Details for the prep exam are given on the Start.htm page. Good luck!

How to Run the CD-ROM

Under Windows 95 and Windows NT, if you have AutoPlay enabled, insert the CD-ROM and choose installation options from the displayed splash screen.

Note

If you have AutoPlay disabled on your computer, the CD-ROM will *not* automatically display the installation splash screen. To browse the CD-ROM manually, double-click on My Computer on the desktop, then right-click on your CD-ROM player icon, and choose Explore from the shortcut menu. By doing this, you can immediately access the files for this CD-ROM.

System Requirements for the Companion CD-ROM

C

The following lists provide you with the minimum system requirements necessary for working with the companion CD-ROM. These requirements are in addition to the system requirements necessary to run Photoshop 5.

For Windows:

Processor: 486DX or higher processor (Pentium preferred)

Operating System: MS Windows NT 4.0 Workstation, Windows 95, or Windows 98

Memory (RAM): 24MB minimum (32MB recommended)

Storage: Hard disk space for shareware and demo programs: 97.5MB minimum

Video: TrueColor (24-bit), 2MB card minimum, TrueColor 8MB card recommended

Other: Mouse or compatible pointing device, CD-ROM drive, Web browser such as Netscape Navigator 4 or MS Internet Explorer 4

Optional: An Internet connection with an Internet service provider (ISP)

For Macintosh:

Operating System: Apple System software 7.5.5 or later (Mac OS 8 recommended)

Memory (RAM): 16MB of application RAM (32MB recommended)

Storage: Hard disk space for shareware and demo programs: 97.5MB minimum

Video: Color monitor with 256 color (8-bit) or greater, plus video card (24-bit color recommended)

Other: CD-ROM drive

Optional: An Internet connection with an Internet service provider (ISP)

Shareware

Some of the programs included on this CD-ROM are shareware—"try-before-you-buy"—software. Independent developers spend hundreds of hours creating, updating, and improving various utilities and tools that make everyone's computing lives that much better. These hard-working souls create the programs or add-on features that retail manufacturers sometimes overlook, yet end users could use. *"If only I could find a program that could..."*

Please support these independent vendors by purchasing or registering any shareware software that you use for more than 30 days. Check with the documentation provided with the software on where and how to register the product. Thank you for your support of shareware!

Windows Installation Notes

To install an application from this CD-ROM, double-click on the My Computer icon on the Desktop, right-click on your CD icon, choose Explore from the shortcut menu, and then double-click on any program folder. Select the SETUP.EXE file, or the file that has the extension EXE. These are the installation programs for the software. Many of these programs will lead you through the installation process. If you have difficulty installing a program, try copying the contents of the folder onto your computer and then double-clicking on the EXE file. Always refer to any documentation that may accompany the individual software.

Troubleshooting Common Problems

The following questions and answers are designed to help you in the event you have difficulties when working with this companion CD-ROM.

I don't see any directories on this CD-ROM. It looks like I have a blank disc.

First, try to clean the data side of the CD-ROM with a clean, soft cloth. If the problem still exists, if possible, insert this CD-ROM into another computer to determine if the problem is with the disk or your CD-ROM drive.

Another cause of this problem may be that you have outdated CD-ROM drivers. In order to view the directories and access the files on this disc, first verify the manufacturer of your CD-ROM drive from your system's documentation.

The CD-ROM doesn't run properly or just spins in my CD-ROM drive.

The usual cause of this is a damaged or dirty disc. Visually inspect the disc for possible flaws or defects, and clean it properly. You should also test another CD-ROM in your drive. This often reveals setup problems that are not disc specific. If these procedures fail, you can contact us to get a replacement disc (contact information is at the end of this file).

The programs run slowly or don't run properly.

Do you have at least the follow amounts of RAM (memory)?

Windows NT: 24MB

Windows 95: 24MB

Macintosh: 16MB

This may sound familiar, but Windows NT/95 programs do not run well on anything less than these amounts. If you only have the minimum amount of RAM, the program may run slowly. Check the individual software installation instructions for RAM requirements for the program you wish to install.

Also, if you only have a single-spin CD-ROM drive, files will be accessed more slowly.

I get an error whenever I try to double-click on an .EXE file included on the CD-ROM.

Many of the programs included on this CD-ROM were created using a self-extracting format or require certain files to be present before installation can occur. Instead of double-clicking on the filename directly from the CD, select the desired .ZIP file, .EXE file, or the entire directory containing the desired application. Copy the file(s) to your hard drive into a newly created folder. Double-click on the filename from your hard drive to extract the files into their own folder. Select the SETUP.EXE or INSTALL.EXE file from within the folder.

INDEX

Symbols

3D
  channels, 249-252
  layering, 282, 285
3D Transform, 38-39
8-bit color, 23, 96
16-bit color, 35, 96
24-bit color, 96-98
32-bit color (True Color), 97-98

A

Acrobat (Adobe), 49
Acrobat Reader (Adobe), 48

actions
  Actions palette, 38, 386-387
  arrows, 387
  Chromium, 391
  Clear Emboss, 388, 391
  color, 392
  creating, 391-394
  default, 387
  dialog boxes, 387
  drop shadows, 391-394
  editing, 395
  installing, 391
  Kai's Power Actions, 386
  Large Rectangular Button, 387
  layers, 392
  multiple files, 394-395
  naming, 392
  overview, 385-386
  recording, 392-393
  running, 387, 391, 394-395
  scrolling, 387
  Text Shadow, 392
  troubleshooting, 386, 395, 469-470
  Type, 388, 391
Actions menu commands
  Insert Stop, 393
  Load Actions, 391
Actions palette, 38, 386-387
Adaptive palette, 99
Add Layer Mask command (Layer menu), 190
Add Layer Mask icon, 257

Q-R

It's where you go to get your pictures processed.

mcp.com

"I consider
book my
...TAL

INSIDE
ADOBE®
Photoshop® 5
New Riders
Gary David Bouton & Barbara Bouton

http://www.TheBoutons.com

The Boutons are back, with all new tutorials and new reference material for the World's most popular image editing program—Adobe Photoshop 5. Get the low-down on new features and get a leg up on photorealistic retouching techniques and more! From novice to accomplished user, *Inside Adobe Photoshop 5* is the definitive guide to advanced graphics work. Availability: *Now*, from really hip book stores! Retail Price: *$44.99 U.S.* Pages: *lots*. Includes awesome Companion CD.

International
Best-seller

By opening this package, you are agreeing to be bound by the following agreement:

Some of the software included with this product may be copyrighted, in which case all rights are reserved by the respective copyright holder. You are licensed to use software copyrighted by the Publisher and its licensors on a single computer. You may copy and/or modify the software as needed to facilitate your use of it on a single computer. Making copies of the software for any other purpose is a violation of the United States copyright laws.

This software is sold as is without warranty of any kind, either expressed or implied, including but not limited to the implied warranties of merchantability and fitness for a particular purpose. Neither the Publisher nor its dealers or distributors assumes any liability for any alleged or actual damages arising from the use of this program. (Some states do not allow for the exclusion of implied warranties, so the exclusion may not apply to you.)

Windows 95 and Windows NT: If you have AutoPlay enabled, insert the CD-ROM and choose Installation Options from the displayed splash screen.

NOTE: If you have AutoPlay disabled on your computer, the CD-ROM will *not* automatically display the installation splash screen. To browse the CD-ROM manually, double-click on My Computer on the desktop, then right-click on your CD player icon and choose Explore from the shortcut menu. From the root of the CD-ROM drive, choose autoplay.exe.

Mac: Once the CD-ROM is displayed on your desktop, open the *Guide to the CD* document for details on the contents of each folder.